"Claar and Klay combine Christian teachings and modern economic analysis in a book that informs both the head and the heart. This book also affords an opportunity to incorporate material on values and social capital into a mainstream course in economic principles."

KENNETH G. ELZINGA, ROBERT C. TAYLOR PROFESSOR OF ECONOMICS, UNIVERSITY OF VIRGINIA

"This book meets an important need for Christians who want to think carefully about economics. Claar and Klay combine sound economics and the moral demands of a lively Christian faith to create integrated, practical advice for all believers seeking to make a concrete difference in the world. This book is a great resource for any Christian trying to make sense of the many seemingly irreconcilable demands of Christian faith and economic analysis."

ANDREW M. YUENGERT, PROFESSOR OF ECONOMICS, PEPPERDINE UNIVERSITY

"This volume presents a balanced view of the respective roles and responsibilities of governments, markets and civil society within a perspective of reasoned hope that is clearly informed by the authors' Christian faith. The integration of Scripture and Christian reflection with economic analysis is careful and well reasoned, and also affirms the positive dimensions of the market process. The book is easily accessible to undergraduate students, and approaches the major stewardship issues of our time not only in terms of individual choice but also from the standpoint of the family, the church and the broader communities to which we all belong. It makes creative use of a variety of examples and addresses the primary economic challenges of our time."

PAUL R. KOCH, PROFESSOR OF ECONOMICS, OLIVET NAZARENE UNIVERSITY

"Books like this one are far too rare. Claar and Klay explore a broad range of compelling issues, write clearly and winsomely, think from a well-reasoned historic Christian perspective, and above all else are seasoned mainstream economists who know what they are talking about. We seldom get a book that considers natural revelation and special revelation simultaneously, and does so with respect for those who come to different conclusions. While making their conclusions clear, Claar and Klay consistently explain their framework of thought in such a way that those who disagree can clearly identify why and where they disagree—a wonderful gift to a long conversation about faith and economic affairs that has too often been polarized and uncharitable."

KURT SCHAEFER, PROFESSOR OF ECONOMICS, CALVIN COLLEGE

"Victor Claar and Robin Klay have given us a sensible discussion of contemporary economic policy issues with some Christian commentary. They emphasize the usefulness of mainstream economics to Christians working in the world."

PAUL OSLINGTON, UNIVERSITY OF NEW SOUTH WALES AND ST. MARK'S NATIONAL THEOLOGICAL CENTRE, CANBERRA

"Claar and Klay combine Christian principles and economic principles in a useful manner so that readers will think better about these issues and look to better solutions than are currently being proffered. Demonstrating an impressive breadth of vision, they deftly move from the big picture and macroeconomics to the care for the individual and restoring hope for the least of these. Covering a wide range of issues, they deal with microeconomics, macroeconomics, public policy, personal behavior, market failure and government intervention. This is a much-needed book that I will use and think many of my colleagues in the Association of Christian Economists will want to use also."

ERIC ELDER, PROFESSOR OF ECONOMICS, NORTHWESTERN COLLEGE

"This short book has lofty goals. One purpose is to explain the economic process, emphasizing the benefits of free markets and voluntary choice. The second task is Christian reflection on economic involvement from an evangelical perspective. The result enriches economic and biblical understanding."

JOHN PISCIOTTA, ASSOCIATE PROFESSOR OF ECONOMICS, BAYLOR UNIVERSITY

"Victor Claar and Robin Klay provide thoughtful Christians a very useful introduction to the economic way of thinking that is lively, nuanced and challenging. Their description of economics presents the powerful ability of markets to creatively meet human needs within a Christian perspective that takes seriously the claims of Christ over his creation. It will serve as a valuable entry point to the world of economics for Christians eager to learn how markets, governments and institutions operate in the contemporary global context."

JOHN E. ANDERSON, BAIRD FAMILY PROFESSOR OF ECONOMICS AND ASSOCIATE DEAN, COLLEGE OF BUSINESS ADMINISTRATION, UNIVERSITY OF NEBRASKA-LINCOLN, AND FORMER SENIOR ECONOMIST WITH THE PRESIDENT'S COUNCIL OF ECONOMIC ADVISERS

"Claar and Klay ask how Christians with shared values can affect outcomes in a market-based democratic economy. They expand traditional economic analysis of self-interested consumers, profit-seeking firms and elected governments to include groups of individuals with common interests such as churches and faith-based organizations. They illustrate that the latter, by pooling resources, can influence the production and delivery of desired services such as feeding the poor, sheltering the homeless and healing the sick, locally, nationally and globally within established economic structures."

ROBERT H. RASCHE, PROFESSOR OF ECONOMICS EMERITUS, MICHIGAN STATE UNIVERSITY

ECONOMICS IN CHRISTIAN PERSPECTIVE

Theory, Policy and Life Choices

VICTOR V. CLAAR & ROBIN J. KLAY

IVP Academic

An imprint of InterVarsity Press
Downers Grove, Illinois

InterVarsity Press
P.O. Box 1400, Downers Grove, IL 60515-1426
World Wide Web: www.ivpress.com
E-mail: email@ivpress.com

InterVarsity Press® is the book-publishing division of InterVarsity Christian Fellowship/USA®, a student movement active on campus at hundreds of universities, colleges and schools of nursing in the United States of America, and a member movement of the International Fellowship of Evangelical Students. For information about local and regional activities, write Public Relations Dept., InterVarsity Christian Fellowship/USA, 6400 Schroeder Rd., P.O. Box 7895, Madison, WI 53707-7895, or visit the IVCF website at <www.intervarsity.org>.

Scripture quotations are taken from the Holy Bible, New Living Translation®. Copyright ©1996, 2004. Used by permission of Tyndale House Publishers, Inc., Wheaton, Illinois 60189. All rights reserved.

"Cuyahoga" words and music by William Berry, Peter Buck, Michael Mills and Michael Stipe ©1986 Night Garden Music. All rights on behalf of Night Garden Music. Administered by Warner-Tamerlane Publishing Corp. All Rights Reserved. Used by permission of Alfred Publishing Co., Inc.

Table 10.1, "Poverty Rates in Six Advanced Economies Over a Six-Week Period," from Howard Oxley, Thai Ghanh Dang and Pablo Antolin, "Poverty Dynamics in Six OECD Countries," OECD Economic Studies 30 (2000-2001):14-15, © OECD, 2000, is used by permission.

Table 10.2, "Net Government Expenditure as a Percent of Wealth-Adjusted Comprehensive Income (CIW)," from The Distributional Effects of Government Spending and Taxation, edited by Dimitri B. Papadimitriou (New York: Palgrave Macmillan, 2006) is reprinted with permission.

Design: Cindy Kiple

ISBN 978-0-8308-2597-4

Printed in the United States of America ∞

Library of Congress Cataloging-in-Publication Data

Claar, Victor V., 1965-
  Economics in Christian perspective: theory, policy and life choices
 / Victor V. Claar and Robin J. Klay.
      p. cm.
  Includes bibliographical references and index.
  ISBN-13: 978-0-8308-2597-4 (pbk.: alk paper)
  1. Economics—Religious aspects—Christianity. I. Klay, Robin
  Kendrick, 1947- II. Title.
  BR115.E3C555 2007
  261.8'5—dc22
                                                                          2007016670

| P | 21 | 20 | 19 | 18 | 17 | 16 | 15 | 14 | 13 | 12 | 11 | 10 | 9 | 8 | 7 | 6 | 5 | 4 | 3 | 2 | 1 |
| Y | 25 | 24 | 23 | 22 | 21 | 20 | 19 | 18 | 17 | 16 | 15 | 14 | 13 | 12 | 11 | 10 | 09 | 08 | 07 |

For my parents.

V. V. C.

To my father, for the example of his life as a lawyer—

practicing justice and mercy—

and to my son, Nathan,

for his tremendous personal support

and attentive reading of our book.

R. J. K.

CONTENTS

Preface

This book addresses issues of economic policy, not only from a Christian perspective but also from the perspective of its authors—two mainstream economists who are also Christians. While several currently available books approach economic issues from a Christian perspective, most are unconcerned with basic notions of economic theory. Often written by noneconomists, such books consider no framework for thought beyond a particular Christian perspective. Economic theory does not inform their writing. As a result, their authors often make radical recommendations for policy based on their particular viewpoints. Unfortunately, due to their failure to consider economic theory and evidence, their policy recommendations are sometimes dramatically inconsistent with the essential, orthodox principles of economics.

We hope that this book will be of use to anyone who would like to know more about how economics can inform the views of Christians on major economic issues. Any Christian interested in thinking about issues of economic policy should learn at least a bit of economics along the way. This does not mean that our book contains dozens of supply-demand diagrams. The book does, however, provide the interested reader with a clear presentation of the principles fundamental to economic analysis of any issue or problem.

Therefore, we do the following:

1. Distill the basic facts of each economic issue considered. We include diagrammatic illustrations wherever possible. For example, we illustrate our macro chapters with graphs of unemployment and inflation rates. We also illustrate our chapter on the environment with figures showing recent environmental trends. We want our readers to have a very clear view of each issue considered, since it is easy to be misled by those who unfairly minimize or overdramatize such problems.

2. Explain the mainstream views in economics of the nature of each problem and its corresponding policy prescription.

3. Critically evaluate, from a Christian perspective, the views and recommendations of mainstream economists on each issue. Whenever possible, we use Scripture to inform our evaluation, meaningfully and faithfully. We also challenge our readers to apply the conclusions in the pursuit of their individual callings and vocations.

Our guiding conviction is that Christians who are serious about problems like environmental damage, unemployment and poverty cannot afford to ignore the achievements that economists are making with these issues. Mainstream economics helps Christians understand economic problems and respond as good stewards of God's creation. Moreover, Christian economists like us can serve as guides for Christians who are wary of the policy recommendations of mainstream economists. Hence, we have tried to write a book that is accessible to anyone, faithful to Christian teaching and responsible to our academic discipline.

The opening chapter alerts readers to the approach we take throughout the book, as we make connections between economics—theory, policy and life choices—and living out the Christian faith. A just and prosperous society depends for its continued success on maintaining the right balance of power and responsibility among three principle spheres: democratic governments, market-organized economies, and strong moral and cultural institutions. Thus the guidance we offer for addressing economic problems flows from identifying points at which markets, governments and institutions (like churches) are especially apt to make a difference for good or ill. We articulate a set of Christian principles and values needed to undergird economic and social action in order to produce a just and prosperous society anywhere in the world.

Chapter two describes how markets function in societies like ours. Unique to our book is clear exposition—using familiar examples, without graphs—to build a case for consumers, workers and producers exercising Christian values in all sorts of markets. We show that markets neither require selfishness nor cause materialism. Instead, they offer unique opportunities for Christians to apply their talents and values in ways that benefit people around the world, while also caring for their own families and communities. Furthermore, we illustrate how the perpetual change that characterizes markets need not threaten our values or livelihoods.

In the first two chapters, we make the case that the role of government should be a limited one. Nevertheless, there is a proper role for government in the economy. We need government. Chapter three considers, from both

Christian and economic perspectives, the ways in which government can help to improve on the outcomes we would observe if unbridled market interaction were the only available avenue for the provision of goods and services in a society. We provide a careful discussion of cost-benefit analysis: how the proposed benefits of any project must be weighed against the alternative possible uses of the resources that are consumed in pursuit of the project.

In three of the four Gospel accounts Christ teaches us how to respond to the authority of government; we are to give to Caesar what belongs to him, and give to God what belongs to him. But what exactly belongs to Caesar has varied widely across time and place. Even in the United States, the tax burden of the average American has risen from about 10 percent of his or her salary to over 30 percent during the last seventy years. In fact, many economists have compared the government to the Old Testament Leviathan—an insatiable serpent. We use chapter four to consider the ways government may exercise good stewardship in tax-policy design. We also discuss whether the biblical injunction to tithe is affected, now that government performs so many of the tasks traditionally undertaken by the early church (caring for the poor and sick, etc.).

Many environmentalists hate Christianity. In a 1967 article published in *Science*, Lynn White stated, "By destroying pagan animism, Christianity made it possible to exploit nature. . . . [W]e shall continue to have a worsening ecologic crisis until we reject the Christian axiom that nature has no reason for existence save to serve man." In chapter five we dismiss White's claim that God's plan for the relationship of humans to nature necessarily leads to environmental degradation. Instead, we assert that Christians, called to be good stewards of all of God's creation, must exercise caution and wisdom in the pursuit of environmental goals. Further, we show that modern economics has much to say about responsible care for and cleanup of the environment.

In chapter six we consider the ways our federal government can influence our macroeconomy—our overall national economy and its interactions with the still-larger global economy. Unemployment rates, inflation rates and national income: these are all macroeconomic issues because we do not normally evaluate them at the local level. Instead, we account for them at the larger, national level. We consider four variables and measures that policymakers have used—both officially and unofficially—as goals of macroeconomic policy: (1) the growth of national income per capita, (2) unemployment rates, (3) inflation rates and (4) stock market values. We include several diagrams, reflecting where the economy has been, is now and may be headed in the future. We also discuss the limits of each of these as measures of overall societal well-being.

In chapter seven we summarize the current state of macroeconomic knowledge today. In particular we discuss the ways the discipline has evolved since the Keynesian economic revolution of the 1930s. Macroeconomic understanding since Keynes has evolved in such a way that Keynes's prescriptions for active policy have become less and less credible. Instead, it appears that a steady, deliberate, less reactive approach to economic policy may lead to the best, overall, long-term path for the economy. Attempts to use *discretionary* monetary or fiscal policy actions to stabilize the economy may, instead, be destabilizing—and even deceitful. Indeed, Adam Smith's invisible hand may be just as powerful in the macroeconomic realm as in individual markets for particular goods and services.

Chapter eight addresses seductive myths about globalization that plague many popular discussions regarding the moral aspects of trade. We start with a case that pits well-meaning Californians, concerned for the environment, against poor Montanans, planning to commercialize new oil fields. Similarly, well-meaning but misguided Westerners often insist on trade restrictions to "protect" poor foreigners from being exploited in world trade. From there, we consider the changes needed for Third World countries to grow their economies and thereby reduce poverty. Finally, we discuss ways that Christians—as individuals, churches and members of secular organizations—can work alongside Third World people to reduce barriers to higher living standards. We continue to urge intellectual and spiritual discipline in the practice of "reasoned hope"—a virtue identified in earlier chapters—which requires long-term commitments and strong faith in God's active involvement.

In chapter nine we present a biblical and theological basis for the Christian conviction that work is meant to be both a blessing and a means by which God's gifts to each person are "called out" to meet their own needs and those of the wider community. Labor markets serve as effective channels through which this happens. We use examples that illustrate how earnings differences among persons, across professions and over time reflect decisions people make about training, job risk, location, responsibility and so on. We emphasize that such decisions involve much more than monetary rewards.

Chapter ten undertakes a special challenge by investigating whether current income gaps ought to concern Christians. Is it only absolute poverty that Christians are called to mitigate, or must they also decry the high pay top executives receive? What is the nature of male-female wage gaps and black-white income gaps? To the extent that persistent gaps result from a mixture of personal choices (about education, family, etc.), the regulatory environment and changing markets, what can be done to ensure more equal opportunity? Is it possible for governments to take actions in this regard without unduly interfering with the ability of competitive markets to produce widespread abundance, and while preserving the freedom of choice markets afford?

Since the time of Adam Smith, and especially over the past two decades, a strong case has been made for the importance of moral values and institutions to every country's economic success. Obviously, where moral values are relatively widespread and influence most members of society (even those who are not associated with any religious tradition), the benefits to society are tremendous. They include the greater likelihood that employees will put an effort into all their tasks, even when supervisors are not likely to monitor them; that companies will more often serve customers than cheat them; and that citizens will buy more things than they steal and pay taxes rather than hiding their lights and incomes under bushels. In chapter eleven we discuss the means by which societies can invest in building more social capital as well as roles played by churches in this endeavor.

To close the book with something very practical, we present "Nine Big Ideas from Economics That Can Help You Be a Good Steward Every Day," culled from lessons presented throughout the book. This brief section serves as a reminder that we can all honor God while practicing good economics.

There is a crucial need for conversation about economic policy in which moral concerns are introduced along with sound economic analysis, whether the ethics arise from religious or secular perspectives. Indeed, the authors' development of the subject is open to application and adaptation by non-Christian and secular individuals and groups. For example, Muslim and Jewish scriptures also give prominence to caring for the poor and strangers. Furthermore, commitments to such values as honesty, dedication to community well-being, and work—all key to the quality of life and material abundance in any economy—spread beyond the boundaries of traditional religions. Although the reference point for much of this book's discussion is explicitly Christian, the authors hope to inform non-Christian readers and to inspire other economists to show the many useful connections between economic policy and moral values emphasized in other religious and secular traditions.

To aid in the clarification of the book's presentation, we enlisted the help of our students at Hope College as readers and critics of the completed chapters. Our readers have included students who have taken no economics, some who are majoring in economics and others who lie in between. This strategy has provided useful feedback from students who differ widely in their exposure to the study of economics.

We are thankful for the help and support of our friends, families and colleagues as the project progressed. It was a delight to work with the experts at InterVarsity Press, including Gary Deddo, Elaina Whittenhall, Taryn Bullis, Jeff Crosby and Ruth Curphey. At American University Armenia, Anna Hakobyan, Varduhi Hyusisyan, Armen Petrosyan, Astghik Melikyan, Edouard Antonian, Lilit Vardanyan and Lucig Danielian provided pivotal assistance during Claar's Fulbright year there. We appreciate Julia Hollenberg, at Hope College, for her help with editing. Careful and extensive comments from reviewers Tom Head at George Fox University and Stephen L. S. Smith at Gordon College improved the final product. We especially thank Rowene Beals for her patient reading and editing of the initial manuscript. She was our perfect "interested reader," as we tested out ideas and honed themes for greater clarity and impact. In addition, Ro fielded pieces of data coming at her from at least three directions with accuracy and grace. We could not have done this project without her support and encouragement throughout the three years in its making.

1

CHRISTIAN FAITH IN RELATIONSHIP TO ECONOMIC ACTIVITY

Framing the Issues

C hristians are commanded to conduct every aspect of their lives in response to the call and grace of God in Christ. Clearly, many dimensions of their lives are interwoven with markets. As a result, Christians seek to buy and sell, and to save and invest, in the light of gospel values. They must do so with an awareness of their own limitations, trusting that God will bless and use their lives. Though their ultimate motivations may differ from those of non-Christians, Christians must deal with the same physical, psychological and economic realities as everyone else. Throughout this book we intend for our examination of economic forces and moral values to also engage those outside the Christian tradition.

One of the fundamental assumptions economists make about human activity is that we are limited in our choices by scarce time, resources and knowledge. Christians acknowledge that reality. Like others, they cannot be in two places at once, know the price of everything or provide for themselves and their families without working, saving and carefully considering their budgets (e.g., how much and what to purchase, in keeping with their values). Furthermore, although Christians are called to have "faith that can move mountains," they are taught not to defy gravity or tempt God by jumping from rooftops (recall Jesus' refusal of that temptation [Mt 4:5-7]). Likewise, they would court physical and spiritual danger if they ignored real limits to their material and financial resources.

While painfully aware of their human limitations, and recognizing the pervasiveness of sin, Christians maintain *reasoned hope* for themselves and for the world. Securely founded on the life, death and resurrection of Jesus Christ, their hope transcends the evil they encounter. Their hope ultimately transcends material scarcity, but they live without any pretensions of treading somewhere above the earth-bound paths of non-Christians. They trust in God's promises of blessings on earth and in the completion of his perfect love in the kingdom of God, which is already here yet still to come in fullness.

Throughout this book we propose to equip readers with an understanding of the economy within which they make dozens of daily choices, and to affirm the spiritual values required to live out their decisions about work, as well as buying and saving, in ways that please God. We do not presume to map out precisely how every Christian or group of Christians should deal with all economic matters. We make use of different traditions for their useful insights regarding how Christian values can be put to work in the economy.

We emphasize the points at which reflection on Christian truths and values is most appropriate and useful for illuminating economic activities. We show how Christians can faithfully interact within the market system without caving in to materialism (see chap. 2 for the development of this point). We also acknowledge that the very limitations of markets open up places for collective action, organized in the private sector, by churches and other associations. We discuss the roles of governments at all levels, which constitute another key realm of human social activity. We show governments acting in ways that may either enhance the creative energies and expertise within the other two realms or weaken their capacity to address big social questions.

The Pillars of a Just and Abundant Society

Traditional economic textbooks portray economies along a continuum, in order to illustrate various degrees of government power relative to the market. Thus, at the far left is a combination of central economic planning and government ownership of all property—best illustrated by the former Soviet Union, present-day Cuba and North Korea. At the far right is minimal government and freedom for markets to deliver any goods and services people are willing to pay for (including morally inferior products, like pornography). Hong Kong is the best example. At this same right-hand end of the spectrum, governments are expected to avoid trying to reduce income disparities between the rich and poor, because it is assumed that the primary social value to be defended is freedom of individual choice, not equality.

Today, nations are located at various points along the left-right spectrum. Thus, to the left of the mid-point is democratic socialism (represented by

Sweden and several other countries in Western Europe), a system in which markets play the key roles in production (i.e., there are few state-owned enterprises). Nevertheless, their governments are expected to deliver health care and education, and to lower poverty levels by taxing high incomes and spending on many public services. To the right of center are large and small countries, like the United States and New Zealand. New Zealand maintains a very limited role for government. By comparison, the size and activities of government in the United States are large and extensive—putting the United States to the left of New Zealand. However, compared to most nations in Western Europe, the U.S. government plays a more restricted role in the economic sphere—as evidenced by a largely private health care system, lower spending on poverty programs and unemployment benefits, and lower tax rates that are intended to encourage investment and entrepreneurship.

In this book we discuss relationships between governments and markets (at local and national levels) that conform to Christian teaching and respect economic insights about such things as improving efficiency. We emphasize relationships that do not require a prominent role for churches in promoting legislation and shaping policy. Instead, we describe a third realm of social power and influence: institutions of private, collective action (like churches, schools and museums) that are free to fund, teach and exercise their values for the benefit of society. We picture society as a tripod, supported by three poles, each of which must have the size and integrity to enable people and their communities to thrive. These poles are democratic government, the market economy, and strong religious and cultural institutions. Novak (1982) masterfully develops this theme.

We propose to illustrate how societies that are based on healthy relationships among the three poles produce a rich variety of solutions to meet social, economic and spiritual needs, even as these needs evolve over time. In small and poor societies, for example, families are the main source of education and health care as well as the chief "employers." In other societies, religious associations—like mosques or churches—provide most education. In richer and more diverse societies, pre-university education takes place mainly in government-funded schools, while spiritual needs are addressed by religious organizations.

To remain healthy, societies must be vigilant regarding the rights and responsibilities of the three sectors—governments, markets and private/voluntary organizations—so that none unduly encroaches on the domain and responsibilities of another. During the second half of the twentieth century, in Europe and the United States, governments grew to meet new social expectations, such as provisions for unemployed workers and retirees. In later chapters we examine what economic theory and Christian teaching have to say about how expansion of some government responsibilities and budgets can impair the ability of markets and private voluntary organizations to perform their functions well.

Recognition of problems in the regulatory role of government has prompted waves of deregulation throughout the industrialized world over the last three decades (in banking, transportation, etc.). More recent efforts to expand collaboration between governments and private voluntary organizations (e.g., via President George W. Bush's faith and community-based initiative) require careful study. It is still an open question whether such partnerships, using tax money, can achieve the desired social outcomes without violating basic church-state separation or compromising the holistic missions of religious organizations (see chap. 11).

In modern societies a balanced relationship among governments, private voluntary organizations and markets leaves individual and group participants in each realm relatively free to exercise their unique talents, insights, resources and values. Thus, for example, we point out the relative advantage to society of governments setting out minimal standards for environmental health, but doing so in ways that preserve access to resources and relatively free choice by individuals, businesses and private voluntary groups regarding their use of water, air and land (see chap. 5). Such economic freedoms, we argue, are absolutely essential for a majority of people to utilize and develop fully their talents and other resources for the sake of personal, social and even spiritual good.

The choice a society makes is, however, not between government action (based on a specific set of moral principles) and completely free, individual action disregarding social benefits and moral values. Even with democratic governments, free markets *and* strong private voluntary associations in place, the ultimate course of any society depends on the continual exercise of personal responsibility in commitments shared with others and based on fundamental values. Christians would add that the future course of any society also depends on effective Christian witness. Spirit-empowered witness and the resulting deep religious conversions, alone, have the power to infuse the realms of government, markets and private voluntary institutions with godly motives, and to guide their activities in the light of truly great visions for life on earth.

One of the reasons we emphasize the crucial roles of moral and cultural institutions is that when they are strong (partly as a result of being given legal stature), such institutions are able to undertake a huge variety of tasks by making use of voluntary contributions of time and money. If, instead, governments assume primary responsibility for providing education, arts, health care and help for needy people, their control results in too little innovation and too many one-size-fits-all public services. One reaction to this inherent problem in education has been the creation of charter schools and support for school vouchers. Both reflect a keen interest by many people to see educational innovation benefit from vigorous competition among many different models, so that excellence builds in places where it has sadly lagged (e.g., especially in poor urban neighborhoods, but also in the whole U.S. public school system).

Finally, in countries where the only funds to support public services come from tax revenues, much less can be achieved. Many citizens of such countries consider their primary duty to society to be fully exercised by paying their taxes or by engaging in political activism on behalf of tax fairness and particular government spending priorities. By comparison with Americans, for example, the French expect much more of government and less of the private voluntary sector. Measured in terms of employment, the U.S. private voluntary sector is almost twice that of France (3.7 percent of the population versus 2 percent in the mid-1990s) (CIVICUS 1997, pp. 49, 150). An interesting comparison can be made between France and the United States regarding the respective roles of private and government sectors in their aid to Third World countries. In 2002, U.S. citizens privately donated on average five cents per person to Third World assistance, and thirteen cents through their government. On the other hand, French citizens privately donated an average of one cent per person, but twenty-five cents per person through their government (Foreign Policy 2004). The Center for Global Development publishes a weighted Commitment to Development Index (CDI). Besides aid, other factors affecting international rankings include trade policy and investment. France and the United States shared seventh place in the 2004 rankings of twenty-one nations, with the Netherlands and Denmark in first place, Australia, the United Kingdom and Canada just ahead of the United States and France (also tied with Germany and Norway for seventh place out of twenty-one countries), and Japan in last place.

Concentration of social goals in the domain of government, especially when undertaken by national governments, can have the unintended side effect of undermining personal moral action and leaving untapped the skills and community resources that could be used to meet crying social needs. Chapter four presents a careful consideration of the domains in which governments can be expected to enhance public welfare, and of the economic principles that suggest appropriate boundaries around that sphere of public life.

The histories of Western societies differ with respect to the relative powers and responsibilities of governments, markets and private/voluntary organizations. A comparison of France and the United States provides an example, but does not explain how or why those differences occurred. After his visit to America in the early 1800s, Alexis de Tocqueville wrote *Democracy in America*, in which he marveled at the ways that Americans organized themselves in every town and hamlet to deal locally with problems they identified—rather than expecting governments to assume primary responsibility for their solution. This, he thought, was the reason why democracy worked in America. By contrast, the French government actually prohibited private organizations from providing services to meet social needs until the law was changed at the end of the nineteenth century. The state was to be the sole provider.

Some of those who have supported recent efforts in the United States and elsewhere to constrain government powers, in favor of markets and private/voluntary organizations, argue that governments gradually took over many functions that could be performed better by the other two sectors. Those who continue to favor a large government role in the provision of social services, including education, health care and retirement benefits, argue that government is the only sector capable of coordinating services and distributing them fairly, because markets (they believe) undermine communal responsibility.

On the other hand, some religious leaders insist that governments have stepped into social gaps because moral values—such as personal and communal responsibility, charity and love—were being eroded by materialism and other secular values. They often argue that the first line of religious offense against social ills is spiritual and moral renewal. Only then are people and communities empowered to change their social environments through loving service. Throughout this book we discuss all of these possibilities, beginning in chapter two, where we examine the claim that free markets promote increased materialism.

In addition to the otherwise untapped resources made available to society through the work of moral and cultural institutions, those same institutions often have an advantage over governments in meeting local and individual needs. Many are grassroots organizations by virtue of their proximity and experience, who understand unique local situations and make intelligent use of local networks (sometimes relying on subsidies from public funds). For a parallel reason John Stuart Mill's ([1859] 1974) influential essay *On Liberty,* as well as recent governmental reforms around the world, highlights the benefits of allowing as much state and local autonomy as possible in the design and delivery of public services. (See chapter 8 regarding the importance of political and economic reforms in the Third World.)

CHRISTIAN PRINCIPLES AND VALUES UNDERGIRD A FLOURISHING AND JUST ECONOMY

It is hard to think of any Christian principle or value that is irrelevant to economic activity. Consider teachings on the importance of prayer and how best to pray; or contemplate God's invitation to each person to entrust themselves to Christ—as their Savior, friend and Lord. If somehow such practices and commitments were strictly spiritual, they would have no connection to the economy. However, the Bible and the church consistently teach that attempts to love and pray to God are meaningless unless they cause Christians to behave differently in the "real world" than they would without spiritual moorings.

James wrote in his epistle that "faith by itself isn't enough. Unless it produces good deeds [expressed in love for neighbors and strangers], it is dead and useless" (Jas 2:17). Furthermore, the first petition in the Lord's Prayer—"may your Kingdom come soon" (Mt 6:10)—cannot be realized without collaboration among "little Christs" (from which we get the word *Christians*) and with Jesus Christ, whose life on earth demonstrated how to live fully. Likewise, the petition to "give us today the food we need" (Mt 6:11) is rightly understood to entail both human work and God's blessing of the earth, with all its potential to bring forth plenty. It is also a prayer for spiritual food, without which work cannot achieve its full potential for people and their communities (for more on this, see chap. 9 about work and vocation).

Although some biblical teachings may be a step removed from direct economic application, the themes that most relate to the economy can be gathered under five broad headings. We offer these without extensive justification in the form of biblical texts or theological writings, although we will provide abundant suggestions for further reading. Most principles appearing below are discussed in Donald Hay's (1991) book *Economics Today: A Christian Critique*. With some modification we make use of his choices because they reflect both Catholic and Protestant thinking about these matters, and they do so with clarity and brevity. The basic Christian principles on which economic life should be organized are revealed by certain attitudes and actions in response to God's creation and gifts to each person and community, namely, delight and gratitude, stewardship and work, creativity and caring.

God provides an abundant and dynamic creation, over which *humans are given the calling and responsibility of stewardship.* Stewardship extends to the use of individual talents (witness the parable of the talents [Mt 25:14-30]). The responsibility of stewards is to manage resources, over which each has been given oversight, in the best interest of the owner (in this case, God) and in service to others.

Humans are created to enjoy creation and to show gratitude for it, as many of the psalms beautifully illustrate. We are to respect God for the gifts of creation by avoiding careless waste or plunder (see Deut 20:19) of resources. (In chap. 5, dedicated to environmental issues, some care will be given to define waste relative to efficiency and in the light of noneconomic goals.)

Biblical sources describing proper human relationships to creation can be found throughout Scripture. The Garden of Eden portrays the abundance of creation. God presents creation as a gift of plants and animals, over which humans are given the responsibility of stewardship (see Gen 1:28-31). Men and women are to continually give thanks to God for his gifts in the created world (see Ps 95). They are to share the produce of the land (their "incomes") with those in need, as prescribed in the Old Testament tithe. Indeed, one part of the tithe was meant to provide food and wine for rejoicing in God's presence at the temple in Jerusalem; another part was meant for the support of widows, orphans and strangers; and the rest was devoted to the support of priests (see Deut 14:22-29).

Human beings have an obligation to work, and their societies must afford them many opportunities to do so, since work is the principle means for exercising stewardship. The importance of work in Scripture is evidenced by proverbs that commend it (see Prov 10:3-4) and by the apostle Paul's insistence that Christians must work if they intend to eat (see 2 Thess 3:10). Work is more than a job or profession, however. It is a calling in which men and women apply and expand their God-given talents, thereby reflecting the image of God (who was at "work" in creation). Through work, people have an opportunity to meet their personal and family needs as well as those of the community. Through work, we collaborate with each other in the stewardly production and use of resources. Indeed, the writer of Ecclesiasticus (38:39, Latin Vulgate) says that our work is our prayer. (Chap. 9 expands on the sense of work as a calling.)

Personally and collectively, *society must make provision for the poor* (as well as the sick, orphans and those otherwise severely disadvantaged)—people who are unable to take care of their basic needs through their work. The Old Testament tithes were a kind of communal tax meant to care for the poor in their midst—both Jews and foreigners. God's concern to prevent intergenerational poverty is evident in the Old Testament law, which provided for land to be redistributed back to the original families every fifty years (the Jubilee). Furthermore, farmers were to leave fallen grain for the poor to glean in their fields (recall the story of Ruth). Some laws were aimed at protecting poor people from scandalous exploitation by those who would extract high interest—even on loans of food. Other laws called on employers to pay their workers every evening (see Lev 19:13), so that they could buy their daily bread.

In the New Testament, Jesus taught his followers to serve the needy as they would serve their Lord (e.g., Mt 25:31-46). Early church leaders assigned deacons and took special collections to provide for poor believers in their midst as well as others in the Jerusalem church (see Acts 6:1-4; 1 Cor 16:1-4). Throughout the Bible, care for the poor is the premier sign of gratitude to God, who led Israel out of slavery (Deut 8:11-18) and who gave his Son to free all from bondage to sin (Gal 4:3-7).

Women and men are made in the image of God (Gen 1:27). Aspects of that image include the capacity, vision and passion to create new things, to uncover new possibilities, and to explore new dimensions. Because God continuously sustains and unfolds new potential in creation, the gift of human creativity is essential for society to thrive, especially in the presence of continuous change. In their exercise of stewardship, *human beings are called to develop resources and apply their talents.* Consider all the shepherds commended in Scripture, as well as those who worked in bronze and iron (see Gen 4:20-22), in weaving (see the famous wife, mother and business person described in Prov 31), and creating music (recall kings Saul and David).

THE FOUNDATIONS OF A SOCIETY BASED ON BIBLICAL PRINCIPLES IN A MARKET ECONOMY

Based on the biblical principles previously described, certain requirements must be met in any society. In social, political and economic dealings, societies must protect the freedom of individuals and communities to choose among a vast array of possibilities regarding their consumption, production and sharing. Without freedom, there is no responsibility. Furthermore, without freedom, human beings are not accorded their essential status as creatures "made in God's image." They are unable to fully explore partially hidden (and ever-changing) callings within their families, work environments and communal relationships.

Societies built on a foundation of political democracy, free markets and strong moral and cultural institutions respect the freedom of human agency and provide an especially fertile environment for human flourishing under God's care. They also imbed certain social values, like civility and fairness. None of these ways of organizing political, economic and social relations by itself guarantees that the values of the kingdom of God are advanced in human history. However, together they enable Christians to practice and share their faith and love, as God guides them. This balanced tripod of social spheres (recall the three-poled model on p. 17) also ensures that non-Christians are accorded the same freedoms and dignity as everyone else.

First, consider government. The pioneers of democratic government believed that listening to the voices of all citizens was key to a well-run government. Collectively, citizen participation was regarded as a source of wisdom that could not be duplicated by any would-be benevolent dictator. Furthermore, founders of the American republic saw the need to provide for competition (both through elections and in the form of institutional checks and balances) so that any proposals for government action would be tested and constrained at various levels. They did this to frustrate potential tyranny by elites or majorities.

Of course, no such complex system would be needed if each citizen could be counted on to act always with perfect wisdom, knowledge and consideration for others. The Christian view of individual calling and responsibility, along with a keen awareness of sin and human capacity for evil, accords well with various forms of democracy that preserve widespread freedom within certain constraints.

Is it also the case that relatively free markets complement Christian respect for individual callings and stewardship? We believe so. While competition is useful in political democracy, it is even more pervasive and fruitful in free-market economies. Producers compete with each other to meet consumers' demands. Workers compete with each other to get and keep jobs that meet their own objectives for income, opportunity, collegiality and fulfillment of calling—as well as safety, access to transportation and flexibility in hours. Financial institutions compete with each other to provide savers with a choice of financial instruments representing various combinations of safety and good returns. They also compete with each other to earn profits through their charges (interest payments and fees) on loans to individuals and enterprises, determined after careful assessment of borrowers' abilities to put the money to productive use. Finally, owners of resources—land, minerals, machines and patents—compete with each other, either to get the best possible prices when selling them, or to earn the greatest income streams possible from their ongoing use.

Within and among all economic entities, competition ensures individuals and groups the widest possible opportunities to make choices based on their own values. However, no market economy magically ensures adequate competition and fairness in all dealings. As a consequence, governments can contribute to the health of an economy, in large part, by establishing fundamental rights and rules that promote both competition and fairness. Thus the protection of private property rights and the enforcement of contracts are essential government tasks. Legislatures, police, courts and prisons are all involved in defining and defending the rights of persons over themselves and their property.

There are other potentially useful roles for governments to play in an economy, which we describe and evaluate in upcoming chapters. For example, we consider the need for a government role in protecting the environment and in providing certain public services that individuals and communities might have difficulty producing for themselves.

Clearly, free markets alone are not sufficient for humans to flourish. While markets *do* generally provide growing opportunities for the exercise of professional callings, they do not directly fund callings to the ministry or support soup kitchens. Nevertheless, free markets and democratic societies make it legal and possible for people who earn incomes in the for-profit sector to pay the salaries of missionaries and to fund religious retreat centers and camps. Furthermore, free markets enable churches, museums, orchestras and schools to buy the materials vital to producing the services they sell either at reduced prices or give away.

Finally, strong moral institutions, like churches and families, are essential to the functioning of a healthy society. Without strong moral convictions, even normally law-abiding people sometimes cheat when they are unlikely to be caught (consider music "sharing" through Internet sites). They use time at work for personal purposes; they hide defects in the cars they offer for resale; they cheat their families of the time and attention needed to raise the next generation; they spend most income on themselves, leaving few funds or productive resources for the future; and they weaken their communities by not offering their time and money to support and equip people who lack strong families and adequate resources.

Christians are painfully aware that they fail their communities and their Lord in many of the ways just mentioned. By themselves, they cannot triumph over sin. Along with all humanity—no matter the education level, culture, economic or religious status—they are subject to sin. As producers, government officials and consumers, their motives, actions and justifications are tainted. Confession, forgiveness and restoration—provided by Christ through the church—constitute spiritual remedies.

However, given the way that sin (even forgiven sin) can leave permanent scars on lives, people who acknowledge the great potential for evil usually favor a three-pole system of democratic government, market economy and strong religious/cultural institutions. Each of these spheres operates by rules aimed at providing equal rights and responsibilities under the law—for the citizens, who vote, buy and sell, maintain families, worship and play. Furthermore, competition within and among these spheres sets some limits on the ability of any one person, self-righteous group, government leader or firm to abuse its power.

Societies lacking strong moral and cultural foundations are forced to devote scarce resources to police officers at *every* corner, soldiers along *every* border. By contrast, people living in societies that are strong in terms of democracy, markets and morals are freer to use their finite resources for better things than huge police and military forces—like food, medicine, entertainment and even church services. When Christians in any society act out their collective calling to be the "salt of the earth," they help preserve their societies and continually open them to receive new life, by God's grace.

FOR FURTHER READING

Bandow, Doug, and Schindler, David L., eds. 2003. *Wealth, poverty, and hu-*

man destiny. Wilmington, Del.: ISI Books. A collaborative effort between the Intercollegiate Studies Institute and the John Templeton Foundation, the purpose of this edited volume is to consider whether (1) market forces are mostly good and rarely bad, or (2) market forces engender in everyone a tendency toward individualistic behavior that leads away from relationships held in community with others. To promote balance in the presentation, the commissioners recruited two editors, one to represent each point of view.

Britton, Andrew, and Sedgwick, Peter. 2003. *Economic theory and Christian belief.* Bern: Peter Lang. Organized around the outline of an introductory principles of economics course, Britton and Sedgwick have designed a book that will help economists understand better—for each major topic—what Christianity has to say, and help theologians understand better what economics has to say. Each of the first ten chapters consists of two major sections: economic theory and Christian belief. Following a brief introduction the economic theory section of each chapter provides a whirlwind tour of the basic economic concepts relevant to that chapter's topic. The Christian belief section spells out for the laity some primary scriptural insights relevant to the topic at hand. Each chapter concludes with a brief summary and discussion section of the preceding two sections.

Hay, Donald A., and Kreider, Alan, eds. 2001. *Christianity and the culture of economics.* Cardiff: University of Wales Press. This volume considers whether markets are a net plus or minus. On one hand, it is possible that markets reward selfish behavior and over time elicit it. Alternatively, markets may merely be a neutral tool that delivers the goods a society desires. In the final chapter, Hay discusses the role of a Christian economist.

Novak, Michael. 1982. *The spirit of democratic capitalism.* New York: Simon & Schuster. This is a classic that should be read by anyone wanting to understand the genius of capitalism, not as a matter of market power but as a dynamic system with great creative power. Better than anyone else, Novak explains why the Christian understanding of God, human beings and God's purposes in the world fits best with free markets. He also shows the danger of governments, markets or moral/cultural institutions trying to usurp power from the others, since each has a distinct role to play in society.

2

MARKETS

Mechanisms for Creating Good
and Exercising Christian Responsibility

In later chapters of this book we carefully consider limitations to markets and
ways that governments and moral/cultural institutions can complement markets without impairing their capacity to allocate resources and produce abundance. Here our first task is to understand what markets accomplish that cannot be done well by any substitute, such as an elite group of economists,
senators or church leaders. Alternative economic systems fail on the grounds
of inefficiency, restricted freedom of choice for groups and individuals, and
relatively poor living standards. In this chapter we not only describe what markets accomplish and how, but also show that they are not primarily vehicles for
rampant materialism. In fact, they support the highest forms of cultural and
spiritual expression.

Consider the marvel of a beehive, with all its complex social organization,
signaling dances and triangulated maps pointing toward the nearest source of
nectar. Contemplate the adaptations by species to changing conditions and
the systematic ways that tropical floras organize themselves in order to get access to light. Meditate on the place that both microscopic entities and moving
heavenly bodies have in the dynamics of the universe. Marvel at what joins the
tectonic movements of eons past with spaces occupied and resources used by
all life on earth today.

Some early scientists who were Christians, like Johannes Kepler (1571-
1630), broke into song in the middle of their treatises because they saw natural
wonders as products of the mind of God. You will search high and low, however, to find an economist (even a Christian economist) breaking out in psalms
of praise while describing how markets work to meet human needs, to direct

human potential and to serve human goals that range from the simple to the profound. Their professional reserve and lack of training as poets may hold economists back. Although they understand and even marvel at the work of markets in the service of humanity, economists find it difficult to convey this to the general public—especially to moral critics who advocate some alternative. We invite our readers to join us on a trip to discover and marvel at markets, and to discern responsible Christian interaction within them, especially as consumers.

SCARCITY—A PRODUCT OF SIN OR AN OPPORTUNITY FOR CAREFUL CHOICES ABOUT CONSUMPTION?

Let us begin with a visit to a small farm community in Iowa, where the dark, overturned soil smells fertile. The farmers work hard, manage carefully and assume the risks of entrepreneurship whenever they invest their savings in new buildings and equipment to raise productivity on their farms. By contrast with similar communities in parts of the Third World, these Iowa farmers and the local town are not poor. However, they too face the inevitable scarcity that underlies the human condition everywhere. They cannot spend any given hour twice—first on their family and second on planting. They cannot buy the latest air-conditioned combines at a time when farm incomes are low. And they cannot go to Florida in the winter if it would mean failing to make payments on their production loans.

Economists often say that *scarcity* is the fundamental fact of human life with which their discipline deals. Thus they model the behavior of consumers and producers as one of deciding how to use limited (hence the word *scarce*) resources like time, money and land. Such models illustrate the case of Tim, a college student setting out to buy some shirts. He is guided in his choice among stores and brands by their prices and quality as well as by his style preferences. Because his income is limited he cannot buy twenty cool shirts. Furthermore, Tim must consider the time he has available to shop around, since he could do other valuable things with that hour and might be inclined to save time by buying online (even at the risk of a poor fit).

Tim must be careful and thoughtful about his shopping because his resources are limited. He may be pictured as trying either to get as many nice shirts as possible with the $100 he has apportioned to the summer clothes budget, or as trying to get the three shirts he needs at the lowest cost (so that he can take his kid brother out to a movie with what he saves by shopping carefully). Clearly, Tim is guided by his self-interest, but he is not selfish. After all, he thinks not only of his brother but also about what shirts would be appropriate for church on Sundays in the summer heat.

So the first stops on our journey—in Iowa and with Tim—serve to illustrate how producers and consumers make choices in light of comparatively scarce means, and that they do so by consulting their self-interest. However, their self-interest does not generally entail selfishness. Instead, it includes careful regard for family, work needs, appropriate dress for worship and the desire to avoid falling asleep during long sermons.

The scarcity that all individuals and groups must take into account when using markets to meet their needs, and to reach certain goals, does *not* result primarily from sinful decisions. This seems obvious in our examples. Nevertheless, many Christian writers have concluded that market behavior is so inextricably mixed with the sin of selfishness that the only way to address the scarcity resulting from sin is to practice simple living and to share all surpluses with others.

Scarcity, in its economic sense (namely, limits on financial and other means that require careful consumer and producer choices), is not something that can be *solved* by simple living and generosity. Quite the contrary, the Swarts, a Christian family living simply on an organic farm near Las Vegas, may be stretched even to give a tithe to their church, since the local market for organic fruits and vegetables is quite limited. The Christian love they show others has to take alternative forms, such as inviting urban kids to spend time on a real farm.

Like everyone else, the Swart family has to make careful decisions about how to use their time and money, even to meet quite ordinary needs. For example, should they sew their own clothes, or buy them, and can their own fruit? No one but this family (prayerfully attending to God's leading and perhaps in consultation with other like-minded Christians) can make such decisions. None of the above choices is obviously selfish or less Christian than others—neither was their choice to farm, despite the fact that both parents are college graduates.

Those who disparage consumer and producer decisions that are based, in part, on the individual's (or family's or church's) consideration of self-interest misunderstand the Swarts' story. When critics assess markets, they usually do so detached from the millions of individual choices that are routinely informed both by self-interest and concern for others—as close as one's family or as far away as the Haitian village where a mission helps people start up small businesses.

Furthermore, personal acts of kindness, the creation of beauty and the search for wisdom—all of which transcend material motives—nonetheless depend for much of their success on very material industries. Catholic economist Peter Danner (1995) writes that

> [those industries] require high labor skills, enormous investments, and ever developing technology . . . [including] a vast education program, serving untold millions, a flood of books, plays, and musical compositions, and architectural temples both to commerce and divinity. (p. 30)

Moreover, markets cater to a wide range of both virtuous and vicious motives:

> Social impulses like friendship, compassion and understanding; and oppositely, enmity, envy and indifference motivate much buying and selling. Life goals of power, popularity, prestige, and the intense desire for truth, beauty and the divine are strong spiritual motives which affect mightily what is produced, exchanged, consumed. (p. 30)

Although it is clear that consumer choices expressed through markets are informed by self-interest (though they need not be selfish), Christians must bring their moral and spiritual values with them into markets. For example, those values exclude the purchase of pornography (whose definition is subject to personal judgment and informed by Christian teaching). They preclude rampant materialism—which often entails an emphasis on showy things, instead of helping others or making purchases that advance intellectual, artistic and spiritual purposes. As an example, most Christians gladly include books, tuition fees, art and spiritual retreats in their spending, but would likely counsel a church family against spending all their discretionary income on the latest home entertainment systems.

In the early twentieth century Thorstein Veblen, a decidedly non-Christian economist, critiqued some consumer habits. He coined the expression "conspicuous consumption" to capture the habits of people who buy the most expensive and flashy products in order to advertise their wealth and attract the admiration or envy of others. Clearly, that is the spirit of the "sinful nature" run amuck (Gal 5:19-21)!

Christianity is not a "Lone Ranger" religion. It depends on vibrant personal faith, love of strangers and deep connections within the Christian community. Even though markets are not themselves the cause of selfishness, they respond as readily to consumers whose motives are morally suspect as to those who carefully consider God's will as they spend, save and give. Christians are not immune to temptations offered by the smorgasbord spread out before them by markets. As a result, they do well not only to pray and gather for regular worship but also to uphold each other as they ponder how to honor God in their purchases, as in every other area of their lives.

The Church of the Savior in Washington, D.C., lay religious orders and Richard Foster's (1998) book *Celebration of Discipline* have something in common. They all offer Christian teaching and communal support for those who understand their personal callings to include a simple lifestyle, closely shared with the needy. Such a life is not every Christian's calling, but it certainly deserves their prayerful consideration and perhaps their financial support.[1] Others serve God best by making music in Carnegie Hall (like Marian Anderson and Wynton Marsalis) or by building a successful company (like Max De Pree of Herman Miller Furniture or Francois Michelin of Group Michelin).

In Michelin's (2003) book *And Why Not?* Michelin shows how business is one of the highest callings. The mystery of God's collaboration with human beings in the business world lies behind the scenes. Corporations are nothing less than the dynamic creations of employees, shareholders and customers working together in concrete ways to make goods and services. But their creation has a deeper meaning, as innovation "frees the imagination and encourages risk-taking—going to the limits in order to see what happens" (Couretas 2003).

Furthermore, it is possible for Christians to commit themselves together (sometimes with non-Christians) to purchase products and services that show regard for humanity and its diversity. For example, a group of Christians might decide to frequent Dave's Digs—a restaurant providing a few quiet corners for the hearing impaired—even though they themselves have hearing as acute as dolphins. Although Dave's Digs supporters have a modest preference for the prices or menu next door, they patronize Dave's just so that there is a pleasant, public place for people living with hearing loss.

Having visited some Iowa farmers, college student Tim and the Swarts living just outside Las Vegas, we are ready to stop by Uncle Don's apartment in a New Haven Christian retirement center. For Don, and everyone else, markets "work" because they produce prices and generate income opportunities that signal those who own resources to produce valued products and services.

---

[1]See Michael Schut, ed., *Simpler Living, Compassionate Life: A Christian Perspective* (Denver: Living the Good News, 1999) for a variety of readings on simple living. See also "The Simple Resource Guide" <www.gallagherpress.com>.

For example, most senior citizens who show up at the local drug store demonstrate their willingness and ability (with insurance) to buy the latest drugs to treat their ailments. A few years ago, some ailments—like prostate cancer or impotency—simply would have had to be endured.

This is a good place to take note of how markets inform (but do not dictate) decisions by Christian consumers trying to exercise good stewardship of their money and other resources. If you brought a gift for your Uncle Don, you probably did not buy a Western string "bolo" tie, even though it was on sale, because nobody born after 1935 would wear one! That would be cheap, but still wasteful, because even Uncle Don would not wear the tie. Neither did you bring him a new computerized toilet that washes and dries off the user (only in Japan are these toilets standard in homes) with the push of a few buttons. Good stewardship of your uncle's resources (for whom you are the designated trustee) suggests that you wait a few years until market competition has cut their price in half. After all, Uncle Don is still a spry seventy-year-old.

For Don and others with good medical insurance, drug companies meet their needs for medicine because their purchases are sufficiently large to encourage pharmaceutical companies to develop drugs targeted to treat thousands of ailments. New drugs and medical procedures can also extend the years of full marital intimacy and enhance the appearance of older persons. For this reason Christian economists do not casually accept accusations that for-profit drug companies are failing to meet health needs. Obviously, they are satisfying a vast array of the public's health needs.

The challenge for Christians, and all others concerned about the high cost of some drugs, is to devise measures that extend access to medicines to many not now covered by insurance. However, these measures can be successful only if they do not compromise the ability of markets to continue serving the vast majority of First World people (we will discuss related Third World issues in chap. 8). No wholesale revolution in health care that seriously constrained market forces could solve the problem of uncovered families—unless, of course, we were willing to sacrifice some other clearly important needs like safe travel, education and policing. Furthermore, no single system could meet all needs for medicine without in some way impairing further private-sector development of drugs to meet current and future needs here and elsewhere.

Christians who want to engage intelligently in public debate about how governments, private firms and voluntary agencies should collaborate to meet the health needs of priority groups—especially those with low incomes, including some seniors and families with young children—must weigh expected benefits against costs. (See chap. 3 for more on cost-benefit analysis.) To the extent that governments take on a greater role, the costs must be covered by collecting more tax revenue from households and businesses (who have other legitimate priorities). The costs may also produce adverse side effects for the very people a new prescription drug program is meant to serve.

For a parallel example, consider the paperwork and fee schedules required by the federal government for doctors who treat Medicaid recipients. Those burdens have led many physicians, reluctantly, to stop taking new Medicaid patients or to leave poorer areas altogether. A statement made to the Practicing Physicians Advisory Council, the American College of Physicians, reports that 30 percent of all family physicians refuse to accept new Medicaid patients, and according to a 2002 survey 24 percent of responding physicians either have lowered the number of Medicaid patients they are willing to treat, or plan to do so within the following six months (American College of Physicians 2003, pp. 5-6).

Whenever community needs are not fully met by markets and existing government programs, Christians should consider how to bridge the gaps—whether for basic drugs or childcare. They have done this since the church was founded in Jerusalem and deacons were ordained to look after poor widows. Christians have the calling, the means and the gifts to provide services ranging from education to care for persons with physical and mental limitations. However, Christians do not, by virtue of their faith, have solutions to fill all the gaps. Neither do Christian economists have a special corner on shaping the best systems.

The issues of unmet needs require Christian involvement at grassroots levels and in government posts, but can never be programmed away. In a famous quotation from the Old Testament law Jesus said, "You will always have the poor among you" (Mt 26:11). Everyone who heard him say this also could recite the rest of the original verse, "I am commanding you to share freely with the poor and with other Israelites in need" (Deut 15:11).

THE POWER OF DYNAMIC MARKETS

One of the persistent criticisms of markets—by Christians and others—has been the way they appear to churn out new goods and jobs at the expense of old crafts, social habits, communities and faith. Karl Marx applauded the great power of capitalism, saying, "It [the bourgeoisie] has accomplished wonders far surpassing Egyptian pyramids, Roman aqueducts, and Gothic cathedrals; it has conducted expeditions that put in the shade all former Exoduses of nations and crusades" (Tucker 1978, p. 476). However, he condemned capitalism for its tendency to treat workers as tools and to make them vulnerable to massive unemployment. Marx mocked capitalists for their claim that capitalism offered "freedom." The hiring of women and children by industrialists, their "enslavement" of workers in inhumane factories, and their payment of subhuman wages suggested to him anything but freedom.

Unfortunately, Marx attracted a huge following, without ever mapping out an alternative to markets that would not degenerate into government tyranny in place of markets and personal freedom. Those who led Marxist revolutions in Mexico (the first such revolution, but one that did not lead to the confiscation of all private property), Russia, China and Vietnam had to ad-lib to build their economies without adequate market signals. Changing market prices would have allowed producers to respond to changing demands and encouraged them to increase efficiency—thereby raising living standards. Instead, without the benefit of either market signals or a popular voice in government, these societies wasted precious resources on extraordinarily inefficient factories and corrupt officials.

The rest is history, since none of those nations still adheres completely to a communist economic and political system. Communism is incapable of providing high living standards using top-down directives. Citizens paid dearly for a system that failed to utilize the tremendous energy and knowledge that are embedded in ordinary people everywhere, and can be released only if people freely make their own choices about buying, selling and working. Because it relied on plans and orders, their system had no way to induce people to fully engage themselves in innovation and production. Furthermore, communist propaganda aimed to replace religious motivations and broad self-interest with "worship" of the "Dear Leader" and rewards for those who turned their neighbors over to the authorities.

The plain truth is that no nation can achieve material, cultural and moral greatness unless it offers extensive freedom of choice to workers, consumers, producers and voters. Freedom is a worthy objective in itself. After all, virtues like saving, sharing and hard work are empty without freedom to choose between these and the alternatives—overspending, stinginess and loafing on the job. The moral superiority of political and economic systems that offer lots of room for choices by individual and groups is matched by their superior outcomes in terms of efficiency and living standards. This is so because consumers, businesses and workers are free to respond to changing market prices based on intimate knowledge of their own values, desires and local resources. Higher gasoline prices, for example, provide the most effective incentive to cut down on gas purchases, in favor of alternatives ranging from more fuel-efficient cars to alternative fuels. A rise in gasoline prices also creates strong incentives for producers to adopt newer, fuel-efficient technologies and bring alternative energy systems on line (ranging from wind to nuclear power).

Price changes create incentives that encourage innovation and substitution. However, when governments rely more on regulation than on rising market prices—for example, by requiring the purchase of bio-mass fuels or setting standards for average fuel efficiency of auto company fleets, the overall rate of innovation in the energy industry slows down. Such methods fail to channel consumer choice away from rising gas prices toward substitutes; they simultaneously reduce the power of profit incentives to elicit faster development of alternatives by businesses.[2]

Markets allow for free choices by consumers, producers and workers. The resulting incentives, presented by changing prices, favor innovation and higher living standards. However, freedom always means change—and change creates some losers (especially in the short run) as well as winners. For example, some older citizens are unable to adapt easily to rapid physical, cultural and economic changes—especially those that affect their ability to stay close to friends, get to grocery stores and support themselves. Those who do not like market-driven changes often yearn for a return to the "good ole days." The good ole days are often misremembered. One of the unintended consequences of the 2002 PBS *Frontier House* series—in which modern families took up homesteading for a period of six months—was that most viewers lost any rosy sentiment for the "homey" and "earthy" life of earlier times. The children of each generation accept the challenges and new opportunities that come with social-economic changes, just as their ancestors bravely left the "known" world for the frontier. For the children, home is for memories, not

---

[2]An example of inherently inconsistent government rules (interfering with price incentives) are the billions of gallons of blended corn-based ethanol-gasoline fuel now mandated by Congress, plus expensive tax credits providing almost a 50 percent subsidy to ethanol producers, at a time when those options are made even more expensive by trade barriers that prevent import of much cheaper sugar-based ethanol from other countries. See James Surowiecki "The Financial Page Deal Sweeteners," *The New Yorker*, Nov. 27, 2006, p. 92. See chap. 5 for more reflection on government regulation versus price-based methods for addressing public concerns about energy and the environment.

necessarily a reason for staying put.

Since 1870 huge changes in America have reduced farming from half of all employment (Heilbroner and Sincer 1984, p. 245) to a mere 2.5 percent of the labor force by 2000 (U.S. Bureau of the Census 2001, table 593). Those changes left some towns without any young people and put urban populations more out of touch with nature. Nevertheless, the dramatic increase in farm productivity lowered food costs from about one third of the family budget in 1909 (U.S. Bureau of the Census 1975, pp. 416-94), to 13.4 percent in 1999 (U.S. Bureau of the Census 2001, table 657) and allowed millions of farm families to find employment in higher-paying manufacturing and service industries. Some industries that today employ hundreds of thousands were unknown at the time, for example, home insurance and small loan companies, television, aerospace, music recording, laser surgery, windsurfing, instant news service and dot-coms of all kinds.

If Americans were to say a blanket "no" to changes that bring new possibilities but also disrupt comfortable patterns, they would not enjoy currently high living standards. Students would be unable to explore an increasing array of possible callings through their future careers. Middle-aged and older Americans would not have the time and money for lifelong education. The U.S. president would certainly not have been able to propose, in his 2003 State of the Union message, that Congress double annual U.S. foreign economic aid to developing countries by 2006 (see chap. 8 on globalization). Everyone would have fewer choices in all aspects of life—jobs, schools, food and religious practices. We would not be free! We would be prevented from fully honoring God with our unique gifts to imagine, build, think and collaborate in love and service to our neighbors far and near.

It is easy to subscribe to freedom when thinking about the material, intellectual and spiritual benefits. But we are often tempted to propose limits on change with the hope of preserving certain jobs, protecting comfortable lifestyles and isolating people from their worst temptations. For example, some Christians and others support laws that limit urban growth (through minimum lot sizes and other regulations). The result, however, is often gentrification of city neighborhoods, thereby reserving urban amenities to those who can afford houses costing $500,000 or more (Vous 2003). The cost of the "good life" for a few is that many families must move to the suburbs and face maddening commutes, while poorer families pile up in older, rundown neighborhoods.

There are many other examples of well-meaning people urging lawmakers to protect certain values and situations from change. The measures employed all have the effect of limiting choices and reducing the dynamism of an economy. Thus, for example, barriers to trade with other countries protect some American jobs while simultaneously reducing the expansion of newer, cleaner and better-paid jobs.

Laws limiting foreign competition violate several of the Christian principles for economic life with which we began this book (for more on this subject see chap. 8). They undercut measures to provide jobs for the world's poorest people, and they fail to honor the unique and changing callings of every person. Furthermore, they show lack of respect for the personal freedom to exercise stewardship over one's resources according to conscience and personal taste. Trade barriers are un-Christian also because they impose government decisions on domestic consumers about what they may buy—preventing them from choosing the prices, qualities and styles that best meet their family needs.

Why should you be prevented by trade restrictions from acting on your understanding that Mexican mangoes are better for your allergies than Florida oranges? Why should your parents have to order Californian Chalk Hill Cabernet (at $50 per bottle) for your sister's wedding when their tastes and budget suggest a Chilean alternative, Chateau Los Boldos (at $10 per bottle)? Why should your poor Cambodian neighbor be kept from buying cheaper imported clothes and shoes for her children by strict quotas on imports.

In Holland, Michigan, where we live, the only LifeSavers plant in the country was recently closed and production was moved entirely to Canada. Was this a disaster for the community and unfair to workers? Many said so. The truth is that sugar from poor Caribbean nations is kept out of the United States in order to protect U.S. sugar beet and sugar-cane growers. As a result candy companies have to pay twice the world price for sugar—whose cost they pass on to consumers. Because Canadians do not discriminate against foreign sugar producers, sugar (the key input in candy) is much cheaper there. That fact alone made the relocation a no-brainer for LifeSavers' executives.

On the one hand, this example shows how trade barriers hurt foreign producers, Michigan workers in the food industry and candy junkies (including smokers trying to quit) throughout America. Import restrictions also keep the U.S. candy industry from being competitive in world markets. On the other hand, workers who lost their jobs at the Michigan LifeSavers plant started considering new opportunities. One woman, for example, decided to follow a dream to be in business for herself by opening her own sandwich shop. She went from bank to bank to locate one that would lend her the needed financing; she researched various franchises. None of this was easy, but she is having the time of her life! Think what she would have been doing without LifeSavers' move and if she did not live in an economy able to grow new jobs and businesses, year after year.

A former LifeSavers employee, who is my (Robin's) neighbor, has thrown herself back into the classroom, at age forty-five, to pursue a new career in physical therapy. The *Grand Rapids Press* reported many other instances where workers laid off during the slow economy of 2003 started new and better careers. Of course, better opportunities for some workers do not directly offset the pain felt by those who are not in a position to change occupations at their age or cannot relocate. But dynamic markets—always churning out new products, services and jobs—also grow the financial resources used by churches and communities to help job losers adapt and discover new and satisfying futures. It is an exciting fact of expanding market economies: they open up unimagined vistas for people who have been trapped in jobs with low potential to develop their talents and use their energy (see chap. 9 on rate of job growth).

Recalling the model we introduced in chapter one, a society that balances political democracy, free markets and strong moral/cultural institutions has at its disposal a multitude of ways for people to respond to inevitable changes without squelching progress or limiting freedom. Indeed, private voluntary organizations are particularly good at meeting immediate needs for shelter, budget counseling and help finding employment for those whose market opportunities and personal support networks are limited. They usually operate at the community level, where their knowledge of individuals and local resources allows them to tailor the help—so that it empowers rather than supplants personal initiative. For some purposes public monies as well may usefully be funneled through private community organizations.

In 1999 George W. Bush campaigned for the presidency on a proposal of "faith-based initiatives." Black, Koopman and Ryden (2004) provide an excellent evaluation of the issues surrounding these initiatives. Though somewhat vague, Bush promised to initiate legislative action that would enhance the longstanding practice of the federal government funding some social services through private voluntary groups (including religious groups). Supporters argue that religious groups often are more successful than government at meeting certain needs (e.g., help for poor people) because help from religious people is more personalized. Furthermore, it includes an emphasis on faith and values, on which more successful lives can be built.

At the time of the writing of this book the faith-based initiative has to be judged as only partially successful. Once elected the Bush administration was not able to formulate legislative proposals that could gain enough Democratic support in Congress for passage. As a result the president issued several executive orders, which required changes in the way federal funds are allocated. Specifically, whenever tax monies are channeled through private organizations, religious groups must be treated equally (in terms of eligibility) with nonreligious groups, so long as the faith-based groups do not use the funds received for specifically religious purposes.

Those who oppose this approach—including some religious and secular voices—argue that there is no way to prevent federal funds from being used for strictly religious purposes. Even though earmarked federal funds might not be used for evangelism, they enable churches to shift some of their own funds toward strictly religious activities. It is quite likely that the American public, Congress and the courts will continue to debate the constitutionality and accountability of tax-funded social services provided by religious groups. Furthermore, some religious groups (including colleges) are unwilling, in principle, to accept federal funding for their social outreach. They fear that government controls that come with funding could make it difficult to conduct their ministries in ways that allow faith to permeate all of life (see chap. 11).

In Holland, Michigan, a multichurch network was created to help recently unemployed people search for jobs and prepare themselves to qualify for openings. Not all jobs would be found locally. In another example, one of our friends, a local Hispanic teacher, was welcomed into the homes of a Texas Christian family to help her search for new opportunities there for herself and her husband. If she had not lost her position at a charter school in Michigan, she would never have met those Christians or discovered a chance-of-a-lifetime for her husband to train for a new vocation as a high school teacher (instead of continuing to languish in Michigan as a factory worker with a college degree)!

Market change is part of what Christians mean when they say "God does not close some doors without opening others." Most Americans would not choose to live in a society that routinely gave preference to a safe status quo over chances for people to realize big dreams by undertaking risky challenges. (In telling the "parable of the talents"—which regards spiritual matters—Jesus appears to encourage careful, forward-looking investments of one's life and finances, trusting in God to reward efforts made in his service; see Mt 25:14-30.) A society that undergirds free markets with strong moral and cultural institutions has the best of all worlds yet attempted in history. The challenge for Christians and others is to uphold this threefold system and to infuse it with high values—reflected in their votes, spending and collaboration with others to meet outstanding material and spiritual needs.

IS ECONOMIC GROWTH GOOD FOR PEOPLE?

By now Tim and the Swarts are a distant memory on this chapter's trip to illustrate the ways that markets work for the good of participants, as long as Christians and others are allowed to operate relatively freely (i.e., without burdensome regulations) and use markets as channels for putting their resources to work for God's glory. Our next stop is west Michigan, just after World War II. Muskegon, a lumber town, had boomed during the late nineteenth and early twentieth centuries, but the lumber business in west Michigan gave way to furniture and other industries. Men have work, families enjoy peacetime pursuits again, and lakeshore artists have earned a national reputation after depending initially on the patronage of rich lumber barons.

It is such a good time and place that many people expect the future to seamlessly stretch out before them with more picket fences, green lawns and new church plants. What they do not know is that wooden office furniture will give way to furniture manufactured with manmade materials and designed to fit different body shapes and style preferences. Even many office walls will be gone by the late twentieth century.

Eventually, local foundries and small furniture businesses will close, and some fathers will bemoan the fact that their sons can no longer expect lifetime employment with high school degrees or less. Only later will they discover that their more educated sons have found better jobs, including designing and selling new office furniture in markets as far away as China. Indeed, some sons will do this without leaving western Michigan, while others will take up new careers that require further education but also allow them to follow their dreams. Their daughters will surpass their sons in attendance at local universities, go on to jobs around the world and do some of their work over the Internet from their homes.[3]

According to critics of economic growth the above picture is an example of

---

[3]This example was inspired by Roberts (2001).

insatiable appetites for luxuries and a corrupted faith. Decent furniture is one thing. But who "needs" an ergonomic office chair? Christian daughters seemed happy enough as stay-at-home mothers. And if the 1950s produced rapid church growth, wouldn't more wealth simply be a temptation to materialism? Today Christian critics of growth add, Who needs fresh vegetables out of season, when families could buy local produce and can food for the winter. Who needs a new toy, DVD or trip to Disney World? Isn't economic growth just a vehicle for materialism—at the expense of displaced local workers, the environment, society and our souls?

Since the late twentieth century, worries about the negative spiritual effects of economic growth (like those above) have been augmented by concerns about the ability of the earth to sustain economic growth. A popular image is one of the "earth groaning under the weight of our foolishness" (Bouma-Prediger 2003). In addition, many Christian commentators suggest that what the world needs is a more equal distribution of existing incomes—to be made possible by holding down present living standards in the West and sending more aid to the Third World. (We will deal with this latter question more fully in chap. 8, about globalization and the Third World.)

Swedish statistician Bjørn Lomborg (2001b) offers a stunning response to doom sayings about the purported connection between economic growth and damage to the environment. After studying the most reliable public data available, he concludes:

> We are not running out of energy or natural resources. There will be more and more food per head of the world's population. Fewer and fewer people are starving. In 1900 we lived for an average of 30 years; today we live for 67 (averages for the entire world). According to the UN we have reduced poverty more in the last 50 years than we did in the preceding 500, and it has been reduced in practically every country. Nor will we lose 25-50 percent of all species in our lifetime—in fact we are losing probably 0.7 percent. Acid rain does not kill the forests, and the air and water around us are becoming less and less polluted. (p. 4)

Apparently, the sky is not falling. Lomborg goes on to say that just because things are getting better does not mean that we should do nothing.

> The food situation has vastly improved, but in 2010 there will still be 680 million people starving, which is obviously not *good enough*. The distinction is essential; when things are not doing well enough we can sketch out a vision; fewer people must starve. This is our political aim. But when things are improving we know we are on the right track. Although perhaps not at the right speed. Maybe

we can do even more to improve the food situation, but the basic approach is not wrong. (p. 5)

Lomborg's book made such an impression on public dialogue that it has been followed with a book (Lomberg 2001a) in which Nobel Prize-winning economists and other experts discuss how best to prioritize public efforts to address what they identify as the ten greatest global challenges: climate change, infectious diseases, hunger, access to water and so forth. This is exactly what needs to happen whenever societies face serious collective problems, namely, to examine the costs and benefits of successive measures to address each problem and to establish a priority for implementation based on the relative urgency of each problem compared to the cost of known means to address them.

If the earth is not groaning due to rising incomes and wealth, perhaps souls in the First World have been made sick. Data could easily be gathered to support that judgment: widespread use of pornography, high divorce rates, violence and the like. However, there is also counter evidence. Violent crime in the United States actually fell over the last two decades of the twentieth century—from 5,950 in 1980 to 4,267 in 1999 per 100,000 people (U.S. Bureau of the Census 2001, table 291). At the end of the twentieth century, 68–70 percent of Americans reported themselves to be religious (unchanged since 1980), while 44 percent (an increase of four percentage points over 1980) attended church at sometime during the previous week (U.S. Bureau of the Census 2001, table 66).

In the year 2000, 89 percent of U.S. households made charitable contributions, with the average contributing household giving $1,620 (i.e., 3.1 percent of their income; church attendees gave more than twice as much as nonattendees). In the same year 42 percent of the U.S. adult population both gave money and volunteered, with volunteers averaging twenty-four hours per month of time given to formal organizations (Independent Sector 2001). Especially encouraging are rates of volunteering by U.S. high school students, which rose to a fifty-year high of 67 percent by 1996 (Independent Sector 2002).

We are aware of no study that has demonstrated a connection between economic growth in America and any downward social trends. Economic growth is neither good nor bad in itself. The same observation is often made about medical and other technology. Medical discoveries can be used for the good of reducing pain and extending life and its quality, or to endlessly remove the signs of age from the faces of the wealthy. Engineering skills can be used to build bullet trains or to make terrorist bombs invisible to screening machines. The same is true of education: it can be used to prepare students for service or to initiate them into worship of the mind. Economic growth, as well, enhances the opportunities for good and bad. Most economists favor economic growth because, overall, it increases choices available to consumers and workers in terms of different goods and lifestyles. The Las Vegas Swarts are an example. They are able to live a simple life and farm organically precisely because more people can now afford higher-priced organic fruit and vegetables than before.

Economic growth makes it possible for us, Victor and Robin, to be professors while others repair our roofs, manufacture our computers, publish the international news we read and provide quality care to our bedridden relatives. What we do with the enhanced opportunities is always a spiritual challenge. With the help of a computer we could use the time we save to gamble or to visit a grandmother in a nursing home. We could immerse ourselves in international news and domestic political debates and forget about being good neighbors. We could be seduced by a desire to show off with expensive sports cars or by putting our advanced degrees on display in conversations with others. Alternatively, we could teach our students about connections between economics and Christian faith and also worship in a largely blue-collar congregation.

Christian churches and their members have a challenge: to understand modern culture, scientific discoveries and political and economic issues, and to help people meet the new opportunities and temptations that come along. We believe Christians should be slow to condemn whole trends and reluctant to paint them as necessarily mateialistic, secular and outright evil. A better understanding of the complex workings of markets helps, but must never lead to moral arrest. As this book unfolds, readers will encounter constant challenges to undergird markets with faithful reflection, careful choices and loving action.

There is a long history of critics blaming markets for causing materialism, undermining spiritual values and disrupting communities. The well-known economist and political scientist Charles E. Lindblom (2002) has written an excellent summary of those criticisms and of efforts to test them against the facts in real market economies. He points to recent research that attempts to track the possible influence of markets on personality and culture. The research finds that "societies [*sic*] aspirations for a challenging job, friendships, and the pleasures of children and family rank higher than do aspirations for more money or more market products" (p. 199). Despite fears that markets undermine communities and convert human relations into opportunities for individuals to profit at the expense of others, the research shows that "participants in the market system interact with and enjoy a wider circle of interactions than did their ancestors in premarket societies" (p. 201). A recent study of fifteen thousand Americans (*Grand Rapids Press* 2006b) reports that less crowded suburban neighborhoods are correlated with increased time spent conversing with neighbors. These findings hold across racial, educational and income differences. They run counter to frequent criticism of urban sprawl, namely, that it has led to a sociologically less "rich" American culture. Apparently, one of the outcomes of rising incomes—movement into suburbs—is actually good for knitting people together!

Furthermore, writes Lindbloom:

> when whole societies become relatively wealthy, as in Western Europe and North America, they tend to develop in their members the kinds of personality traits that Western thought has long prized: higher levels of moral reasoning, self-reliance, sense of responsibility, and capacity to handle cognitive complexity. . . . Some research makes an even stronger claim: that not only wealth but market participation itself tends to produce these and other qualities of character. Market participants, engaged as they are in never-ending choices, see themselves as in control of themselves and their lives. They see their own decisions as making a difference to both the near future and to live aspirations. (p. 209)

These results confirm our own observations and understanding of markets. They offer more abundance, opportunity and freedom than any alternative, and they depend for their effectiveness on the widespread practice of certain virtues, like honesty and the willingness to work hard for one's dreams. By themselves markets do not produce either virtue or depravity. As Christian economists we believe that God, not the market system, is the ultimate source of virtue, meaning and happiness. For precisely this reason our vision of a good society is one in which democracy and market exchanges are undergirded by organizations and communities of faith (see chap. 11 on social and moral capital).

By producing higher incomes, economic growth offers unprecedented opportunities for giving as well as consuming. One of the Christian principles for economic life presented in chapter one is that societies should find ways to provide for the poor and disadvantaged. In addition to opportunities for work, many people need better access to education and health care in order to live more meaningful and productive lives. Throughout this book we insist that

Christians must never avoid their biblical calling, and God's command, to give their time and money in support of thoughtful efforts to help those in need.

To the surprise of many, a recent economic study provides extensive and convincing evidence that religious conservatives (who tend to live in traditional families and reject a prominent role for government in income redistribution, through taxation and special programs) are much more generous givers than secular liberals (who tend to support a strong role for government in income redistribution). And religious conservatives' giving is greater both to religious and to secular charities (*Grand Rapids Press* 2006a).

To what extent is it possible to be faithful in one's obligations to the needy and also enjoy many aspects of material progress? This is the subject of an excellent book by John R. Schneider (2002), *The Good of Affluence*. We are convinced by his study of the Scriptures that one way Christians may affirm the grace of God is by enjoying new possibilities that higher productivity and rising incomes afford them. For an American Christian family, a higher income may allow them to visit Hawaii, something that only the wealthy could do in the "ideal" 1950s. For a Mexican Christian family, a higher income may allow them to send their children to college, something that was impossible for poor families in the 1960s. For a rich Ethiopian entrepreneur, in partnership with a committed Catholic doctor, it may be possible to create a small U.S. research company dedicated to producing an AIDS vaccine that will be affordable to most of the thirty million Africans infected with HIV (an actual case involving a family member of one of the authors). For all of them, higher incomes may mean occasional feasting to celebrate a new job, wedding, graduation or holiday. Better vacations, education, vaccines and feasts only become possible as people everywhere use their God-given talents to produce more valuable products and services and thereby earn higher incomes than did their parents and grandparents.

Churches should help people understand that God wants us to be grateful, to enjoy and to share—all three. If we cannot enjoy (as well as share) higher incomes and new opportunities, we will have misunderstood God's intentions to bless his people in a myriad of ways, including materially.

MARKETS AND PROVIDENCE

In this chapter we have used a trip motif to illustrate certain aspects of markets. They direct resources (which are finite at any one point in time, and therefore scarce relative to our wants) to their optimal use. Thus, as wants and production technologies change, markets induce movements of workers and materials toward new places and uses. The capacity to induce innovation and respond to change is built into the nature of markets. Such change often involves both general advances and some unpleasant side effects, like unemployment for those whose jobs have moved to some other city or country (see more in chap. 8 about globalization).

We argued that change is inevitable and that markets generally serve as inducements for changes that ultimately serve the vast majority of consumers, workers and their communities. We suggested that most efforts to use the law to hold back economic change are misguided. They interfere with the essential liberty of persons and groups to evaluate and act on their own priorities, and they close off new horizons.

The market system, like other social and biological systems, operates without a central command. Nobody has to tell someone in Wisconsin to send building materials to New Orleans after a hurricane destroys homes and businesses there. The rising demand for materials provides an incentive to those who can supply the needs. Of course, for Floridians without insurance or federal assistance to rebuild, national charities and churches may lend a hand. The bulk of the rebuilding, however, takes place because markets interact in ways to make it happen.

Markets elicit new ideas, create jobs, solve consumption problems and grow incomes that may be dedicated, in part, to helping others. The inherent freedom, creativity and ability to coordinate collective action—made possible in market economies imbedded in democracy and supported by strong moral/cultural institutions—are marvels to behold. Adam Smith, the eighteenth-century "father of economics," was the first to portray markets as amazing mechanisms for directing resources to benefit the common man. His famous "Invisible Hand"—at work in markets through competition—depended for its success on the presence of a strong moral climate and the rule of law.

Market economies are not the creation of any one person or culture. They are not the servants of one sort of society or the weapons of a few great powers. They are dynamic, open-ended and overwhelmingly democratic in their response to personal choices. Higher prices call forth resources to bring them down. Jobs with the potential to fit changing callings and meet responsibilities tend to replace those that are static and limited.

We believe that markets are, as Klay and Lunn (2003b) have argued, one way in which God's providence works to sustain and bless humankind. The biological world and celestial dynamics call forth a sense of wonder. They inspire poets and hymn writers. We marvel at the ability of species to adapt to new conditions and thereby save their descendants from extinction. Even so, when populous regions are devastated by natural disasters, we do not doubt that God's providence is still at work everywhere through nature, calling forth untold blessings. As the prophet Isaiah declared, "The LORD's arm is not too weak to save you" (Is 59:1). Likewise, although human beings may use markets to pursue evil, as well as good, we do not doubt that, under God's providential care, markets coordinate billions of free decisions that ultimately bless many.

FOR FURTHER READING

Sacks, Jonathan. 1999. *Morals and markets.* London: Institute of Economic Affairs. In this book, chief rabbi and professor Jonathan Sacks asks whether free markets can be moral. Relying on insights of Austrian economist Friedrich August Hayek, the author acknowledges the role of morality in sustaining free markets and their limits—when market forces intrude in other domains of human life. Three important commentaries in his essay are provided by others interested in the impact of religion on markets and vice versa.

Stapleford, John E. 2002. *Bulls, bears, & golden calves: Applying Christian ethics in economics.* Downers Grove, Ill.: InterVarsity Press. This book provides a good survey of biblical teaching about caring for the poor. It also explores a variety of concrete suggestions regarding ways to alleviate poverty, including possible partnerships between governments and faith-based organizations. Though not all equally sound, the author's suggestions should provoke good discussion and further thought.

3

PUBLIC FINANCE

The Role of Government in
the Provision of Goods and Services

In earlier chapters we suggested that markets facilitate order even through the apparent chaos of individuals pursuing their mutual benefit. Economists believe that individuals should be free to conduct voluntary exchanges that are mutually beneficial—as long as others are not harmed in the process. That is, most economists believe that it would be inappropriate to impede voluntary transactions between two individuals for any reason short of negative spillover effects, like air pollution, onto others. Accordingly, if there are opportunities for two people to make themselves better off through exchange, without harming others in the process, economists want to encourage such transactions, believing that they lead to unambiguous benefits to society.

Further, economists rejoice when their neighbors are able to make themselves better off without harming others. Moreover, Christians should also celebrate their neighbors' good fortune in such circumstances. Of course, this is one of the hardest things for us humans to do joyfully. Nevertheless, we must be happy for our neighbors, and not be like the brother of the prodigal son. Failing to rejoice in others' good fortune can only be a reflection of our own envy or jealousy.

For these and other reasons, we have made the case that the role of government should be one that improves on the outcomes arrived at through market forces alone. But the design and implementation of new policy requires a thorough consideration of all consequences—whether intended or unintended. Often, even if they follow from the very best and most Christian intentions, new policy actions may lead to unfortunate results that surprise even the policymakers themselves. In fact, sometimes new policies can get in the way of the proper functioning of markets—the bringing together of individuals to engage in mutually beneficial exchange.

Therefore, because there is a proper role for government in the economy, we need government. But we also require a thorough consideration of the potential benefits and costs of any policy proposal; careful stewardship demands it. This chapter (and the one that follows) considers, from both Christian and economic perspectives, the ways government can improve on the outcomes we would observe if unbridled market interaction were the only available avenue for the provision of goods and services.

In this chapter we discuss the motivating reasons that a society may rightly choose to let the public sector—rather than private firms or individuals—serve as the provider of some specific goods or services. Government provides a key role in supplying goods that might otherwise go unprovided or underprovided by the private sector.

SPILLOVER EFFECTS

If economic analysis were as simple as described earlier—that society unambiguously improves its well-being as all mutually advantageous trades are exhausted—then economic policy design would also be simple: economic policy should help identify potential mutually beneficial exchanges and encourage their execution. And, to be sure, this is an important role that should be played by policymakers everywhere. Whenever there are low-cost ways to bring potential trading partners even closer together, government should carry them out. This could, for example, include working to bring the unemployed together with potential employers, and also ensuring that there is a high degree of match between the skills of a job candidate and the skills required for a particular job opening. By serving its citizens in this role, government has the potential to reduce search time for the unemployed, provide meaningful opportunities for work and simultaneously encourage longer-term economic growth and stability.

But economic analysis is not that simple. Often, as two parties engage in mutually beneficial exchange, innocent bystanders are harmed. Secondhand smoke is one simple example. When a consumer who enjoys smoking purchases cigarettes and smokes them, the smoker enjoys the cigarette and the seller values the money received more than the cigarettes sold to the smoker. The seller and consumer enjoy a mutually beneficial market exchange. But the smoker and the seller are not the only parties to this transaction. Others near the smoker can be harmed. And the potential harm takes several forms. First, if the bystanders do not enjoy the smell of cigarettes, then they will be less well off than they would be otherwise because of the unpleasant smell. Second, there is a health risk associated with secondhand smoke; even if they are non-smokers, bystanders who inhale the cigarette smoke of others will also face health risks. And third, the smell will probably attach itself to the clothing of the nonsmokers. If so, then the nonsmokers will smell like smoke the rest of the day—unpleasant for them as well as for other nonsmokers they encounter. Moreover, if any of those clothing items require dry cleaning, the nonsmokers will probably take those clothes to the cleaner sooner than they would have otherwise, resulting in an explicit monetary outlay by the nonsmokers.

Therefore, in this case, smoking by some consumers results in a negative spillover onto others not involved in the market transaction—the purchase and sale of the cigarettes.

There are many other examples of how our fellow consumers can harm us when they pursue their self-interest. These include loud music we do not care for, drinking and driving, and smelly perfume.

But spillovers of market exchange onto others are often not bad ones. In fact, they have the potential to be very nice. When your neighbor plants flowers in his or her yard, you might benefit from their beauty as you view them from your house, or you might occasionally enjoy their fragrance when the winds blow in just the right direction. If your neighbor is a master gardener, his or her gardening might even lead to an eventual financial benefit to you: if the marvelous landscaping makes your street seem like a nicer place to live, you might enjoy an increase in the property values on your street.

Therefore, by pursuing their own self-interest other consumers have the potential to harm or benefit you along the way. But spillover effects like these are not limited to the activities of consumers; producers of goods and services may create similar spillover effects as well. Normally, we tend to think only of the harmful spillovers caused by firms, like air and water pollution, noise or an ugly factory. But sometimes we freely benefit from the self-interested activities of firms. When we walk past a bakery, we enjoy the marvelous aroma. Sometimes, because the land is cheap, a firm that wants to put up a new building will buy property that is currently covered with ugly, abandoned, old buildings. If the landscape improves when the firm razes the old buildings and erects the new, everyone in the neighborhood benefits.

Economists have a very specific name for spillover effects such as these, whether positive or negative, or whether they are caused by the actions of producers or consumers. Economists call these spillovers externalities. The late economist Paul Heyne provides a helpful, intuitive definition: externalities are consequences of actions that the actor need not consider when making a decision.

Sometimes externalities are negative (smelly perfume or noise pollution) and sometimes they are positive (nice landscaping or a bakery aroma). In the case of negative externalities the cost of the externality-generating activity to society is greater than the one considered by the firm or consumer causing the negative external effect. That is, while the parties engaged in the market part of the activity (the buyer and the seller) enjoy a net mutual benefit, some of us are simultaneously incurring a cost not borne by either the seller or the buyer.

With positive externalities the total social benefit is even greater than the net benefit enjoyed by those involved in the market part of the activity. Suppose that you replace an old, shabby jacket with a new jacket that really suits you in fit and color. Of course the seller benefits, valuing your money in the cash drawer more than he or she values the jacket in the inventory. And you benefit, since you will feel good about your appearance and will be protected from the elements. But others may benefit as well, if your appearance in the new jacket makes you generally more enjoyable to be around.

An obvious role for government, then, is to improve on market outcomes by encouraging more of the activities that generate positive external effects. If society enjoys a benefit beyond that considered by the parties to the transaction, then a wise government would do well to introduce policies that encourage more of those activities.

On the other hand, negative externalities result when the producers or consumers creating the spillover are not forced to consider the full cost to society of their actions. For example, the reason that firms pollute is because they can use some natural resources (like clean air) to dispose of waste without paying for doing so. If there were a way to make a firm consider the full cost of all of its actions, it would reduce its activity levels. Therefore, just as wise economic policy should encourage more of those activities that lead to positive externalities, it should also discourage the activities that lead to negative ones.

Stated another way, one role of government is to gently nudge the suboptimal outcomes that sometimes result from market outcomes closer to the outcomes we would all hope for given a full accounting of *all* of the social benefits and costs of any activity. Government can nudge markets to provide more of a good when others externally benefit, and nudge markets to produce less when others are being externally harmed.

The remainder of this chapter considers the extreme case of a positive externality: a situation in which multiple individuals may simultaneously enjoy the full benefit of a good or service once it exists, and there is no reasonable way to exclude them. The appropriate role of government is to provide such a good.

BENEFICIAL AND WIDESPREAD SPILLOVER EFFECTS

Markets do an impressive job of moving our precious resources to uses that benefit all of us. But sometimes markets fail too. In the case of negative spillovers, innocent third parties get hurt. The appropriate role of government, then, is to discourage the harmful activity.

Sometimes, though, spillover effects are positive rather than negative. In particular, there are certain goods that, once they exist, may be enjoyed by many individuals simultaneously. One such good is national defense. Nations like Canada and Mexico, due to their geographic proximity to—and friendly relations with—the United States, do not need to provide much in the way of their own defensive capabilities. They are able to enjoy the spillover effects of the vast defensive resources of their friendly neighbor, the United States. In the event of an assault on any of the nations of North America, the United States would quickly mobilize to defend the entire region from the attack—not just the individuals within its immediate borders.

Further, there is no easy, low-cost way to prohibit nations such as Canada and Mexico from behaving in this way. The United States will continue to defend the entire region, regardless of whether Canada or Mexico makes a financial contribution to the effort. As a result, there are limited incentives for nations like Canada and Mexico to mount their own extensive national defense programs.

Economists call goods such as national defense "public goods." In order for a good to qualify as a public good, it must possess two essential properties. First, like national defense, the good must be *nonexcludable at a reasonable cost*. That is, it is cost prohibitive for the owner of the good to try to keep others who have not paid for its use from using it anyway. Second, the good must be *nonrival in its consumption*. This means that, unlike candy bars or sweaters, many individuals may consume the same good simultaneously. All users of the good derive the same individual benefit because there is always enough for everyone.

A lighthouse is another classic example of a public good. There is no good way to prohibit a second ship from using a lighthouse at the same time as another ship. Further, many ships nearing a harbor may navigate their courses using, simultaneously, the lighthouse as a guide. Moreover, one ship's use of the lighthouse does not diminish in any way the benefit of the lighthouse to another ship using the lighthouse at exactly the same moment. Hence, a lighthouse is a public good because it is (1) nonexcludable at reasonable cost and (2) nonrival in consumption. Note that whether a particular good qualifies as a public good has nothing to do with who is paying for the provision of the good.

Due to the nonexcludable nature of public goods, markets fail to induce producers of goods and services to provide the socially optimal quantities of these goods. Why would a private entrepreneur ever consider producing a good or service that could be used for free by anyone who wanted to use it? There is no incentive for entrepreneurs to produce such goods precisely because they are nonexcludable at reasonable cost.

Nevertheless, things like lighthouses, national defense, city streets and streetlamps, sidewalks, and law enforcement services are nice things to have around, even though there are limited incentives for private entrepreneurs to supply them. As a result, we rely on government to provide such goods and services. Since private markets, acting on their own, supply less than the socially optimal quantity of public goods, government plays a pivotal role in supplying the public goods and services that private individuals might not.

When governments at any level—national, state or municipal—decide whether or not to undertake a particular public-good project, they often employ one or more economists to carry out a "cost-benefit analysis." The idea behind cost-benefit analysis is that, prior to the construction of a new street or bridge, government should consider explicitly whether the benefit that will accrue to society from a completed project is greater than the outlays required to produce it.

Cost-benefit analysis is not new. As early as 1900 the United States Army Corps of Engineers employed cost-benefit analysis in order to evaluate various water-resource projects. In fact, since 1981 all proposed federal regulations in the United States must undergo a cost-benefit analysis.

In some ways, the *positive* spillovers of public goods are simpler for government to deal with in practice than *negative* spillovers like pollution. For example, in deciding whether or not to carry out a proposed new project, government need only consider whether society would be better off with it than without it; government will undertake any project for which the anticipated net social benefit is positive. That is, as long at the net social benefit of a specific project appears greater than zero, the project should be recommended for completion. Of course, not all projects that pass a cost-benefit analysis can be completed given the funds available. Therefore, an important second step is the ranking of each project according to its perceived net social benefit.

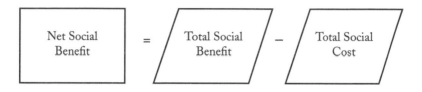

Figure 3.1. Net social benefit

Unfortunately, though, there are also several pitfalls involved in conducting a cost-benefit analysis. While it is normally a very easy thing to calculate the total social cost—the price tag—of a proposed project, estimating the total social benefit can be subject to many pitfalls. For example, if a health care project has been proposed, how do we estimate the value—in dollars—of the health-enhancing services that will be provided? Or if a project has been proposed in the United States that will result in positive spillover effects onto Canadian citizens, should we consider the beneficial effects on Canadians in evaluating the project? Or should the windfall to Canadians not be considered since they will not be paying to help fund the project?

Let's consider five such pitfalls in cost-benefit analysis, revealing how compassionate, thoughtful Christians should responsibly think about them. We will draw upon the work of economists Richard Tresch (2002) and William Trumbull (1990) in describing the pitfalls and also in discussing how we all should approach them. The ways that a professional economist must deal with such considerations are consonant with our biblical principles of economic life.

PITFALL 1: COUNTING JOB CREATION AS ALL BENEFIT AND NO COST

Often, when trying to sell a particular new public-goods project to the taxpayers who will be paying for it, politicians point to the large number of new jobs that will be created to build a new federal building or replace an old bridge.

The politicians are trying to sell us on the idea that job creation is all gain: that it is costless to society.

As any economist would point out, though, nothing ever comes at no cost whatsoever. This is precisely what economists mean when they joke that there is "no such thing as a free lunch." Stated another way, attending a sporting event or the theater for free, even if someone has given you free tickets, is not really free. The cost you incur by attending the event is the value of the time you give up in order to attend. For example, perhaps—instead of attending the event—you could spend that evening relaxing at home, learning to play the oboe, playing with your children or teaching English as a second language. Because there is always something else you could be doing, no activity ever comes at no cost. There is no free lunch.

There is also no free lunch when it comes to job creation. Tresch (2002) refers to the political ploy of selling the jobs created from a public goods project as all benefit—and no cost—as *the labor game* (pp. 823-25).

In economics, all resources that may be used in productive activities of any kind are viewed as precious and limited. Our earth, fresh air, clean water, the creative insights of entrepreneurs, human skills and knowledge that we acquire through education or experience, and humanity itself—all of these are valuable resources to be treasured and not to be consumed arbitrarily. Economists bristle when they overhear someone say that they are "just killing time." For the serious economist, time is too precious to kill. And for the Christian economist, "just killing time" is not good stewardship.

Combining the ideas that all resources—earth, people, time and talents—are precious, and that there is no free lunch leads to a powerful conclusion: job creation is rightly viewed as a cost in cost-benefit analysis. We must not arbitrarily throw our valuable human resources at the first available opportunity for them to keep busy. We must always recognize that every hour a person spends in one task is an hour not spent at some other activity. Someone working to build a new bridge, for example, could always find an alternative use for that time—whether it is leisure, other forms of work or a course of study that might lead to enhanced employment opportunities in the future. This idea is no different from the idea that each tree harvested for timber to build someone's first home is, simultaneously, a tree no longer available to be enjoyed for its natural beauty or to participate in its ecosystem.

Donald Hay (1991) enumerates eight biblical principles for economic life. Among them are "[e]very person has a calling to exercise stewardship of resources and talents," and "[w]ork is the means of exercising stewardship" (pp. 72-74). Such principles are consonant with the view that the new jobs created from a public project must be viewed as a cost in cost-benefit analysis. Failing to take this view diminishes each human and his or her intrinsic value. Doing so reduces a person to something that needs to be "looked after," like a dog or cat when we go on vacation, and not as the creative image of God. Moreover, viewing job creation as busywork ignores the Christian teaching that work is both a calling and an opportunity for stewardship.

Therefore, the labor that will be used to fill the jobs created by a new public-works project must be seen, on both Christian and economic grounds, as a cost in cost-benefit analysis. Workers are precious resources created in the image of God who must be able to consider prayerfully, for themselves, issues of calling, stewardship, leisure and labor.

PITFALL 2: IGNORING SOCIAL CONSTRAINTS

Often, economists are rightly accused of focusing on only physical constraints in evaluating what policy actions might be possible. But the economist charged with performing a cost-benefit analysis cannot afford to be blind to the social constraints that may be present and relevant to the project under consideration. As Trumbull (1990) states, economists who fail to consider the relevant social constraints in making a policy recommendation "are in danger of having their contributions to the decision rejected or not taken seriously" (p. 204).

The implication, then, is that some policy proposals simply cannot be considered viable. Even if they could physically be introduced, some proposals must be kept off the table if they prove contradictory to the prevailing social norms.

In chapter two we saw that unseemly outcomes in markets have virtually nothing to do with the inner workings of markets themselves. Unseemly market outcomes are instead merely a reflection of the values, tastes and preferences of the consumer or producer participants. If we do not like the goods and services we see around us, our complaint lies with the buyers and sellers of such products. The products we see available for purchase are an indicator of the values held by ourselves, our coworkers, our neighbors and our friends.

Therefore, in a market setting the most powerful way to enact meaningful, lasting change is to work toward a renewing of the culture itself. If many individuals do not buy things like child pornography, semi-automatic weapons or narcotics, such products will disappear from our cultural landscape.

Similarly, prevailing social constraints can inform the decisions reached via a cost-benefit analysis. An economist will not recommend any policy action or project that appears to violate prevailing cultural values. Christians then have an obligation to shape those values from within the culture. Christians—as well as non-Christians—can significantly influence both market and public policy outcomes. Whether we work as individuals, share our ideas with our neighbors and friends or form voluntary associations to champion a cause dear to us, Christians can have an important influence on the social norms we choose as a society. In a postmodern culture where most anything goes, we can be salt and light in helping direct what we, as a society, aspire to be. For Christians, evangelism must also play a role in cultural renewal. While less popular in our postmodern age, the Great Commission remains our mandate: "Go into all the world and preach the Good News to everyone" (Mk 16:15).

Thus social constraints must be viewed as legitimate in deciding whether to recommend a particular policy action. Consequently, we must acknowledge our individual responsibilities to influence the forms that our cultural constraints take. In doing so we will be able to influence the direction of public policy in positive ways.

PITFALL 3: FORGETTING ABOUT OR IGNORING DISTRIBUTIONAL CONSEQUENCES

One challenge of cost-benefit analysis lies in the valuation of the benefits of a particular project or policy action. While it is relatively easy to add up the dollar price of a new bridge in mortar, steel, labor and so forth, it is a far more nebulous thing to try to estimate the dollar value to society—the total social benefit—of a proposed bridge. Because comparison of costs and benefits requires a common unit of measure for each, the cost-benefit analyst must quantify both the costs and benefits of a proposal in dollar terms—the only metric available.

The traditional method used in cost-benefit analysis to assess, in dollars, the benefit of a proposed project is called contingent valuation. Contingent valuation requires surveying the potential beneficiaries of a project. The criterion used in such surveys is the willingness to pay. Simply put, contingent valuation consists of asking the potential beneficiaries of a proposed project how much they would be willing to pay, in dollars, for the proposed project. The cost-benefit analyst takes these responses, adds together their dollar values and then compares this total to the total outlays required to complete the project. If the benefit calculated from the contingent valuation exceeds the explicit costs of the project, the project is recommended to the relevant policy-making authority.

Problems arise in contingent valuation, however, when individuals differ in their abilities to pay. Asking a rich woman and a poor man how much they would each be willing to pay to finance the augmentation of law-enforcement services (e.g., more city police) may result in very different responses. Even if both persons hold similar moral standards and values, the wealthy woman will probably state a higher number than will her lower-income counterpart; the woman will report a greater willingness to pay since she has a greater ability to pay. Of course, a very poor person would also benefit from enhanced law-enforcement services. However, the poor person would report a lower willingness to pay because he has less income left than his wealthier counterpart after each has paid for basics like food and shelter. To the very wealthy, law enforcement might be viewed as a necessity; to the destitute, it might be considered a luxury item.

Since willingness to pay varies with the ability to pay, the responsible cost-benefit analyst must keep this phenomenon well in mind in considering alternative public projects. For example, willingness-to-pay reports might lead a city to construct its new elevated mass-transit system so that it passes over every low-income neighborhood. If the poor report that they would pay little to keep the route out of their neighborhoods but the wealthy report that they would pay much, a naive economist might recommend winding the track over every economically depressed section of town because it appears less harmful. Of course, such a course of action would be unconscionable, resulting in the poor being made even worse off than they were prior to the construction of the project. Not only would they be poor, they would now also have a train running right over their heads.

Because willingness-to-pay reports can lead to outcomes that change the well-being of individuals in both positive and negative ways, we must all be aware of such distributional issues in evaluating a project. Christians are called to remember the poor in every circumstance. In the words of our Lord, we are to "invite the poor, the crippled, the lame, and the blind" whenever we host a meal (Lk 14:13). In his letter to the Galatians, Paul tells us that James, Peter and John (who are pillars of the church) suggested "that we keep on helping the poor" (Gal 2:10). Hence, the practitioner of cost-benefit analysis is acting in accord with the Christian vision in taking care not to overlook the ways the poor may be adversely affected. Similarly, when distributional issues are relevant to a policy decision, we must all remember the poor and, moreover, speak for the poor.

PITFALL 4: FAILING TO CONSIDER CORRECTLY WHO HAS STANDING

Prior to relating the parable of the Good Samaritan, Jesus is speaking with a legal expert. After Jesus exhorts the lawyer to love his neighbor as himself, the lawyer replies, "And who is my neighbor?" (Lk 10:29).

Cost-benefit analysis occasions the same question: Who is my neighbor? That is, when we consider a proposed project, who should we take into account in a cost-benefit analysis? In the literature of economics this is referred to as the issue of standing. In a cost-benefit analysis we need to know who our neighbor is. We need to know what individuals should be considered in a cost-benefit analysis. We need to know who has standing.

We must consider who has standing in cost-benefit analysis. That is, we ask who should be counted in assessing the benefits and costs of a public good. In particular we must consider the following three groups: criminals, those affected across national boundaries and future generations.

First, should the proceeds from criminal activities enter positively into a cost-benefit analysis? Economists working in the tradition of Nobel laureate Gary Becker have taken the position that criminal activities and the proceeds from them should be treated as no different from any other activity from which proceeds follow. In this view one could make an argument that criminal gains resulting from a public-policy change—say, a reduction in law-enforcement expenditures—should enter as a benefit into a cost-benefit analysis.

We cannot agree with this view. In light of our earlier discussion regarding social constraints, we must hold that benefits from activities that fall outside of the social constraints codified in law must not be considered at all in conducting a cost-benefit analysis. For these and other reasons, Trumbull (1990) also argues that the proceeds from crime cannot enter into a cost-benefit analysis.

Thankfully, this pitfall is simple to reconcile with our Christian faith. Thievery is wrong (Ex 20:15). Hence, Trumbull's view that criminal gains should not figure positively into any analysis of benefits and costs is an easy one for Christians to embrace.

Whether those affected by cross-border effects should have standing proves a bit more complicated. For example, it is legitimate to ask whether Canadians should be counted among the beneficiaries of a proposed U.S. project that has positive spillover effects from the United States into Canada. After all, Canadians will not help finance the project. Should they nevertheless have standing in a cost-benefit calculation?

This question is more easily answered by considering the alternative case: the case of a negative spillover. That is, suppose that the United States were considering whether to construct a new federally funded waste-treatment plant along the riverfront in Detroit—just across the Detroit River from Windsor, Ontario. Also suppose that the new facility would spawn a broad variety of negative spillovers onto our Canadian neighbors. For example, waste-treatment plants are not well known for their aesthetic beauty. Hence, construction of such a facility in that specific location would worsen the view looking northwest from Windsor to Detroit. Further, because of the negative effects on the view from Windsor, property values in Windsor would decline for any home, apartment building, condominium, office building, library or restaurant with a view of the Detroit River. Like most waste-treatment plants, the facility would also smell bad. Since the prevailing winds happen to blow west to east, Windsor would smell like our proposed waste-treatment plant.

In this example of negative spillovers across national boundaries, it becomes easy to see that we must consider the well-being of those that are adversely affected by a domestic public project. Just like we each individually consider our neighbors in how we keep up our yards, how loudly we play our music or how much foul language we use, the cost-benefit analyst cannot overlook the harm that might result from a proposed project via negative spillovers across national borders.

Hence, foreigners do have standing in cases of negative spillovers. And if we care enough about our neighbors to consider their well-being in the event of deleterious effects, we must also view it as a benefit if a domestically funded project can influence positively the situation of those beyond our borders.

Finally, we ask whether the well-being of future generations should be considered in evaluating a policy proposal. In light of social norms and constraints, we might reasonably assume that future generations should have standing in cost-benefit analysis. If current social mores indicate that we should care not only about ourselves but also our progeny, then perhaps future generations should indeed have standing.

Moreover, Trumbull (1990) argues that social constraints are not the primary reason that future generations must have standing. Instead, Trumbull states that future generations must be considered in any responsible cost-benefit analysis simply because the point of cost-benefit analysis is to assess whether a policy proposal or proposed project will yield a positive net social benefit to all who would be affected by it. Therefore, argues Trumbull, we cannot overlook the impact of a project on some individuals merely because they do not yet exist.

A legal expert asked our Savior, "Who is my neighbor?" In asking this question, the lawyer was seeking a limiting definition—one that would clearly indicate where his obligations ended. Like most of us, the lawyer wanted to know how little he could get away with by finding out who his neighbor is and, simultaneously, who his neighbor is not.

From Jesus' reply we can infer that the lawyer believed that his obligations certainly must end within his own race. Jesus' answer, the parable of the Good Samaritan, conveys quite another message. As Christians, everyone is our neighbor—even those who are different from us. Further, even those who we encounter only briefly or in passing are our neighbors. Moreover, they are neighbors whom we are called, in the same passage and elsewhere, to love as ourselves (Lev 19:18).

Thankfully, the proper approach to issues of standing in cost-benefit analysis is the same as the biblical one. Everyone is our neighbor in the sense that we all participate—or will participate—in the same global society. As our neighbors, everyone must be given standing in cost-benefit analysis. Even criminals have standing, though we cannot view the gains from criminal activities as a social benefit. The unborn, foreigners, people we may never even meet: they all are our neighbors.

PITFALL 5: INCORRECTLY VALUING HUMAN LIFE

How much should a human life saved count for on the benefit side of a cost-benefit analysis? Speed-limit reductions, community hospitals and law enforcement services save lives. But how do we quantify the value of a human life in assessing the total social benefit associated with something like a community hospital? Since the perceived primary benefit of such policies and projects is the preservation of human life, we must therefore attempt to quantify the value of the lives saved in order to compare the total social benefit of a project or proposal to its total social cost. That is, a cost-benefit analyst is charged with comparing—in dollars, no less—the stream of benefits of lives saved by a hospital to the dollar costs involved in building and operating it.

When a lobbyist tries to sell a senator, congresswoman or legislator on the need for a new safety-enhancing policy or program, the rhetoric often turns hyperbolic. A lobbyist might say, "Senator, you must vote for passage of this bill. If even one life is saved as a result of this piece of legislation, it will be worth any expense involved in funding it."

Such rhetoric cannot be correct because it implicitly assumes that each individual human life is of infinite monetary worth. Were that the case, then we should immediately outlaw all driving anywhere in the United States, thereby avoiding thousands of senseless deaths on our nation's highways each year. In 1999 alone, prohibition of driving would have resulted in 42,401 fewer accidental deaths in the United States (U.S. Bureau of the Census 2002).

Nevertheless, we do not outlaw the operation of motor vehicles, and we do not intend to, because we perceive that the benefits of driving outweigh the costs associated with driving. We know that there are risks associated with operating a motor vehicle, but we do not outlaw driving because we perceive that the benefits of getting places by car are greater than the risks of such travel.

Therefore, human life cannot be considered to be of infinite monetary value in a cost-benefit analysis. Nevertheless, we must somehow be able to account for the potentially life-preserving benefits of a proposed policy or project in evaluating its benefits relative to its costs. Let's examine the ways cost-benefit analysts have attempted to value human lives.

Economists have employed at least two methods for determining the value of human lives that might be saved by the introduction of a new public program, policy or project. The first approach uses the wage and salary earnings of individuals as a proxy for those individuals' values to society.

Hence, many economists have argued that the correct method of valuing human lives saved in cost-benefit analysis is to calculate the stream of earnings that an individual could earn over the remainder his or her lifetime should that person's life be saved as a result of a change in public policy. To arrive at a measure of the total benefits of a life-saving proposal, then, the analyst needs to (1) identify the individuals who would be saved as a result of some proposed project, (2) calculate the value of the earnings each person is expected to make over the remainder of his or her natural life, and (3) sum the anticipated income stream across all of the individuals.

Today, most economists reject this method of valuing human lives due to its immediate unseemliness. This technique implies that the lives of Donald

Trump and Larry Flynt are somehow more valuable to society than the lives of Mother Teresa or a public-school teacher. This method similarly implies that the life of an older attorney is of less value to society than a younger one because the younger attorney will earn more over his remaining natural life than will the older attorney. Most economists, especially Christian ones, are not prepared to make such interpersonal comparisons.

Economists have employed an alternative method for determining the value of the human lives that might be saved by the introduction of a new public program, policy or project. This approach stems from the notion that each of us places some value on the reduction in the probability of loss of life that follows the introduction of a new life-saving program or project. For example, lower speed limits reduce the probability that you will die in an automobile accident. Of course, you have no way to foretell whether or not you might be involved in a serious car accident under a higher speed limit; you know only that you are more likely to have an accident in the presence of higher speed limits than with lower ones. Nevertheless, you place *some* value on a proposed speed limit reduction since lowering the speed limit simultaneously lowers the probability that you will be involved in a serious car accident. Consequently, economists attempt to evaluate the anticipated benefit of a life-preserving project by assessing how much the relevant individuals value the reduced risk of death that would accrue from the project or policy.

Individuals already reveal indirectly the value that they place on a reduction in their probability of loss of life. In labor markets, for example, individuals require higher wages to compensate them for working in professions that involve physical risks. Viscusi (1993) estimates that when workers face a probability of a job-related fatality that is twice what workers face in a job with the average probability (1 in 20,000), the workers in the riskier jobs earn wages that are 1 to 2 percent higher.

In determining the value that the relevant individuals place on a reduction in the likelihood of death, an economist would, of course, want to ask them directly how much they would be willing to pay to reduce their risk of premature death. In making such an assessment, though, the economist cannot make such inquiries of identified individuals who would—with certainty—be affected by the new program or policy. For example, we cannot reasonably hope to ask how much someone, already diagnosed with cancer, would be willing to pay to have a new state-of-the-art cancer center built in his or her town. Such individuals would certainly be willing to give all that they have to prolong their lives.

Hence, the analyst must make any inquiries such that the preferences and values of known individuals who would be currently affected by a policy change are ignored. Asking individuals who would be currently affected fails the aforementioned standard that the analyst calculate the value individuals place on their perceived risk reduction that would follow from a new program or project.

The necessity of considering only those unidentified individuals who might possibly be affected in the future by a proposed project or policy is not inconsistent with philosopher John Rawls's (1971) veil of ignorance criterion. Rawls, an emeritus professor from Harvard University, suggests that the only humane way that a person may evaluate a policy proposal is to assess it as from behind a veil of ignorance. For Rawls, the veil obscures a decision-maker's knowledge of the particular circumstances she was born into. That is, Rawls suggests that one must evaluate policy proposals as though one had no information about things like who her parents might have been, what genetic dispositions she might possess, what her parent's income was (or whether she even had parents), or where her family's home was located. According to Rawls, the decision-maker must focus on the impact on human lives in an anonymous way. Above all, the decision-maker must ignore how advantaged or disadvantaged she herself is—or has been—in considering the merits of a policy proposal. Even if her last name is Rockefeller or Kennedy, she must weigh all proposals as though her last name might just as easily have been Guildenstern, Smith, Moukhammad or Khatami.

For the Christian, Rawls's view accords well with Christ's teaching, based on Old Testament law, that we love our neighbor as ourself (Lev 19:18; Mt 19:19; 22:39; Mk 12:31; Rom 13:9; Gal 5:14; Jas 2:8). If we are to consider others with the same regard that we give to ourselves, then we must evaluate the impact that a policy proposal will have by keeping in mind how it would affect us not just in our current stations in life but also had we been born into different circumstances—better or worse.

In conclusion, human life is precious. As a result, we must carefully weigh the costs against the benefits of any proposed program or project that would yield a life-preserving benefit. In evaluating such proposals, we must not jump to the conclusion that any proposal that would save even one life is of infinite monetary value. Instead, the responsible economist will consider how much the at-risk parties would be willing to pay to enjoy the reduced level of risk that would follow from the project. In making this assessment the economist must ignore the preferences of any identified individuals who would, with certainty, be affected by the proposal since they would be willing to spend all they have on the project. Instead, the responsible cost-benefit analyst will consider only the willingness of individuals to pay for the decreased probability of loss of life made possible by the project. In doing so, the economist (following Rawls) treats all individuals equally in assuming that anyone could be subject to a car accident, Alzheimer's or clinical depression.

CONCLUSION

This chapter has introduced the problem of externalities in economics and made the case that government is the appropriate provider of public goods. We have also indicated that, even for such goods, deciding whether or not to undertake a specific project requires a careful consideration of all of the costs and benefits involved in order to ensure the greatest possible net benefit to society given currently available resources.

In chapter four we turn to the less clear examples of externalities. While providing public streets may be a fairly obvious role for government as a public-good provider, we must next grapple with the appropriate and useful role of collective action when it comes to such less clear activities as education, basic research, health care, diplomacy, foreign aid, social insurance and the like. While we do not have room to exhaustively consider all of these possibilities, we use several examples to show that careful policy design requires a thoughtful assessment of the potential benefits and costs of any proposal.

FOR FURTHER READING

Head, John G. 1974. *Public goods and public welfare.* Durham, North Carolina: Duke University Press. A collection of twelve essays written over the course of thirteen years. Eight of the collection deal with public goods. A nontechnical, literary-style discussion.

Mishan, Edward J. 1976. *Cost-benefit analysis.* New York: Praeger. Intuitive, nontechnical presentation of issues in cost-benefit analysis. Not a how-to book, it raises the issues covered in this chapter as well as other relevant considerations.

4

SAVIOR OR LEVIATHAN?

The Role of Government in Our Daily Lives

In three of the four Gospel accounts, Christ teaches us how to respond to the authority of government; we are to give to Caesar what belongs to him, and give to God what belongs to him. But what exactly belongs to Caesar has varied widely across time and place. In the United States, for example, during the last seventy years alone the tax rate paid on the salary of the average American has risen from about 10 percent to over 30 percent. In fact, many economists suspicious of government have compared it to the Old Testament leviathan—an insatiable serpent. Dennis Mueller (1989) gives a good description of the literature in public economics that models government as leviathan.

We use this chapter to consider the ways that government may exercise good stewardship in policy design and management beyond its role as the sole provider of public goods described in chapter three. We also discuss whether the biblical injunction to tithe is affected, now that government performs so many of the tasks traditionally undertaken by the early church (caring for the poor and sick, etc.). Before beginning, though, we introduce two of the most powerful ideas in economics: sunk costs and opportunity cost. Public policy is most effective when policymakers—as well as caring, thoughtful Christians—keep these two ideas firmly in mind for decision making of all kinds.

SUNK COSTS AND OPPORTUNITY COST

When the future need not be constrained by the past: Sunk costs are sunk. It is tempting both in public policy and in our personal lives to believe that our current decisions are constrained by past choices and commitments. For example, when governments set aside wilderness areas and create public parks, it might be concluded that such "investments" should determine future public policy as well.

But what if current scientific work by biologists and economists were to determine that public policy aimed at preserving habitat for endangered species is much less effective (and more costly) than would be private ownership of lands now owned by the federal government? Or suppose that similar research determines that the best way to reduce forest-fire damage is to allow much more extensive controlled burns.

One reaction to the new evidence would be to insist that current policies be maintained because the government, to preserve species in wilderness areas and to suppress fires, has already spent millions of dollars. It requires little thought, however, to see that money spent on a misguided "solution" to such issues is water under the bridge. What policymakers owe to citizens is a willingness to reassess the wisdom of previous expenditures, with a view to better meeting public goals in the future at less expense. Choices made in the past simply are not relevant to today's decisions. The past cannot be changed.

Economists have a catch phrase for this idea: "Sunk costs are sunk." In other words, costs incurred in the past that cannot possibly be recovered are irrelevant to today's decision making. That is, unrecoverable costs are unrecoverable.

Noneconomists have their own catch phrases for this idea. One example is, "There's no use throwing good money after bad." We often use this when we have incurred some unwise cost in the past. Of course, throwing more money today at a bad situation is of no use; sunk costs are indeed sunk.

Another example—nonmonetary in nature, but that conveys the same sentiment—is, "There's no use crying over spilled milk." The milk has been spilled, the money for it has been spent, and no amount of crying will undo the past. The past is past, and sunk costs are sunk.

For good or ill, college students understand this well. At the beginning of each term, each student pays thousands of dollars of tuition money to enroll—and tuition is a nonrefundable, sunk cost. Yet students regularly skip the very classes they have paid thousands of dollars for the privilege of attending. Why? Each Wednesday morning, every student must weigh carefully whether the hour from 11 to 12 o'clock would be better spent in the monetary economics class or doing something else. If the weather is glorious, skipping class might make sense. But if the weather is rainy with temperatures in the low forties, going to class might be the better way to spend that hour. Or a student might cut a class to study for a test later in the day.

Whatever the reason, the point, of course, is that nonrefundable tuition money spent long ago is irrelevant to making decisions today. A wise student will weigh carefully whether an hour is better spent in class or pursuing some other opportunity.

The skeptics among us might argue that students are skipping their classes because the students are not really the ones paying tuition; their parents are. But parents routinely behave the same way, even when the sunk costs are in the form of money they have spent on themselves. We all purchase gym memberships, season tickets or newspaper subscriptions. We all buy them in advance, and we all, at one time or another, decide we have better things to do than go to the gym or go to every single concert or read the entire newspaper from front page to back page.

In deciding issues of public policy, we would do well to remember that sunk costs are sunk and that there's no use throwing good money after bad. The best we can do is to choose today, and choose wisely, what the best option is to pursue among a variety of possibilities.

In the spiritual realm too, sunk costs are sunk. Indeed, Jesus calls us to remember that the past is past. When we choose Christ, we choose to leave behind all the follies we used to put our time, money and energies into. Christ forgives our past—a past that cannot be undone. How freeing it is to be released from the old burdensome activities of the past and come to Christ. It matters not how hard we have worked building up old idols; when we choose today, we wisely choose Christ's glorious gift of salvation, abandoning all else. Christ forgives the past, and we must forget it and live a new, rich life in him.

We cannot pursue every good idea that comes along. Economists are the ultimate party poopers. We have to be. Someone has to remind caring, enthusiastic Christians that we simply cannot pursue every single good idea that comes along.

This is true in our personal lives, in our church's finances and everywhere else. For example, on a really nice spring day, you might like to spend the afternoon fishing. You might also get pleasure from spending the afternoon playing softball. These are both good ideas, and they would both give you satisfaction on a magnificent spring day.

But even though it would be nice for you to go fishing all afternoon, and it would also be nice for you to play softball all afternoon, you cannot do both. You have but one afternoon available to you, and you cannot fish and play softball at the same time!

Every decision in life demands such a realization. In fact, that is precisely why we must decide. We cannot do both. This idea is so fundamental in economics that it has a very specific name: opportunity cost. We say that the true cost of any action is the value of the next-best opportunity forgone. So even if something seems "free," it really is not. For example, suppose someone gives you free tickets to a concert. Going to the concert isn't really free, because by choosing to go to attend the concert, you are simultaneously choosing not to pursue whatever would have been your next-best use of that time.

Scripture reminds us repeatedly that we must make choices. We cannot have things both ways. Consider this famous exhortation from Joshua:

> But if you refuse to serve the LORD, then choose today whom you will serve. Would you prefer the gods your ancestors served beyond the Euphrates? Or will it be the gods of the Amorites in whose land you now live? But as for me and my family, we will serve the LORD. (Josh 24:15)

Or this, from Proverbs:

> Choose my instruction rather than silver,
> and knowledge rather than pure gold. (Prov 8:10)

And in one of Paul's most emotional passages from his letter to the church at Philippi, he agonizes over remaining in this world versus joining Christ for eternity. He would love to be with his Savior; he also feels called to continue his ministry of encouragement here on earth. He is conflicted because it is impossible for him to do both. He writes:

> For to me, living means living for Christ, and dying is even better. But if I live, I can do more fruitful work for Christ. So I really don't know which is better. I'm torn between two desires: I long to go and be with Christ, which would be far better for me. But for your sakes, it is better that I continue to live. (Phil 1:21-24)

In fact, one of the wonderful paradoxes of the great abundance God provides is this: great abundance necessitates making choices. In all things, whether we are blessed with time, talents, spiritual gifts, financial resources or any other resource, the mere possession of a valuable resource occasions a decision: How then shall I use this gift?

Think about your local church congregation. Whether a church is blessed with many resources or few, every congregation must prayerfully consider how to allocate its budget. Soup kitchens are good things. So are educational units. Campus ministries are nice to have in college towns. And giving generously to world missions is important too. But one cannot pursue any of these things without an appreciation that each dollar that goes into building the new educational unit is a dollar that could have been used in the soup kitchen or the campus ministry or for world missions.

Consider world hunger. Suppose you want to give $100 per month out of your family budget to fight world hunger. Good. But where on earth—literally—will you send the money? Face it: for every starving child you help in Indonesia this month, there is another destitute child elsewhere who will not receive your $100.

For the Christian, then, exercising good stewardship—whether resources are relatively scarce or relatively abundant—requires the wise management of our precious resources. For every activity, service or cause we choose to pursue as Christians, we forgo some other valuable alternative use of our time, our talents or our treasure. One way to consider carefully where gifts of time and money should go is to ask, What person or situation do I feel especially drawn to due to my/our experience, closeness to the need, or absence of others to meet the need? (see chap. 11). Having chosen and committed the resources, we can then trust in God to call others (who might be better placed, informed or financed) to meet any remaining needs.

In the remainder of this chapter, we apply this simple concept to an array of "good ideas" that our society could pursue. Thankfully, in every case it turns out that choosing wisely is seldom all or nothing. Instead, responsible stewardship requires wisdom to know how to allocate our resources among all of the good things we could do. That is, there is an important distinction between *effective* policy choice and *optimal* policy choices. In the first case, the benefit of a policy is greater than the cost. And at first that seems good enough. But when we consider that the goal of economic policy is to make society's net benefit as great as possible given the resources available, then *optimal* policy design must be the goal. Otherwise, we fail to be wise stewards of God's rich gifts to all of us.

So what might optimal policy look like? Let us turn to some examples.

WHEN SPILLOVER EFFECTS ARE HARMFUL: THE REGULATORY ROLE OF GOVERNMENT

We teach at Hope College, located in beautiful Holland, Michigan. A picturesque resort town, Holland sits along the eastern shore of Lake Michigan. Historically, Holland has provided residents of places like Chicago a cool, refreshing place to spend part of the hot summer months.

Suppose, though, that a profit-driven firm, Smogcesspool, Inc., builds its flagship factory in Holland. Soon afterward, due to the extremely filthy nature of the manufacturing processes required at Smogcesspool, Holland becomes irretrievably polluted. The air is so dirty that city streetlights burn around the clock. The water is undrinkable. Fish cannot survive, nor can the birds. (This is not unlike the scenario described in Dr. Seuss's *The Lorax*, or the stereotype of places like Pittsburgh, Pennsylvania, sixty years ago.)

Moreover, the entire region becomes spoiled within fifty miles of Holland. The only remaining residents of the Holland area are the firm's employees and managers, actively pursuing pecuniary rewards.

Of course, most of us are frightened and dismayed by such a dismal tale— even a fictional one. We all know that pollution is bad. We all know that "the earth is the LORD's, and everything in it" (Ps 24:1). We all know that it would be a shame to lose Holland as a wonderful place to spend the summer. We fear for those who would need to forsake their families, jobs and homes to move somewhere beyond the fifty-mile range. We are depressed to think that fish and fowl will lose one of their habitats.

But most economists, even Christian ones, would not be so quick to conclude that what we have described is all bad and no good. We need more information. All we have described so far is the costly environmental degradation created by Smogcesspool. But there might possibly be a benefit to society in all of this. In fact, though unlikely, it is indeed possible that the situation we have described may be one that leaves society better off than it would be in the absence of the Smogcesspool facility.

How can this be? The answer is a simple one: an economist would want to know what Smogcesspool is producing. Economists weigh the social costs against the social benefits of any activity. Thus, an economist would need to consider whether our society values Holland, Michigan, more highly as a pleasant lakeshore town or as the location where Smogcesspool produces its output.

But to make this calculation requires knowing what product is being produced at Smogcesspool. Even though pollution is a terrible thing, we cannot simply outlaw Smogcesspool's activities without considering whether the plant's output might be valuable enough to society that we would be better off spoiling Holland, Michigan, in order to let Smogcesspool manufacture its product.

For example, suppose that, for decades, Smogcesspool has been the world's leader in cancer research. After years of successes and failures and clinical trials, Smogcesspool has discovered a pharmaceutical cure for some forms of cancer.

However, because the drug is a new one that is not easily produced, manufacture of the drug proves impossible without a filthy production process.

In such a case, a society might—out of compassion—decide that Smogcesspool should be free to produce its cancer cure. Even though those near Holland, Michigan, will bear some of the costs of the production of the good because they will need to relocate, we might nevertheless agree that such costs appear relatively small when compared to the value to our global society of reducing cancer deaths worldwide. Moreover, we might even be willing to concede that the best stewardship of the earth in such a context might well be to pollute it locally in order to save the lives of those who would otherwise become cancer victims.

Thankfully, we rarely find ourselves faced with such all-or-nothing choices. Most of the time the questions we face are ones of degree. When production of a particular good pollutes the environment, we seldom need to decide whether or not that good should be produced at all. Instead, the relevant question we must ask is, How much of that good are we willing to see produced given the costs to society involved in the production of that good?

In economics the answer is that we should produce the quantity of the good that maximizes the difference between the total social benefit derived from the good and the total cost incurred by society in the production of the good. That is, we must produce the quantity of the good that maximizes its net social benefit.

Figure 4.1. Net social benefit

The relevant social costs of production consist of all resources—including clean air and clean water—used in the production of the good. In fact, the reason firms pollute the environment is because they can get away with it at no cost, unless government intervenes in order to outlaw or regulate the flow of pollution.

In cases where negative spillovers exist, government can help ensure that this socially optimal level of production of such goods is achieved. That is, government can supply essential guidance of markets to ensure that goods are produced at the levels that afford the greatest net social benefit. Historically, government has utilized two primary tools for this purpose: pollution limits and pollution taxes.

Pollution limits. In the case of pollution limits, government decrees the maximum amount of pollution that may be generated. Government does this in order to reduce the overall level of negative spillover effects from polluting activities that would make the air, water and land either less healthy or less able to sustain other activities, like recreation. While pollution limits are indeed effective at reducing overall pollution levels, they do not guarantee that the optimal quantity of each good will be produced since all firms are subject to the pollution limits, regardless of the value to society of any specific good being produced.

Pollution taxes. Because of the shortcomings of pollution limits, economists prefer using a pollution tax to deal with the problem of negative spillovers. Pollution taxes, it turns out, are a more efficient form of government intervention because they address directly the source of the pollution—the productive activity itself. Such taxes are often referred to as Pigouvian taxes in honor of Arthur Cecil Pigou, the British economist who first considered them in the 1920s.

According to Pigou, the reason that firms pollute so much is that they are not required to pay to use resources like clean air and water in the production of their outputs. Unlike other resources used in production (labor, raw materials, machinery, etc.), firms do not pay to use the environment as a resource *because no one owns resources like air and rivers.*

In order to reduce the level of pollution in the environment, Pigou proposed that government charge polluting firms for their use of the environment. In a very important sense, government—speaking for all who are adversely affected—should act as though it were the owner of resources like clean air and water. That is, government should require payment from polluting firms in accordance with the amount of damage done to others via their production processes. Under such a scheme, a firm could be forced to pay for the full costs of production, including negative spillovers onto others, and not merely the costs of resources that it must purchase. Moreover, the amount of the tax should be exactly equal to the amount of harm caused to others by the pollution.

When administered in this way—charging firms for all of the costs to society of the production of their goods—pollution taxes have the potential to yield the socially optimal level of production of each good. To charge any more than this would reduce the net social benefit of the good; society would be losing more in the consequential reduction in production of the good than it would gain via the improvement in air and water quality. To charge any less would also reduce the net social benefit; society would suffer more from the increase in pollution than it would benefit from the consequential increase in production of the good being produced.

Pollution taxes can also help reduce the levels of pollution since they encourage the search for cleaner production technologies that can be introduced at low cost. If manufacturers can discover cleaner ways to produce their products that prove cheaper than paying the pollution tax, then firms that adopt those technologies will generate less pollution per unit produced.

Finally, pollution taxes work well because they address the problem more directly than pollution limits do. In fact, the most efficient forms of government intervention, of all kinds, will be ones that address a spillover—whatever it might be—directly rather than indirectly. Further extending this idea, any tax designed to control a firm's pollution level will be more efficient when the tax is imposed on the amount of pollution itself rather than on the firm's output of finished products.

In the remainder of this chapter, we examine other potential roles government may play in nudging markets along to more socially beneficial, efficient outcomes. In each case, the key is that some form of externality exists, so market mechanisms lead to either overproduction or underproduction. First, we turn to the production of college graduates.

COLLEGE EDUCATION AS A POSITIVE EXTERNALITY

Whether or not to attend college is a potentially life-changing decision. It is also an expensive one. According the to the 2006 edition of the College Board's publication "Trends in College Pricing," average total charges for tuition, fees, room and board at four-year public institutions in 2006-2007 were $12,796. Even adjusting for inflation that represents a 2 percent increase from the previous year, and an increase of 86 percent over the price during the 1976-1977 school year.

In private institutions, real college costs are growing faster still. Among private four-year degree programs, average charges in 2006-2007 totaled $30,367, also an inflation-adjusted increase of 2 percent from the prior year. However, since the 1976-1977 academic year, the inflation-adjusted average total cost of one year of private college has risen 115 percent (College Board 2006, p. 11).

It is not surprising then that families of academically eligible high school students have a serious cost-benefit analysis to do. Even if a student matriculates at a public institution and graduates in no more than four years, the total bill will add up to $51,184 (in 2006 dollars). And for those contemplating a private college or university, the parallel total is $121,468. So every family must weigh the monetary expense of a college education in the form of tuition, fees, and room and board against the expected benefits of a college degree—in the form of personal satisfaction and enrichment in addition to the expected boost to lifetime earnings that a college degree has the potential to provide.

In fact, this is exactly the calculation that every rising college student and his or her parents or guardians must make. And if students and their families were the only ones deciding whether they should attend college, most would consider only the potential benefits of a college degree that would accrue to them personally.

But the individuals who receive a diploma at commencement exercises are not the only parties who enjoy a benefit each time one more degree is conferred. All of us benefit when more people receive college educations. And these benefits come in several forms. First, higher levels of education make our workforce more productive, and more productive workers lead to higher long-term rates of growth for the economy. Second, a nation benefits politically when its electorate is better educated and informed about major issues that affect all of us. College graduates can be wiser critics of the ideas of others and make decisions and vote based on more than emotional appeals. Finally, we all benefit socially when we are all better educated. Public discourse is more profitable, and we even have more interesting times at social events when the range of possible conversational topics is expanded.

Therefore, one way to think about college educations is that they yield a positive external benefit that extends to others besides those providing and receiving college degrees. And this means that the socially optimal number of diplomas awarded each year is a bigger number that the one that would result through market forces alone. Appropriate economic policy, then, would try to nudge upward the number of diplomas per year to one closer to the social optimum.

And thankfully we currently do exactly that using a variety of tools. First, most states operate public colleges and universities subsidized directly through tax dollars. The tuition price charged, then, is a low one in order to ensure a full enrollment. In fact, one reason tuition is lower for in-state residents is precisely because of the perceived benefits to the home state of having more local students enrolled. Second, we make portable grant monies available to students to attend the college of their choice—whether private or public. One way to think about a government-funded grant to attend college is to think of it as a voucher that may be used by students to attend the institution of higher learning that they feel best satisfies their educational needs and aspirations. By subsidizing students in this way, we collectively enhance their ability to pay for college beyond what they could afford based on their personal resources alone. Finally, we pay subsidies directly to private institutions in order to make it financially possible for them to accept a greater number of students and charge a lower tuition price than such schools would if they needed to rely on tuition alone to fund their operating expenses.

Taken together the collective ways that we all encourage more college education are large. The College Board estimates that, on average, full-time students receive about $3,100 of aid each year in the form of tax benefits and grants at public four-year institutions, and $9,000 at private colleges and universities (College Board 2006, p. 4). And these estimates represent only the monies and other benefits received directly by students. The subsidies given to both private and public institutions already make the college costs described at the beginning of this section even lower than they would be otherwise. According to the College Board, total state and local appropriations to public institutions alone for higher education instruction in 2004-2005 totaled $63.3 billion, in 2006 dollars—an inflation-adjusted increase since 1980-1981 of 44 percent (College Board 2006, p. 24).

Of course, simply because a good bears external benefits to others does not necessarily mean that government *must* intervene in either of its roles of provider or "nudger." Often, when it is clear that a good results in a benefit to all of us, caring private citizens exercise their individual and corporate callings to make more of that good available than would be provided by profit-seeking firms.

To see how private choices may influence the provision of college educations, consider two examples. First, the United Negro College Fund (UNCF) supports sixty-five thousand students at approximately nine hundred colleges, including their thirty-nine member institutions. Each year about eight thousand new college graduates have received support from the UNCF. Over 60 percent of those students are the first person in their family to have graduated from college, and 62 percent come from families with annual incomes under

$25,000. UNCF supports students enrolled in both undergraduate and graduate degree programs, and the tuition at UNCF-supported schools is 54 percent less than at other institutions (United Negro College Fund).

Hillsdale College in Michigan serves as a second model of financing college educations. Each year Hillsdale refuses all federal taxpayer funds available to it—currently approximately $5 million. Instead, Hillsdale replaces those funds entirely through the generosity of private contributors dedicated to the college and its mission. Further, Hillsdale offers what many view to be an outstanding education at a remarkable price. In fact, the 2007 edition of the *Princeton Review* counted Hillsdale as one of the top ten college values in the nation (Hillsdale College).

Therefore, whether through taxpayer funds or charitable giving, each year the United States produces a larger number of college graduates than we would observe by market forces alone. And as a result, we all enjoy an external benefit.

Yet education is not the only good that might be underproduced if consumers counted only their personal benefit and providers considered only their sales revenues and operating costs. Consider the socially optimal number of flu shots.

VACCINATIONS AS A POSITIVE EXTERNALITY

When flu season arrives, most of us make a choice regarding whether or not to incur the costs, in the form of pain and money, of a flu shot. But when you receive the vaccine, you are not the only one who benefits. Once you have been inoculated, not only will you not contract the illness; everyone you come into contact with will have their risk of getting sick reduced. That is, flu shots provide a private benefit to you, but they also result in a public benefit—even to those who do not receive the vaccine.

As a result, governments at the national, state and even county level try to encourage more people to get flu shots each season. And they achieve this through subsidizing the provision of the vaccine. Through government subsidies for the provision of the vaccine, we all face a lower price than the one that would have resulted by pure market forces alone. And if more people receive the shot as a result, the benefit extends to all of us.

THE EXTERNAL EFFECTS OF INFORMATION

Magazines like *Motor Trend* and *Car and Driver* routinely rate automobiles. But rarely do they conduct their own crash tests. And even if they do, they seldom conduct both head-on and front-offset crash tests.

One might expect these private publications to conduct their own extensive crash testing. After all, performing such tests would certainly lead to more magazine sales and subscriptions. Their potential readership is very interested in knowing how different vehicles perform in such situations.

Unfortunately, though, the additional revenues that might result from publishing crash-test results do not exceed the cost of crashing the automobiles. This is true for two reasons. First, publishers would need to sell an awfully large number of magazines to pay for crashing expensive new cars. Second, information gives substantial external benefits to those who do not pay for it. In the case of crash-test results in an automotive magazine, it is not a difficult thing to benefit from that information without buying the magazine or subscribing to it. You could borrow the magazine from a friend or see if you can track down the essential facts somewhere on the Internet. Or you could read the magazine for free in the library.

In fact, magazine and journal publishers are well aware of the external benefits generated when a public or college library subscribes to their publications. That is one of the main reasons that publishers normally charge libraries a subscription price dramatically higher than the price of an individual subscription; the publishers are trying to receive at least some monetary compensation for the benefits that will be enjoyed by all of the library's patrons that read magazines or journals free.

Thus it appears unlikely that we can expect many private firms to conduct extensive automobile crash testing on a long-term basis. As a result, because the safety of drivers is important to society, we charge government with conducting careful crash testing, and we pay for it using public monies. Again, because of an externality, the private sector would underprovide a particular service. In this case, because of the external benefits that information gives, we let government conduct the tests on our behalf, then share the results with all of us.

Whether externalities are present or not, often government has the potential to steer society toward outcomes that may lead to enhanced societal well-being. To conclude this chapter, let's consider two such instances: patent law and the income tax code.

THE MIXED BLESSING OF PATENTS

The patent system in the United States is designed to stimulate invention, innovation and job creation. But it also creates temporary monopolies for the inventors of new products. In this section we weigh the benefits of patents (the rapid development of new products) against their costs (relatively high prices due to the monopoly power granted to inventors). We find that patents are indeed a mixed blessing.

Developing and producing a new product is an exciting process. But it is also one that is both very expensive and highly risky. Moving from the genesis of a new product idea to the eventual delivery of the product to the market where consumers can find it is complicated and costly.

At the same time the development of a new product has tremendous potential social benefits. First, successful projects reward customers with a new product they like. The process rewards entrepreneurs and investors for creating and developing the product by correctly anticipating the needs of consumers. And the process stimulates job creation and economic growth throughout.

In the United States we use the patent process to encourage even more invention, creativity and risk-taking by entrepreneurs. By granting a temporary monopoly to a patent holder, the patent process increases the potential rewards that an entrepreneur can reap from a new invention. A patent makes it illegal for competitors to sell a copycat of any patented product for a period of twenty years from the date that an entrepreneur applies for patent protection. As a result, if a hit new product has been patented, then no other firms are permitted to sell the patented product until the patent period expires. Therefore, the patent holder is the lone monopolist supplier of the product.

Of course, one potential benefit to society of the patent process is that it will encourage even more invention and discovery by entrepreneurs. Tempted by the lure of temporary monopoly profits, entrepreneurs and investors will move even more quickly to anticipate the needs of consumers and invent new products that will lead to long-term economic growth.

But patents create monopolies, and monopolies are unambiguously bad for consumers. Without competing firms cutting their prices in order to encourage us to buy from them, a patent-holding monopoly firm will be able to charge a premium (monopoly) price for the product. Of course, a monopolist cannot charge any price; customers do have limited incomes and a variety of other goods they could choose to buy. Nevertheless, a patent-holding monopolist can charge a price that is higher than would be possible in the face of competitive pressure from other firms.

We regularly hear about this downside of patents in the case of prescription medications. When a pharmaceutical company grows close to discovering a new drug, it often applies for patent protection for its imminent discovery. In this way, the company will be able to charge a monopoly price for the drug until the patent expires. In the media we often hear how cruel this practice is: keeping life-saving medications out of the hands of the poorest among us. The greedy pharmaceutical companies care only about money, critics say; they really do not care at all about helping sick people.

But that argument only sees the monopoly-price side of patents. Those who make this argument forget that the reason we discover so many wonderful new drugs so quickly is the incentive that money provides. If pharmaceutical companies had to give away the formula for every new drug they created, and did not have the incentive of a temporary monopoly, the rate at which medicine advances would slow dramatically. Pharmaceutical companies find new drugs quickly because there is money in it. Stated another way, we find new ways to save lives because there is a financial incentive. If there were no patent system in place, medicine would simply not advance as quickly as it does currently.

So there is a tension for us as a society. We balance the benefits of new product discoveries, like prescription drugs, against the temporary cost of higher prices made possible by patents. And like most issues in economics, we must decide the appropriate tradeoff. In the specific case of new medicines, we must ask ourselves how much we are willing to pay in the form of higher prices for medications in order to continue their rapid discovery. Lengthening the patent period beyond twenty years would keep prices high longer but would make new discoveries happen even faster still. Alternatively, shortening the patent period would make new drugs cheaper for consumers, but would also slow the rate at which we learn how to save lives.

Getting government policy exactly right requires careful thought, study and design in order to make sure that the additional costs to society do not exceed the anticipated benefit. The public sector, even with the very best of intentions, cannot pursue a particular policy at any cost; doing so would lead to a less-than-optimal social outcome. So policy must aspire to getting things exactly right.

To further complicate matters, the ways that individuals may respond to a new policy or to a change in an existing one can prove unpredictable. The following example illustrates one such instance.

THE OPTIMAL TAX RATE ON WAGES AND SALARIES

Suppose that in order to fund a worthwhile project a government needs to increase the number of dollars raised through an income tax on wages and salaries. The conventional wisdom says that raising tax revenues will require increasing existing tax rates.

But, as so often happens with economic issues, what at first appears obvious might not be. Consider figure 4.2, which depicts the conventional view of the relationship between income tax rates and income tax revenues.

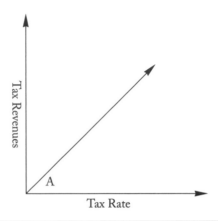

Figure 4.2. The commonsense view of the relationship between income-tax rates and income-tax revenues

Examine point A, where the tax rate is zero. That is, for each dollar a person earns, a worker keeps all of his or her earnings. At point A, where there are no taxes, there are also no tax revenues.

But now consider the opposite extreme. Suppose the tax rate on income were 100 percent. That is, what if workers kept none of their pay but turned all of it in as taxes? Then, at the close of each pay period, workers would examine their pay stubs to discover that all of their earnings had been withheld. At this high tax rate, one might expect very high tax revenues. However, in a world with a tax rate of 100 percent on earned income, it would not be long until almost no one was working. Why should a person be expected to toil all day long, only to receive no reward for his or her efforts?

As the preceding discussion indicates, figure 4.2 is correct to a point, but it is also an oversimplification. Higher tax rates do not always lead to higher tax revenues. Instead, extreme tax rates—whether zero or 100 percent—result in tax revenues of zero dollars.

So how can we improve on figure 4.2? Certainly point A is correct, but where should our line proceed from there? If we know that a 100 percent tax rate also leads to no tax revenues for a government, then we can add a second point, point B, to the diagram. Point B, together with point A, is depicted in figure 4.3.

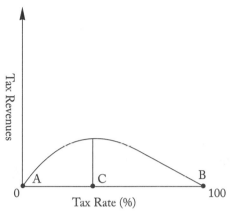

Figure 4.3. The Laffer curve: a more realistic view of the relationship between tax rates and tax revenues

What happens between points A and B? In figure 4.3 we have connected points A and B with a curve known as the Laffer curve. Created on a napkin by Arthur Laffer, the curve depicts the relationship between tax revenues and tax rates. Starting from a tax rate of zero (i.e., no taxes), small increases in the tax rate will not discourage many individuals from working. Thus, beginning from a tax rate of zero, modest increases in the tax rate can lead to fairly rapid increases in the value of tax revenues collected.

However, as the tax rate continues to rise further and further above zero percent, taxpayers begin to change their behavior in three ways that will cause tax revenues to increase more slowly. First, as tax rates rise, workers do not receive the same after-tax income from an hour of work that they used to at lower rates. This realization will cause some workers to choose to work less.

This change in behavior will be most noticeable among workers who were already torn between working and not working. For example, the second-income earner in a two-income household might very well choose to stop working altogether following a tax increase, if doing so would mean that he or she would be free to spend more time at home with young children.

Second, when tax rates are higher, the potential payoff from underreporting income grows. So, as tax rates rise, individuals may begin to understate their earned incomes. As a result, income that might have been reported when tax rates were low goes underreported as tax rates grow—with no taxes collected on any of that income.

Finally, at low tax rates, individuals may not attempt to find clever ways to exploit loopholes in the tax code that can let them keep more of their earned income for themselves. However, as tax rates rise workers contribute an increasingly larger share of each dollar earned in the workforce. As a result, higher tax rates will cause some workers to seek out skillful tax accountants who can help discover legal ways to avoid paying more taxes.

So, consider again points A and B in figure 4.3. At point A, when there are no income taxes, there are no incentives to stop working, to hide income or to work to find loopholes in the tax code. At point B, where every dollar earned is taken in taxes, there is every incentive not to work, to hide income and to find ways to avoid paying taxes. As a result, tax revenues rise initially as tax rates rise. However, revenues eventually fall all the way back down to zero as tax rates approach 100 percent.

Hence, a reasonable question is, What's the best tax rate? According to the Laffer curve, the optimal tax rate lies somewhere like point C. To the left of point C, raising tax rates leads to an increase in tax revenues. To the right of point C, though, *cutting* tax rates will lead to an increase in the number of dollars received in taxes.

Historical experience in the United States confirms the wisdom of the Laffer curve. Prior to the comprehensive income-tax reforms of the 1980s, the tax rate imposed on the last dollar earned by those with the highest incomes was 70 percent. That is, if you were someone already making quite a bit of money, all you kept from the next dollar you might earn was a mere thirty cents. It is indeed hard to imagine that a bright, creative entrepreneur would be willing to work very hard—if at all—to keep a mere 30 cents on the dollar.

By the end of the 1980s, though, we reduced the tax rate on the last dollar earned by those with the highest incomes all the way from 70 cents on the dollar down to a mere 33 cents. Now, if a bright, talented person with a high income were contemplating pursuing some additional creative opportunity, he or she could keep 67 cents of each dollar earned—quite an improvement over the 30 cents at the start of the decade.

So, what happened to tax revenues during this "natural experiment?" Was the Laffer curve vindicated? The answer to this question is crucial. Reducing the tax rates of high-income earners could be perceived as grossly unfair, because wealthy people already make a lot of money. If we really need more tax dollars, then maybe we should *raise* tax rates of those with high incomes to get the needed funds.

But if the Laffer curve is right, and if an economy currently has tax rates that lie somewhere to the right of point C in figure 4.3, then cutting taxes would encourage more work. And more work would lead to higher incomes—incomes that could be taxed.

Looking at the evidence reveals something very interesting. During the 1980s, though taxes at the very top were cut from 70 percent down to 33 percent, tax dollars collected from the top one percent of income earners *rose* by more than 50 percent by the end of the decade. Moreover, the top 1 percent of income earners ended up shouldering a *greater* total share of all taxes paid. In 1980, 19 percent of total taxes were collected from the top 1 percent. By 1990, though, the top 1 percent were shouldering over 25 percent of the entire tax burden (Gwartney, Stroup, Sobel & MacPherson 2006, pp. 101-2). Therefore, in this specific instance, cutting taxes on high-income earners in the 1980s led to a tax system in which (1) more tax dollars were collected overall, (2) more total tax dollars were paid by workers with extremely high incomes, and (3) high-income earners contributed an even greater share of all tax dollars collected.

Of course, had the United States been on the other side of the Laffer curve at the beginning of the 1980s, tax cuts would have produced disastrous results. Therefore, it is crucial for policymakers to appreciate the insight of the Laffer curve and estimate carefully our present position, before deciding whether to raise or lower taxes.

HOW SHOULD I FEEL ABOUT TITHING?

During the last seventy years, taxes paid on the salary of the average American have risen from about 10 percent to over 30 percent. Moreover, the government now performs many of the tasks traditionally undertaken by the early church (caring for the poor and sick, etc.). Further, in nations with relatively high levels of provision of such services and—unavoidably—higher taxes, there appears to be a lower level of charitable giving by its residents as individuals. For example, Brooks (2006) estimates that average individual charitable giving in the United States is about three and one half times greater than in France, a nation with a very large infrastructure of publicly funded social safety nets (p. 120).

As a result, it is legitimate to ask whether the biblical injunction to tithe has been affected by the increasing collection of monies by government to care for the poor and sick. Before considering that question, though, it is helpful to understand the original Old Testament tithe and the history of tithing in America.

Kelly (2004) notes that there is very little source material available today concerning Israel's tithe. As a result, the tithe is not understood well. Despite limited resources, Kelly is able to make several key points concerning what the tithe was, and was not, in Israel's history. First, the tithe was a "rent" paid on land—because the land belonged to God—measured as a tenth of one year's production. That is, it was not an income tax—even though that is how many think about it today.

Moreover, because the tithe was a rent paid according to the yield from land, only landholders were liable to pay the tithe. Even though others had incomes, they were not subject to the tithe, because they did not earn their living from the land. For example, the Levites paid no tithe because they received no land inheritance (Kelly 2004, p. 7).

Today, however, we think of the tithe almost exclusively as an offering to God calculated as 10 percent of our income. But this is a relatively recent notion in the history of Christianity, dating back only to the 1800s.

In early America churches no longer enjoyed the privileged status they had held as state *and* ecclesiastical bodies in Europe. As a result, their sources of funds were no longer as rich and reliable as they had been for centuries. In the New World, then, churches began to explore new sources of revenues. For example, many churches began charging pew rentals. However, by the beginning of the 1800s, such tiny streams of income were no longer adequate to support American churches. Large parish churches began to liquidate their land assets, but such measures were limited. Eventually, many churches experienced a bitter financial crisis in the early part of the 1800s.

In an effort to shore up their finances, churches dusted off the tithing concept during the antebellum period. Much like any other fundraising effort, churches campaigned to compel their parishioners to tithe, and it was during this period that tithing came to mean giving 10 percent of one's income.

Despite this somewhat murky history surrounding the tithe, there are many excellent reasons to give, and give generously, to God, his church and to those who serve him throughout the world. Paul Krupinski, pastor of Trinity Lutheran Church in Grand Rapids, Michigan, provides ten reasons to consider giving generously to God and his church:

1. Give generously, so that it becomes habitual.

2. Give to God first, before deciding what to do with the rest of your income. It will help keep your priorities straight. Don't even think about what you would like to buy until you have first given to God.

3. Give because you believe in the mission and ministry of the church.

4. Give in order to participate in a partnership with other Christians. You can't build a new soup kitchen or Sunday school unit on your own, but it can be accomplished when faithful Christians give together.

5. Give in support of others engaged in the service of God's kingdom.

6. Give to meet the physical and spiritual needs of others.

7. Give as part of the stewardship of your life. Just as we need to be good stewards of the environment and our time, we must respond appropriately to the abundance we are blessed with.

8. Give to express your appreciation for God's blessings.

9. Give because God requires it. Give because of what God asks and because you are probably at your very best when you are giving.

10. Give because it feels good, and it feels right.

So, regardless of what is going on around you, give generously to God. Set aside your offerings to God before addressing the other financial commitments in your life. Let's give God our best and give to him first. We must not let giving to God become a chore or a curse. Instead, we can rejoice in the abundance that God has provided.

And we should not be afraid to prayerfully consider increasing our giving over time. For example, see if you can increase your giving by one percent each year. You might be surprised at the abiding faithfulness of God and at the deep, rich joy available to Christians who faithfully, regularly and generously give.

FOR FURTHER READING

Barro, Robert J. 2002. *Nothing is sacred: Economic ideas for the new millennium.* Cambridge, Mass.: MIT Press. Often, modern economic dialogue degenerates into only emotional appeals and demagoguery. Barro brings a cooler head to such discussions, arguing that there can be few sacred cows when society examines ways in which to improve its well-being.

Barthold, Thomas A. 1994. Issues in the design of environmental excise taxes. *Journal of Economic Perspectives,* 8(1), 133-51. Encourages economists— and others—to fully think through the use of Pigouvian taxes. This very readable presentation suggests Pigouvian taxes are merely a starting point.

Blinder, Alan S. 1987. *Hard heads, soft hearts: Tough-minded economics for a just society*. Reading, Mass.: Addison-Wesley. To arrive at first-best outcomes for the most needy in society, economists need to approach related policy approaches with the most clear, careful analysis available. To do otherwise, relying on pure emotion alone, will result in inefficient efforts to help others. A call to be passionate *and* clear headed.

5

CREATION CARE

Exercising Good Stewardship in the Garden

Many environmentalists hate Christianity. In 1966 Lynn White Jr., then professor of history at UCLA, delivered a lecture that made this point painfully clear. In his address, given at a Washington meeting of the American Association for the Advancement of Science, and later published in *Science*, White (1967) stated, "By destroying pagan animism, Christianity made it possible to exploit nature. . . . [W]e shall continue to have a worsening ecologic crisis until we reject the Christian axiom that nature has no reason for existence save to serve man" (pp. 1205, 1207). White argued that by destroying pagan animism, Christians made it morally acceptable to ignore the "feelings" of natural objects like rocks, trees, insects and plants. According to White, "Christianity bears a huge burden of guilt" (p. 1206). And White is not alone in denouncing Christianity as incompatible with an appropriate view of the relationship between humans and the environment. For a fair, detailed chronicle of the ongoing widespread animosity of radical environmentalists toward Christianity, see either Coffman (1994) or Whelan, Kirwan and Haffner (1996).

In this chapter, we dismiss White's claim that God's plan for the relationship of humans to nature necessarily leads to environmental degradation. Instead, we assert that Christians, called to be good stewards of all of God's creation, must exercise caution and wisdom in the pursuit of environmental goals. Further, we show that modern economics has much to say about responsible care for and cleanup of the environment.

In this chapter we first provide a quick overview of the main sources of pollution in Western industrialized nations. Second, we compare and contrast two alternative ways of thinking in economics regarding the appropriate role of environmental policy: (1) the thinking of "environmental economists," whose views are more traditional in economics, and (2) the views of a newer group who call themselves "ecological economists." We also consider the implications of each viewpoint for the conduct of environmental policy. Third, we discuss whether there might be an optimal level of cleanup of an already polluted resource. To do this, we again apply the principles behind cost-benefit analysis in pursuit of the optimal policy action. Fourth, we discuss global climate change and share some reflections on the report of economist Nicholas Stern (2007). Fifth, we ask whether it is humane for Christians and others to hold poor nations to the same environmental quality standards that are affordable to those of us fortunate enough to live in wealthy Western nations. Finally, we reflect on the hope for environmental sustainability that Christians share, even though we live in a post-Eden world.

The overarching emphasis here is on gaining a greater and more informed perspective on some potential global threats. We are called to use God's gifts of creativity and caring to take action in ways and places where we can make a difference.

One word of warning: looking at issues through the eyes of economics requires a certain intellectual patience. This is especially true for Christians who know they should care about big issues. Economic arguments about creation care are never easy, quick and intellectually unchallenging. What this chapter attempts is to contrast ideology with reason, coming out on the side of reason. And, in this case, reason is much more hopeful than ideology. At the very least, Christians reading this chapter are forewarned not to react only with emotion where God's creation is concerned. Caring for the environment is too serious a business for Christians to rely on emotions alone in considering careful policy.

ESSENTIAL FACTS ABOUT THE ENVIRONMENT

According to Steven Bouma-Prediger, the sky is falling. Bouma-Prediger's 2001 book, *For the Beauty of the Earth: A Christian Vision for Creation Care*, is being taken very seriously by Christians who are concerned about the environment and are seeking guidance about what to do. In fact, the book received an Award of Merit in *Christianity Today*'s 2002 book awards. In the book Bouma-Prediger sounds a warning to all of us:

> Exploding population growth, hunger and malnutrition, loss of biodiversity, deforestation, water scarcity and impurity, land degradation, waste production, en-

ergy misuse, air pollution and acid rain, global climate change—such is the litany of ecological woe. The state of our home planet is not good. The earth is groaning. (p. 65)

Bouma-Prediger was equally alarmed in a 1995 book:

> Global warming, holes in the ozone layer, toxic wastes, oil spills, acid rain, drinking water contamination, overflowing landfills, topsoil erosion, species extinction, destruction of the rainforests, leakage of nuclear waste, lead poisoning, desertification, smog—such is merely a partial litany of worry and woe. . . . [T]hat we today are facing a large and seemingly intractable ecological crisis— nightmare some would say—seems irrefutable. . . . [I]nformed observers concur that the earth and its various ecosystems are groaning in travail. The plight of the earth is all too real. (Bouma-Prediger 1995, pp. 3, 5-6)

In the remainder of this section we describe briefly the major sources of pollution today. Our intention is not to give an exhaustive account of how good or bad things are. Instead, we provide just a glimpse of the current state of the world, as well as recent trends. To do this, we rely heavily upon the outline given in Parkin (2005b).

Land pollution. Landfill space, by itself, is not a problem. Lomborg (2001b) estimates the necessary land area required to dispose of all new waste in the United States through the year 2100. According to Lomborg such a site would need to be a square with sides no longer than eighteen miles (pp. 207-8). Hence, the real space issue is a political one—not environmental. That is, we need landfills, and the landfills do not need to be large, but we are unable to agree where the landfills should be located.

A more serious land pollution issue is toxic waste. Surprisingly, this problem becomes more serious when landfill space is not permitted to grow for political reasons. Under proper management, contaminants from landfills do not escape and seep into the water supply. However, as existing landfills become more compacted, these risks grow since increasing pressure squeezes contaminants beyond the landfill space (Parkin 2005b, p. 344).

Water pollution. One of the most headline-grabbing forms of water pollution is accidental marine oil spills, like the 1989 *Exxon Valdez* spill in Alaska. Contrary to popular belief, the *Valdez* spill is not the largest accidental oil spill in history, despite its release of 266,000 barrels of oil. The *Atlantic Empress* spilled eight times more oil in 1979 (Lomborg 2001b, pp. 190, 192).

Even more surprising is the fact that history's single greatest marine oil spill was no accident. During the final days of the 1991 war in the Persian Gulf,

Saddam Hussein began executing his own form of scorched-earth policy as he retreated from Kuwait. On land, Hussein set fire to Kuwait's oil fields. The fires burned so brightly and hotly that firefighters from across the globe were recruited to put them out. Over ten thousand brave men and women fought the blazes for months: the greatest nonmilitary mobilization of manpower in world history (*Fires of Kuwait* 2001).

But Hussein did not stop there. In retreat Hussein jettisoned up to eight million barrels of oil into the Persian Gulf, resulting in the planet's single greatest marine oil spill ever—and it was no accident (*New York Times* 1993). Owing to both the oil fires of Kuwait and the deliberate oil spill in the Gulf, Saddam Hussein should be as notorious for pollution as he is for ethnic cleansing; no contemporary comes close.

While oil spills are dramatic and receive a lot of media attention, they are not the primary form of water pollution. Today, most water pollution comes from fertilizer runoff, dumping of treated sewage into lakes and waterways, and industrial waste dumping.

Air pollution. There is little dispute concerning air-quality facts. Three-fifths of air pollution in the United States is caused by industry and road transportation. Less than one-fifth is due to electric power generation (Parkin 2005b, p. 343).

As nations grow in affluence and are able to afford more things that improve their quality of life, they choose to devote more of their resources to improving air quality. And the air quality in the United States is improving for most substances. As Parkin notes, though, there is much disagreement regarding the consequences of air pollution—even if the facts are indisputable. The two most controversial consequences of air pollution are *ozone layer depletion* and *global warming*.

The earth's ozone layer protects us all from the sun's harmful ultraviolet rays. Most people, based on what they have read and heard in the media, believe that there is a "hole" in the ozone layer over Antarctica. This is not quite accurate. More precisely, there is a seasonal thickening and thinning of the ozone layer over the South Pole. While it appears that the annual cycle of thickening and thinning corresponds to the passing of the seasons, we do not yet thoroughly understand how our industrial activities influence this phenomenon. Graedel and Crutzen (1993) give a good introduction to the phenomenon of stratospheric ozone depletion.

Global warming is just as controversial as ozone layer depletion, yet even less well understood. No one disputes that the earth's temperature is higher than it was a century ago. However, it is difficult to understand why most of the increase in temperature occurred prior to 1940. If road transportation, industry and electric power generation really are to blame, then we would certainly expect the most rapid increases in temperature to have occurred since 1940, not before. Moreover, scientists—using evidence from tree rings—estimate that the earth may actually be cooler today than it was during the first half of the last millennium (*Tampering with Nature* 2002). That is, the earth may actually have been hotter as China's Tang dynasty concluded, the period of the Vikings came to an end and the Reformation began.

Airborne substances are less controversial, especially since their concentrations are declining in the United States. These 189 currently-identified substances can lead to lung cancer, emphysema and other ailments.

What lies ahead. But what do economic theory, as well as the existing data, indicate? Is there reason for hope? Or for despair? Many economists are very hopeful —even enthusiastic—concerning the future prospects for the environment.

A much more vocal minority, though, does indeed believe that the sky is falling. They offer little reason for hope. They prize nature above humanity. And they are the ones who have the ear of many well-intentioned Christians.

TWO VIEWS OF ENVIRONMENTAL SUSTAINABILITY

What would you think if you were told that there were only 531 billion barrels worth of crude oil remaining beneath the earth's surface, and that—each year—we consume 16.5 billion barrels of the stuff? You would certainly think that we would exhaust the earth's oil supply—and soon: in just a little over thirty-two years. And many thought exactly that when they considered these numbers—back in 1970.

A little arithmetic in 1970 led to concern that we would run out, completely out, of oil. We started turning down thermostats from 72 to 68 degrees. We began importing smaller, more fuel-efficient cars from strange places like Germany and Japan. We aired TV commercials to encourage even more people to turn down their thermostats and drive smaller, more fuel-efficient cars. We went vigilantly from room to room in our homes to make sure no light bulb needlessly burned.

How is it that a 1970 estimate—that we would have burned though the entire planet's supply of oil by the early spring of 2003—turned out to be so far off? Not only have we not run out of oil but gasoline continues to be relatively cheap. This indeed seems surprising, since goods are supposed to be expensive when they are in both high demand and short supply. While it is true that gas prices have risen sharply in recent years, the inflation-adjusted price of gasoline has exhibited a broad overall downward trend over the last century. In fact, in terms of the 2005 value of a dollar, the price of a gallon of gasoline at the end of 2006 was about fifty cents cheaper than it was in the early 1980s. Figure 5.1 depicts the inflation-adjusted (real) price of gasoline, together with the nominal (that is, the unadjusted price), for each year from 1919 forward. Notice that the overall trend is a downward one.

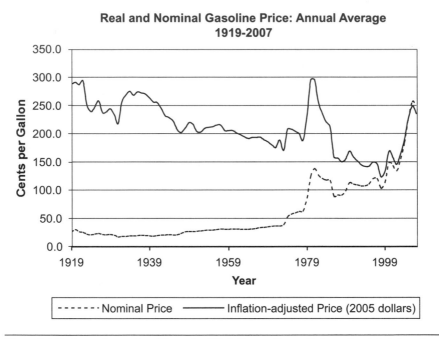

Figure 5.1. Real petroleum prices (November 2006). Source: Energy Information Administration, U.S. Department of Energy (December 2006 and 2007 projected)

We face a puzzle. Some tell us that we will inevitably run out of oil—a non-renewable resource. But the long-term trend of gasoline prices suggests something different. After all, scarce resources are supposed to have high prices. The Hope diamond, Tom Hanks's unique acting skills and oceanfront real estate: all of these are scarce resources, and we expect to pay a high price for them. In fact, price is the tool by which we ration out the available supply of these scarce commodities.

Yet gasoline is still relatively cheap—cheaper than the bottled water we all like to drink. Can economics explain this apparent contradiction?

The answer, it turns out, depends on which economists you ask. Many economists, operating in an area traditionally referred to as "environmental economics," believe this question has a promising answer. Other economists—who call themselves "ecological economists"—have a tougher time reconciling this apparent contradiction of scarce resources and falling prices. In "Environmental Economics" (see below) we outline the fundamental differences between economists working in the environmental tradition and those in the newer ecological school. Environmental economists are hopeful that—given the right conditions, actions and policies—tomorrow will be at least as bright as today, while ecological economists are more alarmed over the state of the planet tomorrow.

Because the specific strategies to address environmental concerns have become thoroughly divisive in recent times—even among compassionate, thoughtful Christians who care genuinely and deeply about the fate of the planet—this section demanded extra care on our part. As we discuss each of the following two schools of thought in contemporary economics, we follow closely the descriptions of each of these two schools provided by Goodstein (2005), a textbook covering economics and the environment, now in its fourth edition. By faithfully following Goodstein, we hope that we will not unfairly or inaccurately portray anyone working within either tradition. Economists in both schools care deeply about the environment; if they did not, they would be working in some other dimension of economics. Moreover, we hope that interested readers will consult the relevant sections of Goodstein's work for themselves. Chapter seven of Goodstein's text is especially helpful in this regard.

Environmental economics. In contrast to the views of ecological economics, environmental economists hold out great hope for the sustainability of the planet and its resources. Their hope stems from two sources: historical economic evidence and economic theory. We consider each in turn.

Recall our earlier example of how inflation-adjusted gasoline prices have largely fallen throughout the last century. If oil is a nonrenewable resource and the population is growing, then the price of gasoline should be rising. In fact, that is one of the primary functions of prices: prices serve as a tool to ration out the remaining quantity of a commodity in limited supply. Thus the price of most commodities, renewable or otherwise, should be expected to rise over time in the face of an increasingly consumption-minded, ever-growing population.

But the available empirical evidence seems to suggest something else. Although prices of particular commodities can rise for sustained periods, for all kinds of reasons, we are unlikely to observe sustained increases in all commodity prices over time. Moreover, commodity price increases, when they occur, are helpful in responding to scarcity—even if they cause some temporary inconveniences.

In a famous bet, economist Julian Simon offered to bet $10,000 that the price of any basket of commodities—to be picked by the other party—would drop in price over the course of any time interval longer than one year. Not only was the other party free to pick the mix of commodities in the basket; the other party could also pick the specific time interval.

The famous environmentalist who took up the bet, Paul Ehrlich, working with physicists John Harte and John Holdren (Ehrlich's colleagues at Stanford), selected five commodities: chromium, copper, nickel, tin and tungsten. At the end of the ten-year time horizon selected by Ehrlich, if the inflation-adjusted price of the basket rose—as predicted by many at the time—Ehrlich would receive the $10,000 prize.

Ehrlich lost. And he could hardly be expected to have won. Most commodities, even nonrenewable ones, tend to become cheaper over time—not more expensive.

Of course, just because something has happened in the past does not explain why it can be expected to happen again in the future. In this case, the fact that commodity prices have tended to fall, on average, over time does not explain why this happened.

For environmental economists this historical phenomenon has a theoretical explanation. Price serves an important role as a tool to ration out the existing supply of any good or commodity. When a commodity grows increasingly scarce, and its price rises accordingly, price begins to fulfill a second important role: inducing a supply response.

That is, as scarcity in the face of an ongoing demand for a particular commodity drives the price of that product ever higher, profit-seeking entrepreneurs begin to undertake two new activities *that will reduce the rate at which the scarce commodity is consumed.* First, entrepreneurs invest in new technologies designed to renew the resource. The most obvious example of this in modern times is reforestation. Entrepreneurs in the lumber and paper industries realize that they will be out of work if they do not take great care to ensure the long-term survival of the earth's forests. Hence, they use modern forestry science to exercise stewardship over each region under their care, renewing our supply of timber for each generation.

Second, as the price of one commodity rises, profit-seeking entrepreneurs begin the search to find other commodities and technologies that serve as substitutes for the increasingly scarce good. As a result, consumers, over time, are able to switch away from the commodity that had a high price to the new and often superior alternative. One of the most recent examples of a new technology-as-substitute is the widespread popularity of hybrid automobiles that combine gasoline and self-generated electricity within one car. In this case, it is the innovation of a car that runs, in part, on self-generated electricity that represents the substitution of technology for gasoline. The Toyota Prius and the Honda Civic Hybrid have become such big hits with consumers that car dealers cannot keep up with consumer demand in some markets.

Meanwhile, engineers at General Motors are working at the frontier of alternatives to the gasoline-powered internal-combustion engine: hydrogen fuel cells. GM has "established extensive hydrogen fuel cell research and development facilities both in the U.S. and Europe." Researchers at GM have produced both AUTOnomy, "a concept vehicle that captures the vision and potential of hydrogen fuel cell technology" and the Hy-wire, which has no internal combustion engine, but instead runs on emissions-free power supplied by a hydrogen fuel cell (General Motors).

In October 2004, Jetcar—a German company—participated in the EU's "Energy in Motion" conference in Amsterdam. At the conference Jetcar shared its advanced car concept with European ministers of traffic and the environment. Since then Jetcar has begun production of a vehicle that can travel over 110 miles on just one gallon of diesel oil (Jetcar).[1]

It would be naive to think that the entrepreneurs behind such developments as the hybrid car, the nascent hydrogen fuel cell and Jetcar have been motivated primarily by altruistic, environmentally friendly reasons. Instead, it is because they seek profits for themselves and their stockholders that entrepreneurs rush to develop and bring to consumers lower-priced alternatives to relatively scarce commodities. New products like these, ones that work better and cost less than their old counterparts, are always a big hit with consumers. And as long as entrepreneurs, inventors and engineers are able to work within

---

[1]This information is based on data from the Jetcar website and our own calculations.

strong market-based economies, there will always be incentives to supply a better product at a lower price to consumers.

In fact, oil firms in Qatar, right in the middle of the oil-rich Persian Gulf, are working to turn abundant natural gas into a clean-burning alternative automotive fuel that they hope will rival anything the oil industry can provide today. This new clear fuel could be used in diesel-powered trucks and cars worldwide. The project is not without financial risks for these groundbreaking companies; but they are willing to assume such risks in exchange for the eventual rewards they hope to receive in the marketplace for delivering to consumers a cheap, clean alternative to gasoline.

Therefore, even though oil is a nonrenewable fossil fuel, it appears unlikely we will drain every drop from below the earth's surface. By the time oil becomes so scarce that no one can afford it, no one will want to buy it anyway because we will soon be discovering better, cheaper, cleaner technologies that will allow us to abandon oil as an input in many of our world's economic activities.

Ecological economics. Where the environment is concerned, ecological economists tend to be a bit more worried about the eventual fate of the planet than their environmental school counterparts. The International Society for Ecological Economics serves as headquarters for the ecological movement. Founded in 1988, the society was established to foster the growth and development of a new school of economics, the ecological school.

Three main tenets of ecological economics set it apart from its environmental economics counterpart. First, for ecological economists, nothing is more valuable than the natural environment, both at the local and global level, *as it exists today.* To the ecological economist, *preservation* is the ultimate goal; mere conservation is admirable but insufficient. Therefore, it is important to preserve the current level of biodiversity among all species, and to contain or reduce the movements of humans in order to preserve the natural order.

Second, ecological economists believe that resource exhaustion is inevitable. According to this view, there are few good substitutes available—and may never be—for precious resources that occur naturally. So, for the ecological economist, once bituminous and anthracite coal are gone, they are gone. Once oil is gone, it is gone. Any potentially exhaustible resource will be exhausted; the only question is how soon exhaustion will happen.

Moreover, ecological economists contend that two simultaneous, inescapable forces are causing us to accelerate toward inevitable resource exhaustion:

population growth and an increasing taste for consumption goods. Regarding the first force, population growth, the views of ecological economists are similar to the views of classical economists like Thomas Malthus. For Malthus, writing over two hundred years ago, population growth represented the single greatest threat to the advancement of civilization. Prior to the era in which Malthus lived and wrote, the size of the earth's population had always been held in check by four threats: war, natural disaster, famine and pestilence. However, as the end of the eighteenth century approached, it began to appear that the last two, famine and pestilence, were no longer the omnipresent threats they had been throughout human history. Hence, concluded Malthus and his contemporaries, population growth would no longer be held in check; even further, they believed that the subsequent strain of population growth on the planet's natural resources would mean that the standard of living enjoyed by humankind would never be able to rise above a minimum subsistence level.

Of course, Malthus and his contemporaries turned out to be incorrect. While the earth's population has indeed grown as we have reduced problems like famine and disease, the global standard of living has steadily grown over the past two centuries. And even though different parts of the globe have grown at different rates, most parts of the planet enjoy living standards superior to anything Malthus might have imagined. Nevertheless, because ecological economists believe that inescapable population growth represents an ever-present strain on the planet and its resources, ecological economists are often referred to as "Neo-Malthusians." Neo-Malthusians happen to drive much of the current dialogue among Christians regarding the environment. Steven Bouma-Prediger's (see pp. 90-91) and Bill McKibben's (1998) writings represent well the presence of Malthusian thought in modern Christian environmentalism.

But ecological economists do not stop here. For them, population growth is only one trend leading us to eventual calamity. In addition, consumers are never content with the existing mix and quantity of goods available. Instead, consumers have unlimited wants for goods—goods manufactured using earth's limited resources.

Taken together, the simultaneous strains of population growth and increasing consumption demand suggest an ever-escalating state of peril for the earth and its resources. Hence, ecological economists recommend that we curtail, or arrest altogether, consumption of all nonrenewable resources.

The final tenet of ecological economics is that, no matter how much we learn about environmental science, the earth is a precariously fragile eco-system—fragile in obscure, unknowable ways. Consider this quote from the United Kingdom's *Guardian* newspaper:

> The human race is living beyond its means. . . . [L]ife on Earth is being de-graded by human pressure. . . . The wetlands, forests, savannahs, estuaries, coastal fisheries and other habitats that recycle air, water and nutrients for all liv-ing creatures are being irretrievably damaged. In effect, one species [human] is now a hazard to the other 10 million or so on the planet, and to itself. . . . De-forestation and other changes could . . . open the way for new and so far un-known disease to emerge. (Radford 2005)

According to this tenet, then, there may be no way for us to anticipate today what eventual global disasters we may be courting through our current actions. Even further, by the time we realize that we have sown the seeds of our own demise, it will be too late to take corrective action. Hence, the best plan is the safest one.

To review, ecological economics is built upon three fundamental tenets: (1) nothing is more valuable than the natural environment, both at the local and global level, *as it exists today*, (2) the dual pressures of population growth and increasing consumption demands are squeezing the planet toward resource ex-haustion, and (3) the earth is fragile in unknowable ways.

Two implications follow from these three tenets of ecological economics. The first implication is the well-documented *precautionary principle:* we should not use any nonrenewable natural resources until we have either found a suitable replacement or discovered a way to renew the resource. The other implication is that public policy needs to hold us accountable to the precau-tionary principle.

Christian living in a post-Eden world. The implication of the discussion on the environment is clear; both particular examples and the theory behind the work of environmental economists provide substantial reasons for hope re-garding the sustainability of the environment. The ecological view that mod-ern societies are thoughtlessly destroying nature by their very use of it and their development of ever more devastating technologies is, though borne from genuine concern, an incomplete picture.

Furthermore, the deep-seated suspicion of Christianity by ecological greats like Lynn White Jr. completely overlooks Christian affirmation of both scien-tific inquiry and ultimate devotion to God, the Creator, Redeemer and Sus-tainer of all that is good. Traditional Christianity has always been supportive of and open to the discoveries of science. We need not be afraid that the findings of the natural and social sciences—including economics—will eliminate the "need" for God. Neither are we to "worship" the findings of science, as if they release us from our moral responsibilities.

So how can we apply both our compassion for the earth and our call to be wise stewards in all things to creation care? As in prior chapters, we need to channel our energies to make the net gains of our actions as great as possible. And achieving that demands a careful assessment of every cost and benefit of any environmental policy proposal.

THE OPTIMAL LEVEL OF POLLUTION CLEANUP

How much should we clean up a polluted environmental resource? Is the optimal level of pollution cleanup 100 percent? Economics tells us it is not.

Think about a natural resource that has been thoroughly polluted. Perhaps the best modern example is Ohio's Cuyahoga River. By the end of the 1960s the Cuyahoga had become so polluted that it no longer served any real purpose other than as a place to dump waste. In fact, in June of 1969 the river had become so thoroughly polluted that it caught fire just southeast of downtown Cleveland.

So dramatic was this incident that it has been immortalized in products as wide-ranging as popular music and beer. On their 1986 album *Life's Rich Pageant*, multiplatinum recording artists R.E.M. recorded a song titled "Cuyahoga." Here is an excerpt from the lyrics:

> Let's put our heads together, start a new country up,
> Underneath the river bed we burned the river down.
> This is where they walked, swam, hunted, danced and sang,
> Take a picture here, take a souvenir
> Cuyahoga
> Cuyahoga, gone.

Today, the Great Lakes Brewing Company of Cleveland, Ohio, takes pride in producing a beer called Burning River Pale Ale, in remembrance of the 1969 fire on the river.

An important question in economics concerns how much pollution cleanup is appropriate. Let's continue to think about the state of the Cuyahoga in 1969 and begin weighing the benefits of cleaning it up against the costs.

Certainly there are benefits of having a clean river. First, clean rivers do not catch fire. Second, they do not look or smell bad. Third, if a river is clean enough, it becomes possible to do things like swim or canoe in it. Clean rivers are nice to have around.

But how many of society's resources should be used in cleaning up a filthy river? And how clean must the river be? If a river is clean enough, it might be possible for the local residents to brush their teeth in it on the way to work each morning.

Consider the benefits and costs involved in cleaning up a river like the Cuyahoga just a little, say a 10 percent cleanup. To clean the river just 10 percent, you could probably do it very cheaply. In fact, it might not cost society any money at all. If you could recruit volunteers to spend their Saturday mornings working at the river, they could easily address some of the most unsightly problems. They could pull out old tires and washing machines. They could gather up litter and dead fish. They could make these improvements very easily, the river would look much better, and the only cost to society would be what the volunteers might have done instead with their time on Saturday. So it would be relatively inexpensive for society to increase the level of river cleanup from zero percent to 10 percent.

But what about increasing the level of river cleanup further, from 10 to 20 percent? Unfortunately, increasing the level of cleanup from 10 to 20 percent will require more of society's resources than an increase from zero to 10 percent. Going from total pollution to a cleanup level of 10 percent required no resources other than volunteers picking up garbage. Improving things further might require the use of chemicals to treat the water. It might also require society to hire cleanup teams with specific expertise.

This phenomenon of increasing cleanup costs is inescapable. Consider how expensive it would be to take the river from 90 percent clean to the sanitized, pollution-free, toothbrushing-safe level of 100 percent clean. And think of all the other things that could be accomplished with the same resources. Therefore, society must again weigh carefully the benefit of additional pollution cleanup, at any stage, against the cost to society of that additional cleanup.

All of us make such calculations every day. We decide the optimal level of cleanup for our cars, our bathrooms, our bodies and our pets. In almost no circumstance does any of us make the decision to clean anything perfectly. We decide that it's not worth the time, trouble or money. We all clean up messes until things are "good enough," and then we move on to more pressing matters.

Society must make such a calculation as well. The optimal level of pollution cleanup for a society is not zero. Neither is it 100 percent. The optimal level of pollution cleanup lies at the point where we decide additional cleanup is not worth the time, the trouble and the money. We should clean up our environment until things are "good enough" and then move on to more urgent tasks.

GLOBAL CLIMATE CHANGE

Recent evidence suggests that the earth's temperature has been rising over the last hundred years or so, and that most of this warming occurred prior to 1940 (see p. 93). Even though this phenomenon is not yet completely understood, the possibility exists that human activity—including road transportation, industry and electric power generation—is to blame.

If so, society faces a difficult choice. On one hand, we must be responsible stewards of all God provides, including all of creation. On the other hand, the activities that may be causing the recent temperature observations are the very activities that lead to long-term prosperity and economic growth for all.

As in other examples we have considered, we do not face an all-or-nothing choice. Instead, the fundamental question becomes how much growth and prosperity society should sacrifice in order to ensure the long-term viability of the planet. After all, slowing the rate of growth will result in a slower rate of increase in the level of per capita national income, both here and abroad. And where the world's poorest people are concerned, this is a very hard choice indeed.

In 2007, Nicholas Stern (2007) released his seven hundred-page assessment of the economic costs and benefits associated with working today in order to slow the rate of increase in global temperatures in the future. Stern is one of the most important figures in modern public economics, and his study reflects an extensive evaluation of this particular challenge. Stern concludes that the economic costs of fighting global warming today, in the form of smaller current incomes and slower long-term growth, are small relative to the potential economic benefits to all of us. Stern employs the most clear-headed techniques available in arriving at this conclusion.

While we have not read Stern's entire manuscript from front to back, we do have a few reflections to share regarding Stern's study. First, the possibility exists that Stern's recommendations have the potential to harm relatively poor people today in order to make life better for the relatively wealthy tomorrow. Since national income in the United States grows, on average, at a rate of about 2 percent per year, and we have no reason to believe this trend will change, then people in the future will have more resources available to them tomorrow than we have available to us today. So one issue raised by Stern's work is one of timing. That is, the decision regarding when to begin address-ing—and paying for—global climate change has serious potential distribu-tional consequences.

In 2006 in the United States per capita income was about $44,000. Un-changed, over one hundred years, a mere 2 percent increase per year would lead to an inflation-adjusted per capita income of roughly $320,000. If we be-gin today to correct global climate change, then, we will be imposing the costs of such programs on the individuals with the smallest ability to pay for it—which hardly seems fair. On the other hand, if the Stern report is correct about the science of global warming, we cannot put off getting started until it is too late, either.

A second consideration concerns how well we understand today which spe-cific strategies are most efficient in reducing global warming. Of course, we would like to see things improve as much as possible at the smallest possible cost. Therefore, we should not begin blindly changing our actions today unless we are convinced that the specific actions we take are the ones that will result in the greatest net benefit for all.

As in other environmental matters discussed here, we must be good stew-ards of all we have been given. And in the case of global climate change, we must carefully consider all of the costs and potential benefits of every specific proposed policy.

FORCING HIGH ENVIRONMENTAL STANDARDS ON THE WORLD'S POOREST PEOPLE

We often use trade barriers as a way to put economic pressure on nations that are engaged in activities we find objectionable. For example, we do not trade with North Korea because of their totalitarian political system. Similarly, we have not traded with nations, such as Iraq, that have poor records regarding human rights. Our hope has been that, under sufficient economic pressures, such nations would begin to institute political or human rights reforms.

Today's environmental activists would like to use trade policies to exert sim-ilar pressure on nations with poor environmental records. That is, they would like the Western nations that have already implemented many new environ-mentally friendly policies to use trade boycotts as a way to bring other nations into line with standards in the West. This disturbing trend was recently high-lighted in the *Economist*:

In his campaign for the American presidency in 1992, Bill Clinton opposed

President George Bush's plan for a North American Free-Trade Agreement with Canada and Mexico, partly on environmental grounds. When elected, he insisted that environmental . . . side-agreements be tacked on to NAFTA. And in 1994, after Congress approved the Uruguay round agreement of the GATT—which gave birth to the WTO—Mr. Clinton promised that future trade agreements would take account of the environment. . . .

But poorer countries are almost all hostile. They fear that environmental issues will be used by rich countries as yet another excuse to adopt protectionist policies. (*Economist* 1999)

Unfortunately, the nations with the poorest environmental records are also among the world's poorest economically. For most developing nations the most pressing issues are not environmental ones; instead, they have more urgent concerns, such as high infant mortality, malnutrition, extreme poverty and inadequate access to safe drinking water and medical care.

For such nations it would be inappropriate to require them to observe the same environmental standards that highly developed nations in the West have been able to achieve. Poor nations should be permitted to first feed, clothe and sustain themselves before we hold them to a standard of environmental responsibility that we can already afford. Moreover, it would be immoral to use trade as a way to attempt to change their behaviors. Doing so would only worsen the economic plight of the poorest nations and also send a message that the lives and the dignity of our fellow human beings in poor nations are less valuable than the rest of God's creation. On the other hand, First World people who are concerned about rapid natural depletion in the Third World could encourage preservation by subsidizing adoption of conservation measures in places where the people are too poor to pay for it themselves.

A clean environment is something every nation can afford as it grows in affluence. When a nation is poor it should work on economic development today so it can afford a cleaner environment tomorrow. Thankfully, we have begun to realize how important it is to the development of poor nations to exempt them from unreasonable levels of environmental responsibility. For example, the recently enacted Kyoto treaty does not apply to developing countries (Carlisle and Ball 2005, A16).

Therefore, we should not deny trade to poor nations that cannot yet afford a high level of environmental quality. Instead, we should do everything possible to help them become more prosperous—including promoting free trade with them. Then, as they grow economically through the fruits that free trade brings to all, they will be able to afford to devote more of their resources toward policies and activities designed to renew the environment.

OUR RESPONSE AS STEWARDS OF EVERY GOOD GIFT

Throughout this chapter we have encouraged the compassionate, thoughtful reader to exercise the best possible stewardship in all things, including caring for creation. And doing so demands a thorough consideration of all costs and potential benefits of any proposed action. Relying on emotion alone, while admirable, may produce less than optimal results. Instead, we encourage all interested readers to keep their passion for doing good, but channel that passion into acting with great wisdom and care.

Aside from collective action in the policy arena, concerned Christians can find opportunities to practice active stewardship in whatever situation or circumstance they find themselves. Especially since official environmental policy actions can take years to coalesce, it is especially important for all of us to begin making a difference wherever we may be, and using whatever gifts we have been given.

One direct way we can all make a difference in our local communities, watersheds and regions is by giving generously of our financial resources to nature conservancies. Conservancies use funds to purchase and preserve land from economic development. By directly buying land, conservancies have a powerful, immediate and lasting affect on the environment. Look online or in your phonebook to learn about conservancies in your area, and give generously.

Second, find ways to make a big impact at low cost. For example, Adopt-a-Highway programs are a fabulously efficient way to make roadways look dramatically better with very little investment of time or other resources. See if others in the professional or social groups you belong to would be interested in adopting a highway near you.

Finally, you could use your financial resources to purchase and retire pollution permits where you live. Each year the U.S. Environment Protection Agency issues and auctions off pollution permits—pieces of paper that give the bearer the right to pollute (or not to pollute) a certain amount of a specific effluent. College students at campuses across the country, often as part of their economics classes, regularly purchase some of these permits from the marketplace and retire them. By doing so the students make a lasting difference in the amount of pollution that may be generated by power plants and other firms. In particular, students at Bates College, Hobart and William Smith

Colleges, Yale University and Florida's Stetson University regularly purchase and retire pollution permits. If you are a college student, ask your economics professor how your class could get involved in buying and retiring permits. In 2003 alone, students in the 200-level environmental economics course at Bates College bid on, purchased and retired a permit for the atmospheric release of a ton of sulfur dioxide (SO_2), a pollutant that causes acid rain. The fifty students in the course each put $5 toward a bid for the permit.

CONCLUSION

In the context of this chapter, our theme of reasoned hope continues to be confirmed. We would not expect our loving God to create us in a way that using our creativity and ingenuity to improve on our physical or social standards of life leads to the annihilation of his glorious creation. In fact, what economics has shown about the environment is exactly what we would expect from a God who blesses us with his creation and—made in his image—our own creativity. As a result of the reasoned hope for the planet discussed in this chapter, we do not have to be in moral arrest about the extreme fate of the world. Instead, we can attend to the local, specific tasks where our actions bring promise at the micro level.

FOR FURTHER READING

Dean, Judith M. 1997. Are we turning poor countries into pollution havens? Understanding the trade/environment debate. *Faith & Economics* 30:7-14. A leading Christian economist clarifies issues surrounding potential environmental effects on poor nations that open their doors to free trade and foreign direct investment.

Poterba, James M. 1993. Global warming policy: A public finance perspective. *Journal of Economic Perspectives*, 7(4):47-63. Poterba is skeptical that we are capable of orchestrating an effective global strategy in the face of global climate change. Instead, he examines how pollution taxes might be introduced at the national level and discusses both their design and potential costs to different nations at different stages of economic development. Finally, Poterba suggests some emissions reduction possibilities for poor nations.

6

THE BIG PICTURE

Issues in Macroeconomic Policy

On Monday, October 24, 2005, stock market investors warmly received the news that President George W. Bush had nominated Ben S. Bernanke to succeed Alan Greenspan as the chair of the Federal Reserve (the Fed). During the trading day the Dow Jones Industrial Average, an average of the selling prices of thirty key stocks, rose by 169.78 points, or 1.7 percent, the market's biggest rally in six months (White 2005, D1).

Such an instantaneous response of financial markets to the mere announcement of a coming change is curious. What is it about Fed announcements that can have such a dramatic influence on the behavior of individuals in markets? In this example the dramatic rise in the Dow index means that thousands of individual stockholders were—simultaneously—attempting to buy more shares of companies' stocks. How can an announcement of a coming change drive such widespread, immediate reactions?

In this chapter we consider the ways that our federal government can influence our macroeconomy—our overall national economy and its interaction with the still-larger global economy. Unemployment rates, inflation rates and national income: these are all macroeconomic issues because we do not normally evaluate them at the local level. Instead, we consider them at the larger, national level.

We rely primarily on our federal government to influence such measures, via either *monetary* or *fiscal policy* tools. The U.S. Congress charges the Federal Reserve—currently chaired by Ben Bernanke—with the conduct of our nation's monetary policy. Eight times each year, the Fed's Open Market Committee meets to set target values for the federal funds rate, the rate of interest banks charge each other for an overnight loan, that it believes will gently push the economy in a favorable macroeconomic direction—one of low, steady inflation rates, low unemployment and steady long-term growth. To achieve the target for the federal funds rate, the Fed adjusts our nation's money supply. If, for example, the Fed believes that higher interest rates would help to move the economy in a favorable direction, then the Fed will work to reduce the amount of money available in the economy—thereby raising the cost of loans (i.e., interest rates). On the other hand, if the Fed believes that reducing interest rates is warranted, then the Fed will work to increase the availability of money in the economy—thereby lowering the cost of loans.

Hence, the Fed attempts to use adjustments in the money supply to push, skillfully, interest rates in the direction that it believes will have a favorable impact on such macroeconomic policy variables as unemployment rates, inflation and GDP. Figure 6.1 illustrates this linkage.

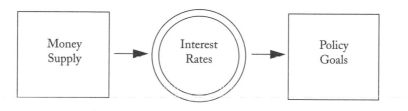

Figure 6.1. The linkages of monetary policy

Via the interaction of the legislative and executive branches of our federal government, the president and Congress together design and carry out our nation's fiscal policy. Through the introduction and passage of legislation dealing with issues such as tax rates, minimum wages and federal spending, fiscal policy can influence the direction of our macroeconomy. Like monetary policy, fiscal policy has the power to be either expansionary (e.g., reducing unemployment rates) or contractionary, though changes through this channel generally take longer than monetary policy changes.

In this chapter we first consider what should be the legitimate goals of macroeconomic policy. Second, we evaluate more specifically the usefulness of monetary policy as a channel for macroeconomic policy. Finally, we consider briefly the usefulness of fiscal policy for guiding the macroeconomy toward favorable outcomes. Governmental attempts at stabilizing the economy may actually be destabilizing. That is, there is certainly a role for government in designing and implementing a nation's macroeconomic policy. However, due to both the dynamic nature of our economy and the power of market forces, the proper role of government in guiding the macroeconomy should be a limited one.

WHAT ARE THE LEGITIMATE GOALS OF MACROECONOMIC POLICY?

Since our federal government is charged with overseeing the nation's fiscal and monetary policies, it is relevant to ask, What are the goals of such policies? We will consider four variables and measures that policymakers have used—both officially and unofficially—as goals of macroeconomic policy.

Goal 1: Long-term growth of gross domestic product. The most popular measure of a nation's macroeconomic success is its national income. The standard measure of a nation's income is gross domestic product (GDP), defined as the total dollar value of all final goods and services produced within a nation's borders and sold within a specified time period, normally one year. Once these values have been adjusted for inflation (so that year-to-year comparisons become meaningful), they provide one important measure of an economy's success. Further, we can divide the total value of GDP by the nation's population to see the value of national income per person, often called per capita GDP. Per capita measures of GDP can be helpful as a quick read of the overall standard of living in a nation and also permit comparisons among nations. Figure 6.2 depicts per capita GDP in the United States during the last century.

As figure 6.2 indicates, when per capita GDP is used as the standard of measure, the United States has enjoyed tremendous macroeconomic success during the last century. National income, in terms of what a dollar was worth in 2000, rose from about $7,000 per person in 1929 to about $37,000 by the end of 2005. That is, the average income at the close of the twentieth century yielded over five times the purchasing power of the average income seventy-five years prior.

But the track record is not a perfect one. Even though inflation-adjusted per capita GDP has risen over the period, sometimes it was rising and at other times it was falling. Economists refer to periods of real GDP increase as expansions. The downturns, though few, are what economists call recessions. Though more precise definitions exist, most people use *recession* to describe a situation in which real GDP has declined for at least two successive quarters. Historically speaking, the most recent recession in the United States was rather small in magnitude and lasted about ten months, from March 2001 to November 2001. And the recession that preceded it was also relatively minor, occurring from July 1990 to March 1991.

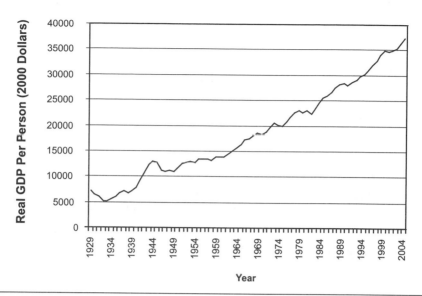

Figure 6.2. Inflation-adjusted per capita GDP in the U.S., 2000 dollars (from U.S. Bureau of Economic Analysis)

Economists reserve the term *depression* for an extremely severe recession. The only depression in U.S. history was the Great Depression of 1929-1939. (We discuss the severity and disruptive effects of the Great Depression in chap. 7.)

Inasmuch as per capita GDP is the primary measure of a nation's economic growth, there is a moral imperative of economic growth for Christians. Economic growth is not some greedy, materialistic aim, although many Christians think so when they consider the often breathless financial reporting on quarter-to-quarter GDP results. Instead, long-term growth is the fundamental driver of sustained material well-being, and is fundamentally linked to job growth and to growth in the incomes of the poor. Using a sample of ninety-two countries, Dollar and Kraay (2002) demonstrate that average incomes among the poorest fifth of a nation's population rise proportionately with average incomes.

However, economists everywhere realize that GDP is a very limited measure of the overall quality of life in a nation. That is, merely adding up the incomes that we all earn from producing goods and services measures our quality of life only imprecisely. Using Parkin (2005a) as a guide, let's consider several of the ways in which GDP is an imperfect measure of our overall societal welfare.

Household production. First, GDP includes no measure of the noncommercial productive activities that each of us performs daily. Every day across the United States we all perform productive activities—for ourselves or others—for which we collect no monetary payment. For example, in our homes we may shovel our own sidewalks, supply the labor in painting our own houses, cut our own lawns, prepare our own meals and rotate our own tires. Although these are productive activities that maintain or improve our quality of life, they are not included in our measure of GDP simply because we are not selling these productive services to anyone else.

Similarly, most of us perform volunteer work at some time in our lives. We volunteer in soup kitchens, teach English as a second language and help paint our local churches. Again, because we provide such productive services without receiving payment for them, this form of production is not included in our GDP measure.

In the area of household production, then, GDP understates our quality of life. Unless productive activities are sold to another, they are not included in our measure of GDP.

Leisure. GDP does an excellent job of indicating how much income we earn as a nation. However, it tells us nothing about the quality of our lives when we are not working. Any precise measure of our national economic welfare should include information about how much leisure time we have remaining after we have earned our incomes. Further, such a measure should also capture the satisfaction we are able to derive from the time that we are not at work.

We (Victor and Robin) enjoy going to church, spending time with our families, reading good books, listening to the radio, traveling to both new and familiar places, walking along the shore of Lake Michigan and conversing with our outstanding neighbors and colleagues. We also enjoy Sunday afternoon naps and daydreaming. We love doing all of these things. They enrich our lives. But GDP captures neither the time we have available for leisure nor the satisfaction we derive from that time. As a result, GDP understates our quality of life because it only considers what we do at work. GDP misses both the time we spend in leisure and the satisfaction we are able to derive from it.

Political freedom and social justice. There is little doubt that the states that constituted the former Soviet Union have not experienced much economic growth since the Union's collapse. In fact, Parkin (2005a, p. 92) estimates that the average rate of GDP growth in transition economies was *negative* during 1992-2002. While less efficient in allocating resources than market mechanisms, the centrally planned command-and-control policies of the communists resulted in a provision of goods and services that was not much worse than the availability of goods today in the former Soviet republics. Hence, were we to look exclusively at GDP as a measure of overall well-being, we might be tempted to conclude that life in the newly independent republics is no better than was life in the same republics under Soviet rule.

But GDP is not a perfect measure of the quality of life in an economy. In the case of the former Soviet Union, measures like GDP do not capture the reforms of the mid-1980s, such as *glasnost* (open discussion of political and social issues and freer dissemination of news and information) and *perestroika* (economic and governmental reform instituted by Mikhail Gorbachev). Not only did such policy reforms improve the quality of life for citizens in the USSR; the reforms also led eventually to the collapse of the Soviet Union, ushering in greater individual liberty than had ever been known in either communist or tsarist Russia. Therefore, because GDP does not capture essential liberties, or related social issues such as racial harmony and religious freedom, it understates the quality of life of a society.

Environmental quality. While GDP is a good measure of most of the outputs of a nation's productive activities, GDP does not capture what may be happening environmentally as a consequence of producing the goods and services included in GDP. If productive processes simultaneously reduce environmental quality, then GDP may overstate the level of well-being in a society.

Indeed, the parallel modernization and industrialization of a society together have historically led, at least initially, to both higher incomes and higher levels of pollution. No one has expressed this idea more succinctly than world-famous architect Frank Lloyd Wright. In the mid-twentieth century, Pittsburgh's civic leaders sought suggestions from Wright about what to do with the polluted steel city. "Wright, who looked down at the river triangle that was more grime than gold, . . . offered this advice: 'Abandon it'" (Dvorchak 1999).

Thankfully, though, once a society has endured the growing pains of industrialization, environmental improvement soon follows. This happens for two reasons. First, as an economy grows in its research into new technologies and new production processes, it uncovers more efficient methods of production—ones that are normally cleaner, safer and more cost effective than their predecessors. For example, nearly all automated car washes now employ sophisticated water-filtering and reclamation systems that recycle the water used to wash one car, so that it may be used to wash the cars that follow. While water reclamation happens to be a very environmentally friendly practice, profit-seeking car wash operators use water reclamation primarily as a way of saving money on a key input: water.

Second, the demand by citizens for environmental cleanliness tends to increase along with a nation's per capita income (see chap. 5). When a nation is very poor, its citizens are much more concerned about where tomorrow's clothing, food and shelter will come from than they are about caring for the earth. Of course, this does not mean that poor nations are uninterested in being good stewards of creation. All it means is that their need for nutritious food and medical care is, today, more pressing than their worries about things like noise pollution.

Eventually, though, as a nation's income grows, its demands for goods other than necessities begin to increase. The demand for a clean environment grows together with demands for goods such as dental care, books and bicycles. Figure 6.3 shows some ten-year trends in air pollution in the United States, illustrating that environmental quality normally improves dramatically as a society grows in both its knowledge of technology and its ability to afford a cleaner planet. The figure depicts concentrations of the Environmental Protection

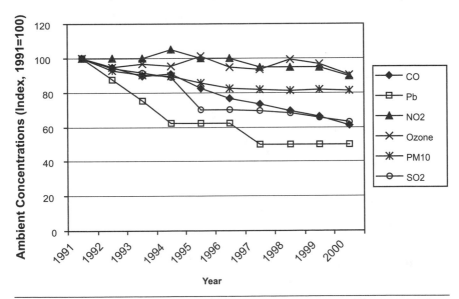

Figure 6.3. Trends in air pollution in the United States, 1991-2000 (from *National Air Quality and Emissions Trends Report, 2003 Special Studies Edition*, U.S. Environmental Protection Agency)

Agency's six principle pollutants: carbon monoxide (CO), lead (Pb), nitrogen dioxide (NO_2), ozone, both coarse and fine particulate matter (PM 10) and sulfur dioxide (SO_2).

Of course, as Murphy (2003) demonstrates using World Bank international data from the 1980s, not all environmental variables improve together with increases in the income of a nation. For example, both municipal waste per capita and carbon dioxide emissions per capita worsen steadily as a nation's per capita income increases. But variables such as these are the exception rather than the rule. Several environmental variables initially worsen as a nation's income grows, but improve dramatically as environmental protection becomes more affordable due to greater increases in per capita income. Urban concentrations of both particulate matter and sulfur dioxide rise initially as a nation develops, but fall to near zero micrograms per cubic meter of air as per capita income begins to rise above $1,000. Other variables get progressively better as a nation experiences long-term growth. Both the percentage of a nation's population without adequate sanitation and the percent without adequate drinking water decline steadily and continuously as a nation grows; these variables never grow worse.

Goal 2: Low unemployment. A second possible goal for macroeconomic policy is keeping unemployment low. The best-known measure of the job market is the unemployment rate, the percentage of individuals in the labor force who have not worked in the past thirty days and have also looked for work during the same period. Figure 6.4 depicts the path of the unemployment rate in the United States during the last half of the twentieth century.

As figure 6.4 indicates, the unemployment rate rose to its highest levels in this period during the deep recessions of the 1970s and early 1980s, when 9.7 percent of the labor force was not working in 1982. The highest unemployment rate in U.S. history, though, was approximately 25 percent, during the height of the Great Depression. Rarely has the U.S. unemployment rate risen above 10 percent. While the rate has never been near zero, it came closest at two times: just before the start of the 1920s and again during World War II.

Regardless of the specific policies in place, our resilient, dynamic macroeconomy creates millions of new jobs each year. Incumbent presidents seeking election to a second term will often claim to have created some huge number of new jobs during their first terms; in fact, though, presidents have little to do with the number of jobs created each year. Profit-seeking entrepreneurs create

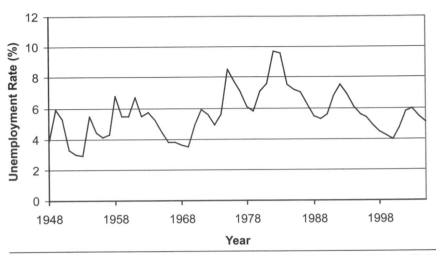

Figure 6.4. The unemployment rate in the United States, 1948-2005 (from U.S. Bureau of Labor Statistics)

nearly two million new jobs every year—both during recessions and during periods of expansion.

Hence, a lack of job creation is not typically the source of rising unemployment rates in the United States. Instead, unemployment increases when more jobs are destroyed in a given year than the two million or so new ones that have been created.

For policy purposes a valid question concerns whether policymakers should pursue a goal of zero percent unemployment. Christians view work both as a calling and as the primary channel through which they exercise stewardship over the earth's resources. In this light, we should advocate policies that generate opportunities for the unemployed to work—to exercise their stewardship of time and talents.

However, as a matter of policy, we should not attempt to reduce the unemployment rate all the way to zero. Doing so would require that workers take any available job opening—regardless of the fit of the opening to the skills and talents of the unemployed individual. In such a world we would have brain surgeons flipping hamburgers and plumbers painting lines on highways. Of course, there is nothing whatsoever that is inherently good or bad about any of the aforementioned professions. However, it is simply not good stewardship of our time, talents and skills to seek high employment rates if doing so squanders precious human resources in the first jobs that become available. A better option is to allow some unemployment as workers carefully search for meaningful employment opportunities.

For precisely these reasons we have instituted—and continue to maintain— a system of unemployment insurance in the United States. We do not want to see a newly unemployed person forced into taking the first job to come along in order to pay his bills and to feed his family. Instead, we provide a system of unemployment insurance to give a newly unemployed worker a chance to search for a job opening that provides a relatively high degree of match with his or her skills, knowledge and talents. To do otherwise would result in an inefficient use of an individual's unique abilities.

Moreover, as Christians we would not want to put policies into place that force unemployed persons to settle for jobs that are not a good match. Were we to do so, we would deny individuals the opportunity to pursue their unique callings—ones in which each person can exercise stewardship to the glory of God—and respond to new callings as their circumstances and interests change.

Therefore, one goal of macroeconomic policy must be to keep unemployment low, thereby affording individuals opportunities to exercise their callings as stewards over creation. However, we should not attempt to reduce unemployment to zero. Instead, we should view some level of unemployment as a good thing if it represents the free choices of unemployed workers seeking meaningful opportunities to pursue calling and stewardship in the labor market.

Goal 3: Low, steady inflation rates. While inflation has not been a cause of great concern at the beginning of the twenty-first century, there are nevertheless at least three reasons that a low, stable inflation rate should be a goal of monetary policy.

Inflation captures the rate at which the purchasing power of a dollar is changing over time. While many assume that inflation has always been positive, that is, that prices have always risen, that is not true. Figure 6.5 presents the inflation rate in the United States over the last century.

In figure 6.5, inflation rates that are positive—and thus lie above the horizontal line at zero—represent periods of increasing prices. When inflation rates are negative and prices are falling, the rates lie below the horizontal line at zero; these periods are referred to as periods of deflation. Note that sometimes inflation rates are falling, yet positive; this phenomenon may be observed in many of the years since 1980. Because the inflation rates lie above

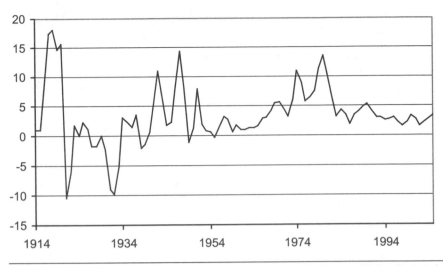

Figure 6.5. Inflation rates in the United States, 1914-2005 (from U.S. Bureau of Labor Statistics)

zero, inflation is still positive and prices are still rising. The falling inflation rates in this period indicate that prices are rising, but that they are rising more slowly than in prior years. Economists refer to such periods of decreasing, yet positive, inflation rates as periods of disinflation, a term attributed to Clark Warburton. Warburton, an alumnus of Houghton College who later completed degrees at both Cornell University and Columbia, pioneered monetarist economics before passing off its torch to its greatest champion, Milton Friedman.[1]

Inflation can prove costly to a society both when price level changes are unanticipated and when they are fully anticipated. Let's look at the costs associated with inflation in both circumstances.

First, and more commonly in Western industrialized nations, inflation proves costly and problematic when changes in inflation rates are unexpected. When one is unable to correctly anticipate fluctuations in the rate of change of the overall level of prices, surprise redistributions of wealth result. Typically, these redistributions take place between borrowers and lenders, and between employers and employees. In both cases, such surprise redistributions are made possible due to the presence of multiperiod contractual obligations in both the markets for loans and the markets for labor.

---

[1]For more about monetarism—the idea that monetary changes are the main source of economic disturbances—and the life and contributions of Warburton, see Bordo (1980).

In the case of loan markets, consider as an example how car loans are ordinarily structured. In May 1999, Victor agreed to purchase his first-ever new car—a 1999 Mazda Protegé ES—by making payments at a fixed annual rate of interest over the five years that would follow. The specific financing terms meant that Victor had to make a total of sixty monthly payments of $320 to Mazda American Credit Corporation until April 2004.

Because of inflation, the real purchasing power of the $320 payment fell during the period of the loan. That is, Victor handed over something to the credit company that was worth less—in buying power—than what he had handed over the month before. Even though inflation rates were low during the term of the loan, inflation rates remained positive, reducing the quantity of goods and services that a person could buy with $320.

Of course, Victor is both a consumer and an economist. Accordingly, before Victor signed the car loan, he had already formed fairly specific expectations concerning how quickly prices would rise during the term of the loan. Stated another way, Victor had formed an expectation concerning how quickly the real purchasing power of the $320 he parted with each month would fall during the five years of the loan. Like most other economists and noneconomists, Victor formed this expectation based on things like the existing inflation rate, recent inflation rates and news reports concerning where the economy might be headed over the following five years.

But Victor turned out to be wrong! While prices indeed rose after May 1999, they did not rise nearly as quickly as he had expected. Consequently, while the $320 he parted with each month was indeed worth less and less, its value did not fall nearly as quickly as he had anticipated. So, Victor ended up parting with more of his purchasing power to finance that car than he had imagined.

Of course, Mazda American Credit was delighted! Each month they received a check for $320 dollars that turned out to be of greater value than they had imagined back in May 1999.

Therefore, because actual inflation rates turned out to be lower than expected, the borrower, Victor, was made worse off, while the lender—Mazda American Credit—was made better off. Had the opposite happened (i.e., prices grew more quickly than had been expected), the author would have been made better off at the expense of Mazda American Credit, because the real value of the $320 would have fallen faster than either the borrower or lender had anticipated.

Thus, when prices change at rates different from what has been anticipated at the front end of a loan period, real wealth can be redistributed between the borrower and the lender. When inflation is higher than expected, borrowers gain and lenders lose. When inflation is lower than expected, lenders gain and borrowers lose.

Similar redistributions can occur between employers and employees as a result of multiperiod labor contracts that guarantee a fixed dollar wage. When inflation is greater than expected, $20 per hour is not worth as much as the employer and employee had anticipated when they signed the contract. As a result, the $20 per hour the employer parts with is not worth as much as anticipated. Simultaneously, the employee cannot afford as many goods and services with the earnings as he or she had expected. Therefore, when inflation rates are higher than expected, employers gain and employees lose. On the other hand, when prices rise more slowly than anticipated—as in the period since 1999—employees gain more purchasing power at the expense of their employers.

Because unanticipated inflation can lead to redistributions of wealth between (1) borrowers and lenders, and (2) employers and employees, a legitimate goal of macroeconomic policy should be to keep inflation rates steady, so that such surprise redistributions do not take place.

Moreover, all parties will be more likely to enter into contracts when they expect fewer surprises of any kind during the term of contracts written in dollar terms. Therefore, steady rates of inflation can also be beneficial inasmuch as they may help markets function more efficiently and smoothly; when parties feel confident about the future, they are more likely to enter into contractual agreements that potentially yield mutual benefits and, moreover, contribute to economic growth.

While unexpected inflation imposes costs in the form of surprise redistributions of wealth, inflation can prove costly, even when fully anticipated. This problem is most common to the Latin American nations that have experienced periods of very high inflation. In some nations, such as Bolivia in the mid-1980s, prices grow so quickly that these nations experience periods of hyperinflation, when prices rise by more than 50 percent per month.

Figure 6.6 compares the annual inflation rates in the United States from 1970 to 2001 with an average of annual inflation rates in members of the newly formed South American Community of Nations (Argentina, Bolivia, Brazil, Chile, Colombia, Ecuador, Guyana, Paraguay, Peru, Suriname, Uruguay and Venezuela) during the same period.

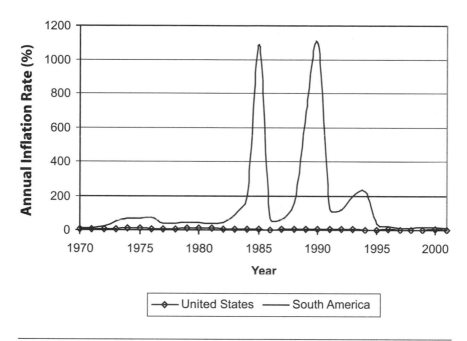

Figure 6.6. Percent per year inflation in the U.S. and members of the South American Community of Nations, 1970-2001 (from International Monetary Fund)

Note that the relatively flat line represents annual inflation in the United States. The other line, with the sharp peaks in the mid-1980s and early 1990s, represents the average annual inflation rate in members of the South American Community of Nations. During the entire period, annual inflation rates in the United States fluctuated between 12 percent and zero percent. During exactly the same period, annual inflation rates in the South American countries twice rose to over 1,000 percent.

When inflation rates become very high, inflation is costly to a society—even if changes in the inflation rate may be predicted perfectly. Economists refer to such costs as shoeleather costs. Consider the case of a hyperinflation. When a nation's prices are rising furiously, the purchasing power of currency in your pocket, paycheck or bank account is dwindling furiously as well. In such a climate no one wants to hold currency unless they absolutely must. Shoeleather costs refer to the ceaseless running an individual must endure during a hyperinflation to ensure that he or she holds as little currency as possible.

For example, in economies experiencing a severe hyperinflation, prices rise so quickly that they are often marked up several times per day. As a result, employers may opt to pay their workers in multiple payments throughout the week in order to preserve—as much as possible during a hyperinflation—the purchasing power of their employees' salaries. Further, as soon as people receive a paycheck, they must move as quickly as possible to the bank to cash it, then onto the stores—before they close—to spend their earnings. They must do this because prices will be even higher tomorrow, but today's paycheck will grow no larger!

Moreover, these people must not save any of the money for future spending. They must spend all of their salary immediately, allocating a large portion of their wages to goods that they may use in conducting barter transactions during the period between today's paycheck and the next. Hence, they will be sure to include, in today's shopping cart, goods that others would be readily willing to accept in exchange for other goods tomorrow. These goods must also be excellent stores of value; fresh fish does not make a good item to buy today for trades later in the week. Historically, many different goods have been used in barter because they possess these properties. People have traded beaver pelts and wampum in the early Americas, butter in Norway, rice in Japan, goats in colonial Africa, and cigarettes in World War II POW camps. Such goods are useful as a store of value, and others readily accepted them in trade. Today, in a nation experiencing a hyperinflation, citizens may buy goods such as cigarettes and liquor with the balance of their paychecks, because they possess the same properties; a person can buy them today and save them to acquire other goods and services tomorrow.

Thus, inflation is costly not just because of its surprise redistributions of wealth. Even when anticipated, inflation is costly due to the phenomenon of shoeleather costs, which drain away our time from the enjoyable or productive activities that we could pursue instead of running all over town before stores and banks close each day.

While these are the primary ways that inflation may prove costly, there is one final channel we must mention. In nations experiencing hyperinflation, inflation rates become less predictable. Hence, in addition to the shoeleather costs of a hyperinflation, high inflation also leads to inflation rates that grow more variable and less predictable. Thus, inasmuch as high inflation can occasion more variable inflation rates, the shoeleather costs of a hyperinflation will be compounded by the greater redistributive costs resulting from unexpected changes in inflation rates in high inflation economies. Balvers and Cosimano (1994) give a careful exposition of this phenomenon, and detail its implications for monetary policy.

Moreover, price instability is particularly harmful to the poor. Levin and Smith (2005) make a thorough case for helping the poor through the pursuit of stable prices. Practitioners and economists should work to prevent these costs from falling heavily on the poor by creating "social safety net policies" directed at those among the poor who need the most help. Developing these policies requires intense study and careful design; nongovernmental organizations (NGOs) and practitioners, with their grassroots-level experience and international connections, can provide vital insights to the development of these social programs. Indeed, there really is a Christian ethical dimension to macroeconomic policy.

Goal 4: Stock market values. Historically, macroeconomic policy has not aimed at influencing the size and direction of stock market price changes. Policymakers have focused exclusively on variables like those previously mentioned—unemployment, inflation and long-term growth of GDP—in setting their policy goals.

More recently, though, it appears that the Fed's Open Market Committee has grown more sensitive to the fits and starts of the stock market in deciding whether to raise or lower its target for the federal funds rate. This should come as no great surprise, due to the growing number of individuals with some stake in our nation's stock markets.

Throughout the past few decades more and more citizens have purchased shares of stock. This new class of stockholders came about primarily from two sources. First, during the buoyant years of the 1990s, many day traders began to dabble in the stock market. Second, an ever-growing number of firms now use stock market mutual funds as the primary method of providing retirement plans for their employees. Taken together, the nation's citizens hold more of their wealth in stocks than ever before. According to data taken from the Flow of Funds accounts produced by the Federal Reserve Board, the total financial wealth of U.S. households stood at $35.7 trillion at the end of 2000. Of this amount, $11.6 trillion (i.e., about one third) was in the form of equity holdings (i.e., stocks).

Hence, in light of the magnitude of these holdings, the Fed began to pay attention to the stock market in deciding how to conduct its monetary policy. The Fed does this primarily due to the economic linkage between an individual's stock of wealth and his or her current consumption spending. During the heyday of the 1990s consumers spent and spent on current consumption, largely because they felt secure regarding the value of their wealth holdings in the form of stock shares. For example, individuals with retirement plans tied to stock performance were largely unconcerned with saving more for retirement out of current income; their wealth in the stock market had appreciated so dramatically that they felt they could spend today with little consequence for tomorrow.

The Fed does not officially pay attention to the stock market in evaluating policy decisions. Nevertheless, due to the aforementioned impact of wealth holdings on consumption, the Fed may seek to stabilize stock values in an effort to ensure that consumer spending stays strong (when there are signs of potential economic weakness). Using empirical techniques, Rigobon and Sack (2003) investigate the specific nature of the relationship between stock-price movements and monetary-policy decisions by the Fed. Rigobon and Sack find a significant response of monetary policy to shifts in the stock market. As stock values fall the Fed typically responds with an expansionary monetary policy change designed to reduce interest rates. They do this hoping to make borrowing more attractive in order to offset any drop in consumer spending caused by falling stock values. If the stock market instead moves upward, at some point the Fed is likely to use contractionary monetary policy to slow the movement in order to forestall an eventual sharp downward correction.

Whether it is appropriate for the Fed to use its policy instruments—either officially or unofficially—to target stock-market price trends is unclear. (We will discuss this issue in chap. 7.)

CONCLUSION

This chapter has described the macroeconomic variables that our federal government currently uses to set policy goals for our economy. (The same would hold true in most developed economies.) Our government pays attention to and tries to influence (1) the growth of national income per capita, (2) unemployment rates, (3) inflation rates and (4) stock market values. In chapter seven we describe current understanding of the monetary and fiscal policies available to pursue such goals. We discuss both the advantages and limitations of these policies in the pursuit of such goals.

FOR FURTHER READING

Howard, Bruce. 1996. *Safe and sound: Why you can stand secure on the future of the U.S. economy.* Wheaton, Ill.: Tyndale House. A marvelous job of discussing issues of both macroeconomic importance and personal financial responsibility. Though now a bit dated, the thoughtful reflections on individual choice and responsibility make the book a profitable read.

7

WHAT DO WE KNOW ABOUT MONETARY AND FISCAL POLICY?

The study of macroeconomics has experienced its greatest advances during periods of economic revolution. Macroeconomics tends to evolve as science in the manner described by Thomas Kuhn (1970). Kuhn's view has given rise to the use of the catchphrase *paradigm shift* in our everyday parlance. According to Kuhn, a scientific paradigm is like a plateau along our path to greater knowledge and better understanding of events and phenomena that we observe today or have seen in the past. Most of the work that researchers do occurs under some current prevailing paradigm: our best guess right now about the overall nature of the world in light of the knowledge that we currently possess. Researchers continue to work within the prevailing paradigm until confronted with facts that so greatly challenge it that a new paradigm must found. The move to the new paradigm—the "paradigm shift"—must be such that the new paradigm can explain both past experience and the new information that occasioned the need for a new paradigm.

In fact, the study of modern macroeconomics itself began during a period of upheaval in macroeconomic events—a time during which none of the old reliable economic explanations and prescriptions appeared to work anymore. During this first period of cataclysm, the Great Depression, our global economy had fallen and could not get up. The best and brightest economists working within the existing paradigm could not come up with the policy recommendations that could lead the world out of its economic malaise and misery. Even in the United States, unemployment rates rose as high as 25 percent during this period; and the depression years stretched on to include the entire decade from 1929-1939.

In his 1936 work *The General Theory of Employment, Interest, and Money*, British economist John Maynard Keynes struck the spark of a paradigm shift.

According to Keynes the main cause of depression—or even recession—in an economy is insufficient private spending by households and firms on goods and services. Were households buying more consumer goods, and were firms spending more on new machinery or new manufacturing plants, then taken together this additional demand for goods and services would lead to greater production of goods and services and, in turn, greater employment at the firms that produce these goods and services.

Moreover, said Keynes, we must not forget that each dollar spent in an economy will be spent again and again. One additional dollar spent to buy a quart of milk, for example, is a dollar that can be spent by the shopkeeper to buy other wares. The producers of those wares, upon receiving payment, can use those funds to pay the employees who helped to produce those goods. Those employees will buy groceries, shoes and plumbing. Faced with greater demand, the grocer, the cobbler and the plumber will need to hire more employees. According to Keynes, this cycle can continue in perpetuity. Hence, just one more dollar spent can result in a multiple overall increase in the quantity of goods bought in an economy, leading to greater and greater employment in an economy.

The point of the Keynesian contribution to economics, then, was that economists prior to that period had not been giving adequate attention to a basic policy option—that government could use policy to stimulate spending on goods and services that was not happening on its own. If recessions occur because households and firms are spending too little, then government should step in and shore up the difference—even if government needs to use deficit financing to do so. That is, government should begin buying more goods and services when households and firms are buying fewer. By doing so, government can keep the demand for goods and services strong, and employment strong in the production of those goods and services.

Historically, it is important to note that Keynes owes much to Nobel laureate Sir John Hicks for interpreting Keynes's *General Theory* for the broader public. Hicks made the *General Theory* accessible to the profession by giving a clear exposition of what Keynes had in mind in Hicks's 1937 article "Mr. Keynes and the Classics: A Suggested Interpretation." When economists today refer to the *General Theory* of Keynes, they are, in fact, describing the exposition of Keynes provided by Hicks.

Hicks's role is vital inasmuch as the *General Theory* was not a book that proved immediately accessible to most readers—even economists—upon a first or second reading. Most regard the *General Theory* as difficult going on two grounds. First, Keynes's writing was not lucid. Second, in order to show the big difference between his new paradigm and the prevailing one, Keynes compared and contrasted his views with those expressed in a 1937 article by Arthur Cecil Pigou. Unfortunately, Pigou was also notorious for his lack of clarity in writing. As a result, much of the *General Theory* consists of the unclear writing of John Maynard Keynes trying to contrast his views with those expressed in another unclear text. Since Hicks's (1937) publication, economists have debated whether Hicks correctly captured the essence of Keynes (1936). In fact, in his later years Hicks himself began to doubt whether he had understood the *General Theory* correctly; see Klamer (1989) for a revealing interview with Hicks.

Contemporaries of Keynes were initially quite skeptical of his prescription for a weak economy—that government should buy more goods and services to offset the insufficient purchases of the private sector. Keynes's critics pointed out, correctly, that such a policy prescription might be the remedy for today's small ills, but it could lead to greater economic disease in the future. According to Keynes's critics, then and now, higher levels of government spending might very well spur the economy today, as workers are called back to their employers in order to meet the additional demand for products. However, in the long run, especially if government borrows to finance purchases today that it cannot fund through current tax revenues, an economy can fall into an even greater malaise. In the long run, debt-financed government spending will lead to escalating inflation, slower long-term economic growth and higher tax bills.

Keynes knew his critics were correct. He had said as much in his earlier *Tract on Monetary Reform* (1923). Keynes realized that any short-term economic palliative could lead to larger, more obstinate economic difficulties later on. However, Keynes firmly held that it was better to use economic policy today to fix today's problems than to let the unemployed remain so today. Hence, Keynes's most famous quote is, "In the long run we are all dead" (p. 65). Therefore, to Keynes, his critics were absolutely correct. They were also irrelevant; the best policy is the one that concerns itself mainly with this generation and not with the next.

Therefore, Keynes concluded that an economic policy that responds quickly and directly to temporary fluctuations in an economy is superior to one that fails to do so. That is, Keynes preferred discretionary economic policy:

policy conducted at the discretion of the economists and others in charge. According to Keynes, policymakers need the freedom that discretionary policy affords, whether fiscal or monetary. And it was Keynes who, in effect, first put the notion of discretionary fiscal policy on policymakers' radar screens.

Keynes's prescriptions marked the beginning of the modern macroeconomic era, a watershed both in terms of the study of economics and the policy actions taken by government. Current college students taking an introductory level course in macroeconomics will encounter Keynes throughout their study. Regardless of the relevance of Keynes to the economy as we understand it today, most introductory courses in macroeconomics are structured around the landmark work of Keynes.

In the remainder of this chapter we will summarize the current state of macroeconomics today. In particular we will discuss the ways the discipline has evolved since the Keynesian paradigm shift. Our macroeconomic understanding since Keynes has evolved in such a way that Keynes's prescriptions for discretion no longer command the level of confidence they once did.

Instead, it appears that a steady, deliberate, less reactive approach to economic policy may lead to the best overall long-term path for the economy. Attempts to use discretionary monetary or fiscal policy actions to stabilize the economy may, instead, be destabilizing. While it is true that modern macroeconomists disagree regarding which specific model describes economic reality best, modern macroeconomics identifies several limitations regarding discretion as the best avenue for maintaining both long-term economic growth and short-term economic stability. Hence, we argue for policy tied to rules (as opposed to policy that is discretionary). This has the benefit of making policy actions transparent to everyone as well as limiting the possibility that a policymaker could make discretionary changes to the economy for mere political gain.

Further, though, these models are not simply arcane mental exercises developed for the pleasure and delight of boring economists. They have deep value to us as we consider whether there is a Christian moral imperative for macroeconomics and the conduct of macroeconomic policy. In fact, there is a fundamental moral desirability of macroeconomic stability. The welfare of the poor, as well as sustained low unemployment, depend on it, inasmuch as macroeconomic shocks are really expensive for families and communities. Therefore, macroeconomic stabilization policies matter—a lot—and to get them right we need to understand the underlying forces that drive the economy.

NEW CLASSICAL MACROECONOMICS

The second major paradigm shift in modern macroeconomics was occasioned by our economic experience from the mid-1970s through the early part of the 1980s. According to the paradigm prevailing at that time, due mainly to Keynes and his followers, we should always expect a stable, long-term tradeoff between unemployment rates and inflation rates. That is, while we might successfully pursue reductions in the unemployment rate, such reductions are not costless. We must expect that increasing inflation rates will accompany any decrease in the rate of unemployment. This long-term tradeoff between unemployment and inflation is sometimes called the Phillips curve tradeoff because it was initially attributed to New Zealand economist A. W. Phillips (1958). Using nearly a century's worth of data from the United Kingdom, Phillips identified a strong, consistent, long-term inverse relationship between unemployment and inflation rates.

Surprisingly, more than thirty years prior to Phillips's publication, Yale economist Irving Fisher (1926) had already related the rate of inflation to the unemployment rate. It was not until the publication of a historical note by Donner and McCollum (1972) that the economics profession became widely aware of Fisher's earlier discovery of an unemployment-inflation tradeoff. In 1973, the *Journal of Political Economy* reprinted Fisher's paper in their "Lost and Found" section bearing the new title "I Discovered the Phillips Curve."

So both Fisher and Phillips had identified an inflation-unemployment tradeoff. Yet, in the 1970s the unemployment-inflation tradeoff appeared to break down. The U.S. economy began to face persistently high levels of both unemployment and inflation rates.

Figure 7.1 depicts this phenomenon. Each point in the diagram represents the inflation-unemployment rate combination for one specific year in the period. The solid line has been fitted to the data points to represent the apparent overall relationship between movements in the inflation rate and in the unemployment rate during the period. As the figure suggests, during the period the two variables exhibited more of a positive relationship than the inverse one suggested by Phillips.

Thus, any long-term inverse relationship between inflation rates and unemployment rates broke down beginning in the early 1970s. During that shorter period, the opposite appeared to be true: unemployment and inflation rates moved together in the same direction—a direct contradiction of the

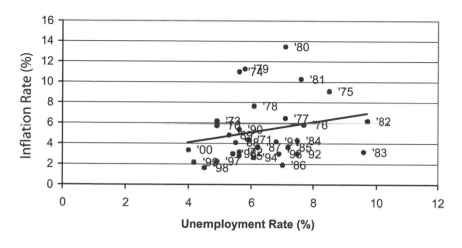

Figure 7.1. Inflation and unemployment rates in the United States, 1970-2000 (from U.S. Bureau of Labor Statistics)

Phillips curve tradeoff, illustrated by the fitted line included in the figure. Unemployment and inflation rates moved upward together at the beginning of the 1970s, downward together in during the 1970s, upward together again to begin the 1980s, and downward together throughout the 1980s. The stage was set for a paradigm shift in macroeconomics.

The shortcomings of the Keynesian paradigm that led to the eventual shift away from it can be more fully appreciated when we understand its basic underpinnings. Recall that Keynes believed that recessions were due to insufficient spending on goods and services by consumers and firms. Hence, Keynes's prescription for low unemployment was that government should step in and shore up the deficiency in private spending by purchasing more goods and services—even if government must borrow to do so. Faced with greater demand for their products, firms would produce more goods and hire more workers in order to do it. Further, firms would be able to charge higher prices for the products they produce in the face of both greater demand and increasing employment across the economy. The resulting combination of greater employment and higher prices is the Phillips curve tradeoff: higher prices combined with reduced unemployment.

Achieving this tradeoff, though, requires one additional, crucial assumption: that firms can hire all of the additional labor they require without paying higher wages for it. That is, the Keynesian paradigm assumes that laborers are willing to work for the same number of dollars per hour, even as the cost of living rises because firms begin to charge higher and higher prices in the face of greater demand for their products.

In the Keynesian view, then, workers are rather naive. Even though they should be aware of the Phillips-curve relationship—that the cost of living will rise even as they are called back to work—workers will not seek higher dollar wages in order to insulate themselves from the inflationary effects that will accompany their increased employment. And as long as firms can hire naive workers at the old wage rates, firms are happy to hire more labor in order to produce more goods that firms can sell at higher prices. What firm wouldn't be?

But Keynes dramatically underestimated the capacity of individuals to anticipate the rise in prices that accompanies governmental attempts—fiscal or monetary—to stimulate the economy. Keynes had overlooked the simple idea that individuals are wise enough to consider all of the information that is available to them about the future in making decisions today that cannot be changed in some future period. Muth (1961) pioneered this simple idea, known as rational expectations. The theory of rational expectations was later augmented by Robert Lucas who, in 1995, was awarded the Nobel Prize for his work with rational expectations.

Simply put, rational expectations says that individuals make economic decisions today by incorporating all information that is available to them regarding the impact their decision will have in the future. Such information can come from a variety of sources. For example, individuals may seek out financial information from newspapers, television, stockbrokers, coworkers or financial planners.

Further, individuals are wise enough that they learn from their past mistakes. If someone has made a poor economic decision in the past, he or she is smart enough to learn from that experience and not make the same mistake again. In the rational expectations view, then, individuals are smarter than Charlie Brown in the *Peanuts* comic strip. In *Peanuts*, Lucy Van Pelt offers—over and over again—to hold a football for Charlie so that he may kick it. Over and over again, Lucy assures Charlie that she will not pull the ball away from him, no matter how fast he runs forward to kick the ball. But over and over again Lucy pulls the ball away at the last instant, and Charlie Brown kicks at only air, becomes airborne himself, and falls to the ground on his back. No matter how many times Lucy and Charlie repeat this exchange, Charlie never manages to learn from his past mistakes. He always kicks at the ball, and Lucy always pulls it away. Charlie Brown never forms a rational expectation of Lucy's future actions; he never learns about the future from his past errors.

Thankfully, we have been created to be wiser than Charlie Brown in his infinite yet charming naiveté. Accordingly, a new macroeconomic paradigm has replaced the old Keynesian one: new classical macroeconomics. New classical macroeconomics combines the wonderful insight of rational expectations with the amazing abilities of markets to allocate resources to their most highly valued uses. In the new classical view, individuals making economic decisions today incorporate all information available to them in assessing how their decisions today will affect them in the future. For example, in the Keynesian view, individuals are assumed to ignore where the cost of living might be headed when they accept a job offer today. By contrast, the new classical view affords a prospective employee the insight to consider not only what a wage offer of $30 per hour can buy today, but also what that same $30 per hour will buy tomorrow, given his or her rational expectation concerning inflation.

New classical macroeconomics has dramatic implications for the conduct of monetary policy. Suppose, for example, that the Federal Reserve has decided that our economy is stagnating and that the Fed would like to provide a stimulus to the economy. That is, perhaps the growth rate of GDP has slowed and, at the same time, the unemployment rate has risen. Recall that, under the older Keynesian paradigm, economic slowdowns happen because firms and consumers are buying too few goods. Hence, the Fed should use its powers of monetary policy to provide stimulus by changing the money supply in such a way that consumers and firms are encouraged to go out and buy more goods and services at a faster rate than their current rate of purchasing. More specifically, the Federal Reserve should pursue monetary policies that increase the money supply and lead to lower interest rates. By directly increasing the rate of growth of the nation's money supply, thereby making the number of dollars more plentiful, the Fed can indirectly cause the price of borrowing dollars—the nominal interest rate—to fall. Faced with the cheaper financing costs that lower interest rates bring, consumers will buy more new homes, new cars, and other goods and services that require financing. Similarly, firms will be more likely to undertake new ventures that appeared too costly at the old, higher rates of interest. As firms and consumers begin to buy new goods and services, GDP will rise and previously unemployed workers will be called back to work in order to meet the new, higher levels of demand for goods and services initiated by the Fed's expansionary policy.

While this all sounds very exciting and promising, such old Keynesian prescriptions suffer from one serious shortcoming: in the long run, bad things will probably happen. As Keynes and his critics both pointed out, policy actions designed to stimulate employment today will lead to greater inflation tomorrow.

Moreover, according to the assumption of rational expectations, everyone knows this! Recall that Keynesian models, instead, assume dense, naive workers. In such models, firms faced with growing demands for their goods and services will be able to hire more labor at the old, lower wage rates because workers are naive; in the Keynesian view, workers are clueless concerning what happens to the cost of living when firms—faced with growing demands for their products—raise the prices of their products. Were workers any brighter, they would demand higher wages upon being called back, knowing that firms across the economy will begin raising prices in the face of higher demand for the goods and services they produce.

In reality, though, firms will not be able to hire back all of the labor they desire at the old, lower wage rates. Instead, given their rational expectation that expansionary monetary policy actions on the part of the Fed should always lead to higher prices of the goods and services consumers buy, workers will begin demanding raises in order to keep their purchasing power from slipping. In response, firms will not hire all of the workers that Keynesian models predict; workers cost too much. As a consequence, employment will not improve over the long term, nor will the production of goods and services. The economy is no better after the policy action than before.

This dramatic implication of the new classical model is sometimes referred to as the policy-ineffectiveness proposition. The proposition states that, due to the ability of individuals to anticipate and respond to active changes in monetary policy, active changes in monetary policy are doomed to failure. As soon as consumers, workers and firms know in advance that the Federal Reserve plans to undertake some policy action, those same consumers, workers and firms will begin to take action immediately in order to insulate themselves from any possible adverse effects that might result from such a policy change. Therefore, active monetary policy actions will always be neutralized as long as citizens know in advance that the policy change is coming. Robert Lucas (1976) is credited with making this dramatic discovery.

For example, suppose that current workers knew in advance that the Fed had plans to increase the money supply over the next two years in order to cause a temporary boom. With this advance knowledge, workers could begin lobbying today for increases in their paychecks over the next two years, since they would know that adding more dollars to the money supply makes the prices of goods and service—the cost of living—rise in dollar terms. Thus, in order to preserve their actual purchasing power, workers would ask for more money in accordance with the anticipated inflation. As a result, workers would remain equally costly to hire and as a consequence there would be no net change in either the number of workers hired across the economy or the level of goods and services they produce.

One obvious implication of the policy-ineffectiveness proposition is the policy changes can nevertheless be effective, as long as they come as a surprise to a nation's citizenry. For example, if the workers involved in labor contract negotiations today had no reasonable way to anticipate that the Federal Reserve had plans to begin to dramatically expand the rate of growth of the nation's money supply, they would later find that they had agreed to work during the contract period for a dollar wage that afforded dramatically less purchasing power than they had anticipated. In such a scenario labor would remain relatively cheap, firms would hire more of it, and the nation's level of output would rise.

But conducting monetary policy in such a manner can only be viewed as deplorable. Christians cannot embrace monetary policy actions that improve macroeconomic variables like the unemployment rate or GDP when such actions are successful due only to deliberate trickery and deceit. Instead, Christian economists advocate monetary policy that is transparent; that is, the Federal Reserve should do its very best to ensure that no policy change comes as a surprise. In fact, under the new classical view of the economy, the best monetary policy is one that never reacts to temporary fluctuations in macroeconomic variables. Given the speed at which freely functioning markets direct resources to their most highly valued uses, monetary policymakers should never seek to actively manage the economy. Instead, the most important thing that the Federal Reserve can do to help the economy improve steadily over time is to make sure that we experience as few surprises as possible. When we feel secure that the Fed will not take any surprise policy actions to jump-start the economy, we can all be more confident as we engage in and interact with the economy. No longer will we need to guess whether interest rates are headed up or down before we decide to commit to finance a new home or new car. Instead, we may with confidence conduct our daily activities in the security that the Fed will not be a contributor to the economic disturbances that we occasionally experience.

Therefore, the new classical economics improves on the old Keynesian paradigm by combining two powerful ideas: (1) markets work well in directing resources to their most highly valued uses, and (2) individuals use rational expectations about the future in deciding what economic actions to take today. Hence, the very best economic policies are ones that facilitate the functioning of markets and that do little to surprise tomorrow those who are making economic decisions today. Consequently, the best monetary policy is one that does not seek to actively tinker with the money supply in response to short-term fluctuations in macroeconomic variables. Instead, the Federal Reserve should grow the money supply at a steady, constant rate each year so that no one can be tricked into taking an action today that, in the light of tomorrow, will turn out to have been a bad idea.

REAL BUSINESS CYCLES

While very popular today, the new classical macroeconomics is not the only compelling macroeconomic story that rose out of the decline of the Keynesian paradigm. Economists today are still somewhat divided concerning which of today's two viable models of the macroeconomy performs better in explaining past economic events and predicting future ones. The real business cycle model provides an alternative explanation to the new classical story of economic recessions and expansions. While somewhat different in its foundations from its new classical counterpart, the real business cycle story nevertheless yields the same policy implication: active attempts to stabilize the economy via economic policy are ultimately destabilizing. Market forces work better to direct resources to their best available uses than can any attempt to fine-tune the economy, using either fiscal or monetary policy.

In the real business cycle story of macroeconomics, market forces are always at work. Incessantly directing resources to their most highly valued uses, market forces ensure that resources are rarely, if ever, underutilized in the economy. Goods markets, labor markets, financial markets—all move quickly to their equilibrium positions so that our economy is always functioning as efficiently as it can at any point in time.

Even under such conditions it is nevertheless still possible for an economy to experience increases or decreases in the level of real output, real GDP. That is, even in an economy where markets clear rapidly in their direction of resources, there can still be recessions and expansions of the economy. And typically, as GDP rises in an economic expansion, employment rises along with it. The reverse tends to be true as well; a fall in GDP corresponds to a fall in employment in the economy. According to the real business cycle model, the primary impetus for such fluctuations is technological advancement.

How can technological advancement occasion both economic expansions and recessions? Let's consider first the more immediately obvious case of how technological expansion leads to economic growth. Typically, our production technologies evolve relatively slowly over time. Pentium chips run faster, we begin using a few self-service checkout lanes in grocery stores, and we learn to make color photocopies. Such discoveries let us be more productive in the workplace. Faster computer chips help us get more work done, self-service checkouts help grocers serve more customers, and color copies make our presentations more impressive to our customers.

With such discoveries comes greater individual productivity in the workplace and, as a result, greater output. Further, as awareness of the new technology develops, demand for the products that incorporate the new technologies will grow, so does demand for individuals who can assemble, distribute, service and produce the parts for the computers, self-serve checkout lanes and color copiers. Therefore, new technology leads to our producing more goods and services, and employing more individuals in order to do it. That is, a technological advancement can lead to an increase in GDP and an increase in employment.

While it is fairly obvious that increases in technology can occasion greater output and employment, it is less clear how a technological advance could result in a recession. According to real business cycle theorists, recession can result from technological advance when the new discovery is so great and revolutionary that much of our existing capital and job skills becomes obsolete. Suppose, for example, that some entrepreneur has been working tirelessly to devise a new product or technology that he believes will revolutionize our society. Forgoing other current employment opportunities, he invests much of his personal wealth, together with his time, creativity and ingenuity, in the pursuit of his eventual discovery. Through starts and failures, he endures. In our American past his last name might have been Edison or Bell or Ford. He puts off current comforts in his drive for uncertain eventual rewards.

Eventually, the discoveries of the light bulb, the telephone and the automobile led to job creation at rates our nation had never seen. Further, our nation became more productive once we were able to harness the light bulb to create second- and third-shift jobs. The telephone let us communicate both more quickly and in a way that let us be better understood than could the telegram. And the automobile revolutionized the transportation industry; through the use of an assembly line, Henry Ford made it possible for many to afford a car—while paying his employees the dramatically high wage of five dollars per day. Moreover, the realization of these discoveries eventually led to the creation of millions of new, better-paying, cleaner, safer jobs for Americans. Without question, such dramatic, revolutionary discoveries eventually lead to fabulous increases in employment and output.

But in the short-term there will be growing pains, in the form of recession, when technological advances are revolutionary. The press sometimes refers to this phenomenon as a cycle of creative destruction. When technological change proves so dramatic that it creates brand new industries, an economy can struggle as it makes its way from the old ways of doing things to the new ones. The main reason for such struggle is that the existing productive resources—and even the skills of laborers themselves—suddenly become obsolete. As the economy evolves through the process of remaking its productive processes and retraining our pool of labor in order to take advantage of revolutionary technological change, we can expect that output—and employment along with it—will temporarily fall. For example, many highly skilled horse-drawn carriage builders eventually made the transition to building cars, but they initially had few skills to contribute in auto production. And the closing of telegraph offices that came with the advent of the telephone left their operators, initially, unemployed.

All such major, revolutionary changes in our technology lead to a cycle of creative destruction. It is precisely because of our ingenuity and creativity that we are able to abandon the old, costly, inefficient, low-skilled, hazardous ways of doing things as we usher in the marvelous new jobs that accompany such revolutions. And such times are exciting with the prospect of what tomorrow can bring. Yes, some labor, machinery and other productive resources are briefly rendered idle through this cycle. But the better jobs that follow such cycles are among the benefits we all gain, even as our old jobs are destroyed and forgotten. In fact, due to the cycle of creative destruction, employment in all twenty of the *Jobs Rated Almanac*'s twenty worst jobs has steadily fallen since 1900. Moreover, job titles like "cooper" or "millwright" are so outdated that most of us no longer even know what they mean.[1]

The policy implications that follow from the real business cycle theory of macroeconomic fluctuations are no different from those implied by the new classical model. Market forces work better to direct resources to their best available uses than can any attempt to fine-tune the economy, using either fiscal or monetary policy. Moreover, attempts to increase employment through expansionary monetary policy can make conditions even worse. For example, in the real business cycle model, the only consequence of adding more dollars to the money supply is higher prices across the economy! Therefore, freely functioning markets create the jobs necessary to maintain high levels of employment in an economy; active monetary policy—no matter how noble its makers' intentions—cannot reliably accomplish it.

PURSUING STOCK MARKET PERFORMANCE AS A MACROECONOMIC GOAL

We concluded the preceding chapter by briefly considering whether the Federal Reserve should use its policy instruments to target stock-market price trends as a macroeconomic goal. In light of the insights of both the new classical and real business cycle models of the macroeconomy, we cannot embrace the pursuit of growing stock values as a proper goal of monetary policy. Regardless of which model more accurately describes the workings of macroeconomies, the implications are the same: activist monetary policies designed to expand or stabilize the economy cannot work.

In the case of new classical economics, individuals are considered wise enough to incorporate all information available to them today in making their decisions for tomorrow. Hence, a key implication of the new classical model is that monetary policy can only be effective when the Fed deliberately attempts to deceive the public. Regardless of how meritorious their aims, monetary policymakers must not actively pursue higher stock values when doing so requires deception.

---

[1]Merriam-Webster defines *cooper* as "one that makes or repairs wooden casks or tubs." De Pree (1987) defines "millwright" in the following manner: "In the furniture industry in the 1920s the machines of most factories were not run by electric motors, but by pulleys from a central drive shaft. The central drive shaft was run by the steam engine. The steam engine got its steam from the boiler. The boiler, in our case, got its fuel from the sawdust and other waste coming out of the machine room—a beautiful cycle.

"The millwright was the person who oversaw that cycle and on whom the entire activity of the operation depended. He was a key person" (p. 7).

Moreover, in the real business cycle case, the economy is always growing, expanding and developing dynamically as a nation's technology evolves and changes. Hence, individuals should be free to act within markets to pursue the mutually beneficial gains resulting from new discoveries. Since such discoveries follow from the incentives provided in a market system, monetary policy should be as predictable as possible in order to encourage creativity and entrepreneurship.

Thus attempts to tinker with the prices of stocks will only divert resources from opportunities that appear less promising today to others that prove less promising tomorrow. Because we rely on stock prices as indicators of the value of a firm and the resources it commands, we cannot afford to let the Fed attempt to manipulate stock prices.

CAN ACTIVE FISCAL POLICY HELP MACROECONOMIC CONDITIONS?

Due to the limited ways in which we now believe that economies respond to active economic policy actions, there is no reason to believe that fiscal policy—the taxation and spending policies of government—can perform any better than monetary policy actions in improving on our attainment of the macroeconomic goals considered in chapter six. Activist policies designed to expand or stabilize the economy cannot work, whether those policies are fiscal or monetary.

In fact, due to the considerable lags associated with the policymaking interactions of the president and Congress, attempts to guide the macroeconomy prove even more dubious than those of monetary policy. In general, the lags involved in the policy process may be divided into three categories. First, there is a period of time that elapses between the genesis of a macroeconomic problem and its recognition. This lag is often referred to as the *recognition lag*. For example, a flood that destroys much of the infrastructure in a nation, like Japan, could have a negative impact on other economies across the globe. The recognition lag is the time it takes for policymakers in another nation to realize that the negative economic effects of the flood could adversely affect other economies.

Second, there is a period between the discovery of a new problem, such as a flood, and the moment when a new policy action is pursued in response. This lag is known as the *implementation lag*. Any implementation lag in the fiscal policy channel will prove dramatically longer than its corresponding lag in monetary policy. For example, the Fed's Open Market committee meets eight times each year, and decides—within two days!—whether or not to make a change in policy. In contrast, the president and Congress cannot decide anything quickly. Even when the same party holds simultaneously the presidency and the majority in both congressional houses, fiscal policy evolves slowly. Due to the tremendous implementation lags of fiscal policy, it is even less useful for macroeconomic purposes than is monetary policy.

A final lag in the policy process, the *reaction lag*, is the time that passes from when a policy action is taken until its effects on the economy may be observed. While the recognition and reactions lags are equivalent for both fiscal and monetary policy, it is the extended implementation lag associated with fiscal policy that makes it even less appealing in the pursuit of macroeconomic goals than monetary policy.

This is not to say that there is no relevant role for fiscal policy. Indeed, there are many crucial ways that government can effect positive change in an economy, and we discussed many of them in chapters three through five. Nevertheless, due to its lengthy implementation lag, fiscal policy proves less reliable in pursuing macroeconomic goals than monetary policy.

CONCLUSION

Macroeconomics is a science subject to paradigm shifts. Our macroeconomic understanding since Keynes has evolved in such a way that Keynes's prescriptions of active policy actions have become less and less certain. Today we are not content with a policy designed around the adage "In the long run we are all dead." Instead, in light of the development of the new classical and real business cycle models, a steady, deliberate, rules-based approach to economic policy may lead to the best overall long-term path for the economy. Attempts to use discretionary monetary or fiscal policy actions to stabilize the economy will, instead, be destabilizing.

Moreover, the welfare of the poor depends on long-term growth and short-term stability. Without sustained long-term growth, we needlessly prolong the plight of the poor, both in terms of daily living standards and in terms of all of the good things that growth can bring (such as cures for cancer and production techniques that cause less pollution).

And without stability, the poorest among us will experience the greatest disruptions. Most of us, from the lower-middle class up, can endure recessions reasonably well. We may experience some slight disruptions, but we'll come out all right.

For the poor and working class, however, their existence is far more fragile. And we bear a moral responsibility to them to grow the economy in the least disruptive and most predictable ways economic science permits.

FOR FURTHER READING

Lee, Susan. 1996. *Hands off: Why the government is a menace to economic health.* New York: Simon & Schuster. Clarifies for the lay person the distinction between Keynesian macroeconomics and its newer alternatives.

Mandel, Michael, J. 2004. *Rational exuberance: Silencing the enemies of growth and why the future is better than you think.* New York: HarperBusiness. Very easy read, covering many related issues in economic growth and macro stability. Would work well to read soon after reading this chapter; the two offer nice complementarities and contrasts.

8

INTERNATIONAL ECONOMIC RELATIONS

Hope for the Third World

Globalization is attracting critics in the early twenty-first century the way the Vietnam War did in the 1970s. The streams of criticism and multiple motives of those who organize antiglobalization protests are difficult to disentangle. Certainly, Third World poverty is one of their concerns. Protest leaders believe that rich firms and large international organizations, like the World Trade Organization (WTO) and the International Monetary Fund (IMF), manage world trade for the benefit of elite consumers and stockholders in rich, industrialized regions like the United States, Western Europe and Japan.

GLOBALIZATION: THE ENEMY OF POOR NATIONS?

Behind the critics' thinking lies a picture of international economic relations in which rich countries enjoy the benefits of economic growth at the expense of poor nations. The critics believe that many international economic dealings—whether in the form of trade flows, bank loans, multinational investments or government aid—constitute exploitation. All those dealings are said to be modern versions of violence and injustice that characterized rich nations' behavior toward the colonies before their independence.

In an effort to persuade all right-thinking persons to join their cause against globalization's mistreatment of the poor, some organizations sponsor protests and circulate litanies of grievous facts comparing rich and poor countries. These "facts" typically include all the following:

1. In 2001, 80 percent of the world output of goods and services was consumed by 16 percent of the world's population—those fortunate enough to live in rich countries (World Bank 2003, p. 234).

2. In the same year, the average per-capita income of people in rich countries was sixty-two times the income of those living in the poorest developing countries; for Haiti and the United States, the comparable figure was seventy-two times (World Bank 2003, p. 234).

3. The income gap between the incomes of rich and poor countries is rising, resulting in even more economic injustice.

4. Multinational firms close plants in their home countries and open new ones in Third World countries without thought for home-country workers, because they earn profits by *exploiting* workers in poor countries. They do so by paying abysmally low wages and avoiding the expenditures needed to provide safe and humane working conditions overseas.

5. Lacking loyalty to their workers and other moral values, the same multinational companies—whether owned by Japanese, Europeans, Americans or now Koreans—eventually shut down the transplants and move to still poorer countries. This happens when rising local wages and pressures from workers make it unprofitable to stay.

6. Consumers of products produced by the foreign plants of multinational companies unwittingly participate in *shark capitalism,* because First World consumers pay exceedingly low prices for imported products, like sports gear, coffee and small electronic goods.

In this chapter we examine these and similar claims in order to understand the extent of Third World poverty, changes needed both inside and outside these countries for living standards to rise, and various ways that Christians can exercise their faith in support of poor people living there. The causes of poverty are complex and the way out of poverty is difficult. A major lesson of this chapter is that effective antipoverty measures rarely take the form of *less* trade, *less* international investment or *lower* spending by consumers on products produced in Third World countries. In fact, the only practical way out of poverty includes *more* globalization, not less.

Globalization—that is, the increased movement of goods, money and people across national borders—is nothing other than an enlarged version of what happens in every town, state and country as markets expand and knit the component parts into a web of interdependence. The marvel of local and international market forces is their ability to coordinate decisions made by individual consumers, producers, workers, savers and investors to their mutual advantage. Without any central directive, markets induce the movement of resources into places and activities where they can do the most to increase output and raise incomes. Furthermore, widespread access to growing material benefits, made possible by such coordination, is founded on the moral bedrock of freedom for all participants (see chap. 2 for the development of this proposition). They should normally be allowed to make their own choices—in pursuit of their own diverse values—as they buy and sell their goods, labor and money.

UNDERSTANDING WORLD POVERTY IN TERMS OF A FAMILIAR, LOCAL EXAMPLE

We can get a better view of the big globalization picture by investigating similar market processes over a smaller geographic area. Imagine that oil has been discovered under a ranch in Montana that you inherited from your grandparents. Because you prefer to continue your career in engineering, you do not plan to take up ranching. You are in the process of deciding what to do with the land. The alternatives include selling it to your grandparents' neighbors, who want to expand their ranching operation; selling it to a developer, because the nearby urban area is growing and, with it, the demand for housing; selling it to an oil company; or leasing subsoil rights to an oil company to extract the oil, while maitaining the legal right to additional uses (like recreation or farming) of land lying above the oil deposits.

Whichever option you choose, the decision process includes estimating future incomes and nonmonetary benefits that you could derive under each option. If you decide to sell to the energy company, will your conscience condemn you because the oil well can be expected to eventually run dry? Probably not. You know that long before this happens, the company will search longer and harder for oil in other locations (all the more so, as world oil prices rise). Nationally, this has led Shell Oil to close its operations in northern Michigan and to start extracting oil in parts of Wyoming for which the technology was not available less than six years ago. Outside the United States, international oil companies are seeking out potential new oil fields in Siberia to replace those that are playing out in the North Sea and Alaska.

Furthermore, you would not have done anyone a favor by withholding the oil in perpetuity, since oil is useful only if it can be extracted and sold in a process that responds to the ultimate users' desires for personal transportation and heating, and for the goods and services produced and distributed with the aid of oil and its derivatives.

Consider what you would think about efforts by a group in California to organize a campaign against the *exploitation* of Montanans. Suppose organizers publish data showing that the average living standard, in the year 2003, in California was more than 41 percent higher than that in Montana (U.S. Bureau of the Census 2006, table 689). They argue that it is "unfair" for Californians to buy oil extracted from Montana because this leaves less for future Montanans. We put "unfair" in quotes since many people who oppose economic change because it is "unfair" do so with strong material incentives of their own. Both unions and companies facing international competition often portray the competition as unfair precisely because the products are produced and sold for less than domestic firms charge. The same charge of "unfair" is not usually made, however, if the low-cost competitor is only across town or located in another state of the Union. Whenever an argument that does not hold water domestically is used to challenge international commerce, a red flag should go up in the listener.

The campaign to protect "Montana for Montanans" calls on the governor of California either to ban all sale of Montana oil in California or to require that gas refined from Montana oil be clearly labeled (perhaps with colored additives), so that Californians can avoid buying cheap gas that "exploits" the dire needs of Montanans and their fragile environment. Given the thought and care you have put into your decision to sell the land to an oil company (including consideration of the welfare of your family, the town and their future), you probably resent Californians' misplaced feelings and activism on behalf of "poor Montanans."

Now, consider a Third World country like Indonesia, Brazil or Cameroon, with oil, wood, orange juice, clothing or small electronic goods to export in world markets. What must their citizens think about antiglobalization protestors (e.g., Seattle in November 1999) who argue that poor nations need to be "protected" from First World greed? What must they feel about efforts to persuade Western consumers to boycott their products? Will they support efforts to get the World Trade Organization to turn away potential buyers from their markets? After all, their export industries are said to be built on exploiting "cheap labor," using up natural resources and getting richer on the backs of the poor.

This is a good place to recall some of the antiglobalization claims already listed (see pp. 143-44). Third World countries, just like Montana, stand to gain from strong sales of their products. The observation that Americans consume more than the Chinese (see claim 2), for example, has no more moral significance than a similar observation that Californians earn and consume more than Montanans. Over time, we expect incomes in Montana to grow as their trade with California increases. It makes little difference to people in Montana that Californians have a higher per-capita income than Montanans. People are poor—in Montana or China—as long as they lack valuable skills, capital or other resources.

Chinese families do not care much about how their living standard compares with that of Americans, as long as it rises over the years and offers better opportunities for their children. The good news is that consumption per capita in China has been rising dramatically. Over the period 1980-1998—about one generation—consumption per capita rose by 144 percent (World Bank 2003, p. 276). This is something to cheer about, even though China's per capita income in 2001 (in purchasing power terms) was still only 12 percent of that of the United States.

Of course, in addition to resources and skills, Montana and Bangladesh, for example, must also ensure certain conditions and enforce basic rules, so that trade benefits people in buyer and seller states (or countries), by creating new production and income possibilities for their citizens. This can happen only if those who work and buy, and those who provide the funds needed to organize production and distribution have the right (and the ability) to choose among employments, purchases and loan opportunities. Trading goods and exchanging money in open markets are voluntary transactions because they are neither forced nor limited by law and custom.

Favorable conditions for marketing Montana oil include, first, a legal system that protects buyers and sellers from fraud and gives landowners considerable freedom to dispose of their property as they choose. With a sound legal system in place, theft of the oil is not an option for the oil company; neither is nationalization permitted (a form of government theft that still affects many developing countries). Second, it is important that no exclusive practice (or law) impede oil companies (or other would-be users of the land) from bidding against each other to buy or lease the land, because such restrictions would lower the revenues of Montanans. Consequently, the state should not have the right to forbid most potential uses of the land.

A third important condition for favorable economic development in Montana or China is that buyers have reasonable access to a variety of funding sources to finance the purchase of a farm in Montana or to upgrade a small shop in China. If, instead, state or federal laws make competition from non-Montana-based banks illegal, a win-win exchange of land for money or capital improvements on the land could be prevented—to the detriment of current and future Montanans (as was the case before federal deregulation in 1994 permitting interstate banking throughout the United States).

The rate of economic growth in China rose greatly as a result of their economic reforms during the late twentieth century. However, the Chinese government still limits access to foreign funds that could be made available through international investment. As a result, China's growth rate could be even more rapid than it has been over the last decade.

A fourth condition for strong economic development is that ranchers in Montana and income earners in China should have the right to dispose of their revenues on the purchase of consumer goods or machinery, or to put their money to work in domestic and foreign stocks, investment funds, or bank accounts. If, instead, a good share of new income is captured by heavy taxes, or if goods coming from other states (or nations) face heavy tariffs, or if local land laws prohibit many alternative uses for land (because of feared environmental, aesthetic or political impacts), then benefits from land sale and improvements will be smaller than otherwise.

Fully aware of the need for reforms in those areas, China worked for many years to gain admission to the World Trade Organization, because their new leaders recognized how much growth they had missed out on by closing their borders to many foreign imports. However, some countries still impose high tariffs on imports, thus making both home consumption and production using imported parts more costly. Furthermore, although some Western countries have strict land-use laws, copying Western measures used to protect environmental resources would be prohibitively costly and premature in Third World countries.

China's citizens look forward to a time when, with continued economic growth, they will be able to provide for necessities (like food) and also set aside funds for environmental protection. Indeed, studies have shown that as per-capita incomes rise above very low levels, environmental quality in poor countries decreases at first, but after a threshold is reached (usually less than $8,000 per capita), the trends reverse. The subsequent environmental improvement is due to a number of factors, such as a gradual shift toward cleaner industries and public pressure on governments to introduce measures to protect the quality of environmental resources like water and air (Lynn 2003, p. 102).[1]

In addition to freedom of choice for buyers and sellers, another necessary condition for creating mutual benefits from land sales in Montana is that it be possible to transport the oil and sell it competitively in markets at a considerable distance from Montana. Montanans benefit from these and other exchanges across state lines when some tax money is used to build inter- and intrastate roads and highways.

In the case of many Third World countries, more highways, ports and railroads need to be built (and better maintained) if their products are to find ready markets in the rest of the world. Foreign sales earn them higher incomes and allow the average person to buy more goods and services. Over the last decade it has become evident that the best results are achieved when governments collaborate with businesses and community groups on such infrastructure projects. Working together, they can keep costs down and ensure that user fees—needed for upkeep and expansion—are collected from all users (*Economist* 2003).

While applying the Montana lessons about markets to globalization issues faced by Third World countries, we have emphasized that private-property rights must be established and protected in order for buyers and sellers (and their communities) to benefit from domestic markets and international trade. Furthermore, we noted the importance of expanding opportunities for Third World countries to sell their resources, goods and services to other countries at competitive prices. This happens when international transport costs fall, world markets are opened (by lowering trade barriers) and private and public investments are made in roads, dams and other physical infrastructure.

One further response to criticisms of globalization should be added, even though we did not mention it in the Montana oil example. The oil company that offered you a good price for the ranch land is almost certainly a company with home offices in one state but also doing business in many states and within several countries. In the latter case, it is referred to as a multinational

---

[1]We have used economic relationships between Montana and California to illustrate those between poor and rich countries. However, this parallel fails to convey important legal differences. Both states operate under federal law, which requires certain conditions, like democratic choice and respect for labor and environmental laws. Supranational law could enforce such conditions on independent nations. Nevertheless, China's failings in these regards have a better chance of being remedied through free diplomatic and economic engagements between China and the West than unilateral dictates or isolation. This is the main reason why China was voted into the World Trade Organization despite China's failure to guarantee high levels of personal economic freedom.

corporation (MNC). There is a reason why Montana may not have its own oil company, operating exclusively within the state. The same reason explains the existence of multinational firms. Starting with success in their home market, the most productive firms ultimately extend their reach beyond political borders because they are able to offer higher prices to sellers of their inputs and lower prices to consumers of their products than could businesses confined to one state or country.

By virtue of the expertise developed in their home market, Sony Corporation, for example, spread its sales far beyond Japan. As chronicled in Morita, Reingold and Shimomura (1986), Sony was quick to design their products to meet different tastes and conditions outside of Japan. While the founder was living in New York City for a year, he noticed teens carrying radios on their shoulders. This inspired him to remove the recorder function from Sony's own small tape recorder, add lightweight headphones and produce the first Walkman. Sony's phenomenal success would be mere history had they not continued to spend large sums on research and design. Their ongoing growth is the result of setting goals to meet high quality standards, serve diverse cultural tastes and offer products at prices the average person can pay. Not surprisingly, Sony now has subsidiaries in more than three dozen countries. Although Japan is no longer a developing country, its rise to First World status serves as a valuable example of how relatively free markets and trade produce remarkable progress in living standards.

Other multinational corporations are able to create markets for their products and for their suppliers because they are supremely qualified in the domains of financing, marketing, technology or exploration. For this reason, both First and Third World countries are generally well served by multinational corporations. Some MNCs only market, but do not manufacture, their products (like machinery and food) in foreign countries. Others sell patents to foreign companies, allowing them to use newer, more efficient technologies. Some MNCs invest directly in production facilities overseas, like car or electronic assembly plants. Still others partner with local firms in joint production. A multinational company may supply outside funds, international outlets and technical know-how, while the local partner provides labor and local marketing expertise. MNCs do not continue in business unless they offer valuable services and products at attractive prices to their suppliers and customers.

Why then are multinational corporations often vilified for exploiting Third World countries (see claim 4 on p. 144)? Perhaps it is because the critics do not understand the key roles MNCs play in getting Third World products to world markets, supplying inputs to Third World farmers and businesses, and financing Third World production. When they are able to sell machinery, consumer goods and certain foodstuffs (e.g., the wheat needed to bake bread) at prices that could not be matched by local producers, MNCs are helping Third World people. They accomplish this, not primarily for charitable reasons, but in the expectation of earning profits. Nevertheless, the nature of uncoerced market exchanges is that they always produce mutual benefits for buyers and sellers.

Third World people sell their products—like textiles, tropical foodstuffs and electronic goods—in international markets because, by selling their relatively abundant and low-cost products, they can buy relatively abundant and low-cost goods from trading partners. (Note that the term trade *partners* much better fits the facts than the common term trade *rivals*.) Whether domestic or foreign firms produce and market the goods, one key to Third World export successes is their low wage scale. Workers take jobs in export industries at low wages (compared to U.S. wage scales), but usually higher than wages paid in the domestic sectors of those economies.

In 2003, National Public Radio reported a story about a foreign-owned textile manufacturer in Africa. Each morning the factory gates were opened and as many workers as needed for the day were allowed to come in to work. Daily, people from the area waited outside the factory gates, long before they were opened, hoping to find work for the day. They did this because, although the wage was low, it was still the best pay they could find in their area. After the number of people needed was allowed in, the gates were closed. Nevertheless, many people could still be found standing, with faces pressed up against the fence. They hoped to earn even part of a day's wage, if only the factory managers would to decide that more workers were needed. (This situation is powerfully similar to Jesus' parable of the vineyards in Matthew 20.)

Although this picture may evoke sympathy in First World circles, what we see here are new employment opportunities for some workers, which give them access to the first rung of an "income ladder" that gradually raises the family incomes of poor people. Furthermore, over time, international competition for workers raises wages in companies producing for export, faster than in other sectors of Third World economies. Rising wages in the export sector eventually spread beyond exports to the whole domestic market.

Korea is an example of a formerly poor country having graduated from low-wage to high-wage industries over time. Whereas their growth success during the 1970s and 1980s was tied to export success in textiles and other low-wage industries, by the 1990s those industries had moved into South East Asia (see claim 5 on p. 144). Korea's export success today is largely in high-tech, high-wage industries like automobiles and electronics. A more general picture of Third World economies can be found in a 1998 Brookings Institute study. They found that between 1960 and 1992 average manufacturing wages in developing countries rose from one-tenth the U.S. manufacturing average to 30 percent (Lukas 2000, p. 8). This is the stuff of hope and progress!

Families and governments in Third World countries tend to invest part of their income growth (made possible by strong export performance) in key sectors like education and road building. Such investments are important since they make it possible for economic growth to spread new opportunities into poorer regions (like Chiapas in Mexico) and groups (like the "untouchables" in India) within poor countries. When sustained growth happens, both skills and living standards rise. As a result, some industries move off to still poorer regions—bringing new opportunities for employment and incomes there. For the region (or country) "losing" certain industries, this is usually evidence of social and economic progress, because new industries (using better technology, requiring higher skills and paying higher wages) simultaneously are attracted to that region.

APPLYING LESSONS FROM HOME TO GLOBAL POVERTY

If the Montana ranch case is so clear and the necessary conditions for mutual benefits are so obvious, why do most First World citizens fail to understand that globalization is, on balance, good for the people of poor and rich countries alike? Why do we fall prey to the simplistic, though tempting, maxim, "the rich are always getting rich on the backs of the poor"?

Apparently, there are some blind spots in our vision, causing us to blame First World institutions and systems for Third World poverty. Selective blindness also prevents us from appreciating how criticisms of globalization may undermine the very forces that are vital to progress against poverty. Economic growth, via expansion of markets (globalization), is essential in order for Third World countries to gradually reduce the proportion and numbers of poor people living within their borders.

A key blind spot is the lack of awareness in First World countries of the centuries of economic, political and technological changes that were required in order to bring improvements in their own living standards. Until the sixteenth century, China's wealth and technology were greater than those of any country in the West. However, beginning in the late eighteenth century economic growth rates in Western countries began to rise. The cumulative result is that living standards in the First World now greatly exceed those in Third World countries, including the previously great Chinese empire. Thus the sources of the "gap" between the richest and poorest nations are the surprising growth rates in the former and stagnation in the latter.

The political and economic challenge today is to discover what conditions and processes would enable people living in today's poor nations to enjoy the fruits of prolonged economic growth. Among the conditions Westerners take for granted are the rule of law, especially in regard to the protection of persons and private property. Those laws—which formed a platform for long-run growth in the West—are either missing or not enforced in most Third World countries. Also absent in many poor countries are honest, efficient and responsive governments at all levels.

Largely as a result of economic amnesia, many First World citizens believe that their own economic success was gained at the expense of Third World countries. Those who wrongly assume this to be true oversimplify the task of development. Several popular—though misguided and misleading—propositions about the causes and remedies of Third World poverty result from oversimplification of the development challenge. These include statements like:

- *Rich countries' aid to poor nations is needed as compensation for unjust gains.* There is no possible "payment" that would fully offset the earlier unjust gains. Nevertheless, more aid must be the fundamental answer to Third World poverty.

- The only fair transactions between rich and poor nations are those that involve sacrifice by the rich in favor of the poor. *For-profit entities are to be distrusted* because they only exploit people and resources rather than create new resources (like capital), incomes or unimagined future possibilities.

- It is always within the capacity of empathetic donors to reverse the course of underdevelopment. Aid donors know the causes and can trust in the expertise and good will of those who purport to speak for poor people (e.g., their governments). *With enough will power and economic aid, First World countries can eliminate abject poverty worldwide in the next twenty years.*

All such claims have the virtue of sounding sympathetic to the plight of Third World people, but they are based on simplistic assumptions. They misrepresent the difficult and lengthy task ahead for poor countries to increase productivity and raise living standards.

BARRIERS TO ECONOMIC GROWTH AND POSSIBILITIES FOR POVERTY REDUCTION

Certain conditions assumed in the Montana example (see pp. 145-52) made it possible to consider various options for the inherited land. Those are the very conditions that are absent in most Third World countries. In most poor countries, if Mario wants to buy land from Hector, the following problem presents itself immediately. First, Hector does not hold a piece of paper documenting his title to the land on which Mario wants to build a one-room carpentry shop attached to his home. Even though Hector does not have a title document to prove his ownership, Mario is willing to accept his word for it and buy the land from him. Mario has no other choice, because he lacks personal influence, time and funds needed to bribe an official for the permit to open his shop. In a famous study, Peruvian economist DeSoto reported that it took up to a year's worth of an average worker's income in Peru—in the form of payments over and under the table to bureaucrats—to get such a permit. In further study, DeSoto documented that it would take "168 steps, involving fifty-three public and private agencies and taking thirteen to twenty-five years" to gain clear title to land a person already occupies in the Philippines (Soto 2000, pp. 18-20). Even in these seemingly insurmountable circumstances Mario hopes for the best and starts building his shop with cheap materials and his own "sweat equity."

A month later, a city planner comes to Hector, telling him that the city intends to bulldoze the slum and offers him money to purchase the land. Of course, Hector does *not* tell the official that he has already sold those parcels to the present occupants. Instead, since his traditional (tribal) rights to the land are acknowledged, and the rights of the new owners are not in writing, he sells it a second time. In the next week the whole barrio—home to hundreds of families living in simple huts they built themselves—is bulldozed down in the name of urban renewal.

Unfortunately, this is a true story with only the names changed. If you were Mario, to whom this has just happened (or any of his neighbors), you would not be eager to cut back on bare-minimum living expenses in order to save for rebuilding your shop somewhere else. Virtually every effort you might consider to raise your family's standard of living is obstructed. In this case, the lack of clear property rights makes it very risky for you to undertake a small family business. Profitable and socially useful economic activities will not happen under these circumstances. Such activities include building housing, providing informal taxi service and selling small items in local markets.

Looking beyond the case of Mario and Hector, we can take note of additional barriers facing poor people who are willing to struggle hard to improve the lives of their families. Consider Maria, who has an administrative job that allows her to set aside a dollar a month in saving, hoping to pay for her eldest daughter to attend high school. Banks in Maria's country are completely unreliable—either because the owners are thieves or because the government occasionally freezes individual accounts (as happened in Argentina in 2002-2003). As a result, Maria hides the cash under her bed, even though she runs a high risk of theft. Furthermore, because almost no one wants to use banks, bankers do not have funds available to make small loans to businesses in parts of the country where the conditions are favorable for small and medium-sized business expansion.

With these two examples, we have barely scratched the surface of obstacles to economic development. In addition, there are three other circumstances that make it especially difficult for many poor countries to grow themselves out of poverty.

First, *accidents of geography*—like a hot climate and steep terrain—limit growth. Tropical climates are notorious for their hospitality to endemic diseases that kill millions and disable still greater numbers every year. For example, malaria alone causes over 1.1 million deaths and a loss of over 42 million life-years annually (World Health Organization 2002). Total figures for the ten hardest-hitting infectious diseases—not including AIDS—are 2.9 million deaths and 92 million lost life-years annually. These are the diseases that especially affect the world's poorest populations.

Many poor countries lack access to water transportation along rivers or the sea, which is much cheaper than land transport. This prevents the creation of truly national markets in which a season's abundance in one region can be shipped to another region facing food shortfalls. When remote areas of a country are inaccessible to goods coming from other areas or countries, due to high transportation costs, goods do not flow back and forth. As a result, people in that country (or a region within a country, like Chiapas, Mexico) are unable to earn higher incomes by specializing in making certain products and investing in new skills, tools and processes.

Of course, many geographic challenges are not immutable. Indeed, mountains make transportation of goods difficult and expensive, but tunnels and more durable road surfaces lower costs. Internet technology now enables production to take place without either people or products leaving centers that are separated by thousands of miles (e.g., the services provided by Indian software engineers, who are the second largest exporters of software in the world). New agricultural techniques and products—including irrigation, fertilizer, herbicides and the hybrid seeds used to produce drought-resistant crops—are all measures that gradually (or sometimes rapidly, as in the case of the 1970s "green revolution") raise production and incomes in poor countries.

Second, *bad government* and *bad public policies* also frustrate economic growth. Bloated and corrupt bureaucracies are one such problem because they burden taxpayers and favor well-connected persons over energetic risk-takers and doers. They also cause inefficient resource use and inflation. Budget deficits are sometimes an obvious sign of bad government. (However, potential budget deficits are masked whenever governments simply print new money to pay for excess spending, instead of borrowing from local or foreign sources—resulting in very high inflation.) Those deficits result from inadequate tax laws, widespread tax evasion and wasteful spending.

One of the ways that Third World governments waste scarce financial resources is by providing water, electricity and rail travel, for example, at low prices that do not cover the costs of production and distribution. The shame is that these services overwhelmingly go to those parts of their populations who could afford to pay. As a result, governments do not make the needed investments for the extension and upkeep of these key public services. For example, in many poor countries cheap piped water reaches rich neighborhoods, while poor families must buy high-cost bottled drinking water.

Third, *excessive government regulations* often stymie entrepreneurship and restrict market size. We noted the effects of bad regulations and corrupt bureaucracy on Mario's inability to open a simple carpentry shop. Furthermore, despite recent policy changes, highly protectionist First and Third World trade regimes artificially reduce market sizes, just as falling transportation costs could be enlarging them.

Another weakness of governments in Third World countries takes the form of poor regulation of the financial sector. In the late 1990s a financial crisis in South East Asia brought suffering to millions of people. That crisis revealed weak financial regulation. Banks had taken advantage of a boom to lend to businesses without commercial promise but with strong connections to local political elites.

STRIKING PROGRESS DESPITE CLAIMS TO THE CONTRARY

There is much to cheer about in spite of challenges and the mistakes made by Third World countries and rich nations. Consider the remarkable improvements in living standards in many Third World countries, especially over the last two decades. In his book *Imagine There's No Country: Poverty, Inequality, and Growth in the Era of Globalization,* Indian economist Surjit S. Bhalla provides stunning evidence of shrinking income gaps between First and Third World peoples, along with closing gaps in literacy, infant mortality, life expectancy, educational achievement and political and civic liberties.

Most remarkable is that the greater share of these improvements has occurred during the era of globalization (1980-2000) compared to the preceding two decades 1960-1980—just the opposite of antiglobalization claims. Such improvement is exactly what economics predicts as the result of goods, capital and people becoming more mobile than ever before in human history. After all, lower wage rates paid for any skill in a Third World country (across the spectrum from semiskilled production workers to highly skilled engineers and programmers) attract domestic and international businesses to those places. Then, increasing demand for less expensive labor in poorer regions and countries gradually raises their wage rates relative to those of richer regions and countries.

It is a tragedy that many vocal groups vilify the dependable mechanisms by which poorer people obtain access to improved opportunities and living standards, calling it profiteering and exploitation. The fact is that no foreign aid program has come anywhere near achieving the level of improved living standards earned and enjoyed by people who are increasingly connected to global markets. For example, remittances (wages sent home) from Mexicans working in the United States exceed the total value of foreign direct investment in that country and far exceed total aid to Mexico.

The trajectory of sustained improvement in many parts of the Third World just described is a powerful reason for hope. In addition to reforms being undertaken in these countries, other forces from the outside have the potential to add momentum for good. For example, the ongoing Doha Round of negotiations among the 150-plus members of the World Trade Organization is aimed at the difficult task of reducing tariff and quota barriers to Third World agricultural exports like sugar and cotton. Part of the difficulty is getting agreement among First World countries to significantly reduce price supports and subsidies for their own farmers. Such favoritism both interferes with the ability of Third World producers to sell at their more competitive prices and hurts consumers everywhere.

In part because global markets do not simultaneously lift all ships, Christians and others who care about the poorest of the poor are called to supplement market forces. Loving and well-targeted assistance can create sustained increases in labor productivity and incomes for those who have fallen behind. They too can have their day in the sun.

HOPE FOR REDUCING POVERTY

Christians are called to *reasoned hope*. This is clear in their personal lives, but it is equally important for their effective engagement with big issues, like world poverty. Faced with the complexity of Third World poverty, people often are drawn to either of the following extreme perspectives:

- The job of helping the poor is seen as too overwhelming. Caring Christians have no alternative but to seek personal righteousness in their lives at work, home and in their neighborhoods, while praying for God to help those whose needs and opportunities most First World individuals cannot possibly know or do anything about.

- Alternatively, caring Christians should set out to revolutionize the world in "solidarity with the poor" by taking on the powers and systems they believe are to blame for world poverty—especially markets, big corporations and international bodies.

Neither of the above options fits well with the exercise of reasoned hope. We have noted that markets and big corporations are not generally the villains, and that both are absolutely essential to the economic growth needed to lift millions out of poverty. International organizations—like the World Bank, the International Monetary Fund and the World Trade Organization—should indeed undertake reforms. However, the need for reforms has relatively little to do with any First World power plays or failure by their economists to condemn exploitation. Instead, the real question is: How can these organizations tailor their help and advice to fit diverse national circumstances without undermining the incentives needed for Third World governments to follow-up with fundamental reforms? Those essential reforms must deal directly with the defense of property rights, taxation, spending, regulation, trade and the financial sector.

The first option for responding to world poverty—retreat into personal piety and prayer—is also unavailable to Christians, who must exercise reasoned hope. Both personal piety and prayer are absolutely essential, but they are not sufficient. Scripture teaches Christians their absolute duty toward the poor (see chaps. 1-2). The first channel of duty is often through the exercise of one's vocation—as a worker, neighbor or member of a family.

Since the beginning, however, Christ founded the church for a wider and deeper mission than can be achieved through local charity alone. We use *charity* here in its fullest sense: real service alongside people in need. Such charity embodies respect for their dignity, unique callings and personal responsibility. The apostle Paul collected offerings from foreign churches to help poor members of the Jerusalem church. Ever since, churches have put feet on the gospel by bringing both spiritual hope and material assistance to people near and far.

Most Christians can fulfill some part of their duty toward poor people around the world through their churches and other Christian organizations. The outlets for engagement include congregational mission trips, denominational mission programs, interdenominational efforts (like Church World Service, which is engaged in relief and development projects) and special-task Christian groups (like Opportunity International, which is active in microlending). As in all their spending, saving and giving, Christians have an obligation to be good stewards. In this case, they should investigate the suitability of the missions and methods of such organizations for meeting their goals, and determine whether they use funds efficiently (e.g., by keeping overhead low as a percent of donations).

Most people cannot dedicate months to carefully examine and compare various charities involved in Third World work. Instead, they have to rely on some combination of internal and external assessments made of several organizations that seem most attractive. Given limits on their time, money and expertise, individual Christians (and their congregations) can exercise improved stewardship by concentrating on a few organizations that are dedicated to special causes or multipurpose missions. Experience over time with the organizations to which they donate time, money and other resources can provide evidence about whether a particular goal—like helping poor people raise their incomes—is actually being met.

One of the purposes of this chapter is to provide readers with an understanding of Third World poverty so that they can discern how best to contribute individually and collectively toward helping poor people. One implication is that Christians generally should not support approaches that reduce the chances for poor people to earn a living (e.g., by boycotting products coming from Third World countries). (We do not deal here with unique, personal callings to sacrificial actions that are born out of prayer and confirmed by other Christians.) On the other hand, they should be eager to support organizations that work with groups of poor people, so that over time their ability to support themselves grows. Some organizations specialize in emergency help; others specialize in community development; but the best organizations either tackle both or work closely with other agencies, so that their efforts multiply the positive outcomes (without duplicating costs). International bodies, secular organizations and foreign governments funnel some aid through Christian organizations because they are known for their long-term commitment to helping poor people in the most disadvantaged areas and for working among minority groups who face intimidation from majority ethnic groups.

Christians may also exercise reasoned hope with respect to Third World poverty by contributing their time and money to secular organizations whose visions and approaches effectively complement Christian efforts on behalf of poor people. Equally important is the support of organizations that study various approaches to economic and political reform (e.g., the International Economic Institute and other policy think tanks)—without which community-level efforts to help the poor are blocked, frustrated or even undone.

The history of economic growth in Western countries—whose takeoff occurred less than two centuries ago—suggests that progress is possible. However, progress occurs over long periods of time, during which living standards rise as a result of small changes that produce and spread cumulative returns. To expect a time frame of twenty years for eliminating poverty in the poorest parts of Africa, for example, would be unreasonable. It could also be dangerous, since First World countries might prematurely decide to take over "bad" Third World governments in whom they lose confidence.

Christians should be especially practiced at thinking in the long run rather than joining calls for revolutionary changes based on misguided messianic expectations. When Christ did not immediately return to establish his kingdom on earth, the apostle Paul consoled the distressed and disappointed Christians. He had earlier strongly criticized those who slipped into immorality, thinking that what they did today (e.g., avoid work) did not matter since the kingdom was due to come at any moment. Paul taught new Christians to act with faith and hope, and to live righteously; they were to be in it for the long haul, until Christ's return.

In more recent times the famous early-twentieth-century missionary Dr. Albert Schweitzer encouraged patient faithfulness in small deeds with the following observation:

> Of all the will toward the ideal in mankind only a small part can manifest itself in public action. All the rest of this force must be content with small and obscure deeds. The sum of these, however, is a thousand times stronger than the acts of those who receive wide public recognition. The latter, compared to the former, are like the foam on the waves of a deep ocean. (Badaracco 2002, p. 3)

CONCLUSION

We have illustrated how crucial it is that buyers and sellers everywhere have access to markets for their products, money and resources. Without access, economic growth will not occur, and poverty will stubbornly persist. As Klay and Lunn (2003b) also argue, we believe that markets are often providentially used to accomplish what no amount of Christian charity or political activism alone could achieve. We also affirm that God's ways of meeting the needs and desires of his people include concerted efforts by churches and institutions dealing with educational and health concerns. Often, one of the most useful roles for governments is to coordinate local antipoverty efforts in keeping with necessarily limited funds and in response to shared priorities.

We affirm that God calls specific individuals and groups to do some things that contradict the means and motives most visible in markets. Thus we believe that St. Francis and his followers have been called to live simply and to preach good news to poor and rich people alike. They do not deserve to be criticized either because they refuse to buy middle-class staples (like shoes) or because Francis left his mission in Egypt (where he had hoped to bring peace between Christian crusaders and Muslims) to minister again among his own people. The Franciscan calling is unique. The wonderful truth about the Christian understanding of *calling* (the subject of chap. 9) is that God calls each person (often mediated by their faith community) to tasks that are uniquely suited to his or her endowments of faith, character, talents and surroundings.

We challenge readers who have yet to settle on a career or are contemplating a career change to consider ways that their work might dovetail with efforts to meet the needs of poor people in Third World countries. Private voluntary organizations offer some career (and short-term) opportunities for Christian service. However, businesses—small and large—are the single most powerful agents of the economic growth needed to reduce the scourge of poverty. Foreign direct investment by itself represents almost three times the total amount of economic aid given annually to Third World countries (World Bank 2003, pp. 240-41). As a result, any exploration of careers as callings should include business. This holds true especially for those who are alert to the needs of Third World people.

The reasoned, energizing hope of Christians is that God always answers the prayers of poor people throughout the world and continues to guide the church to do what is within its power and calling to accomplish, in partnership with brothers and sisters who lack material goods but who are often rich in spirit.

FOR FURTHER READING

Dean, Judith M., Schaffner, Julie A., and Smith, Stephen L. S. 2005. *Attacking poverty in the developing world: Christian practitioners and academics in collaboration*. Waynesboro, Ga.: Authentic Media. Copublished by World Vision. Written by Christian scholars and practitioners, this book explores many aspects of poverty reduction—domestic and international. They evaluate the effectiveness of various approaches and policies in terms of their impact on the poor—ranging from education and trade to debt relief and global policies.

Dean, Judith M., Schaffner, Julie A., and Smith, Stephen L. S. 2006. "Global poverty: Academics and practitioners respond. *Review of Faith and International Affairs*, 4(1):13-20. In this article, Christian economists talk about what constitutes good stewardship on the part of governments, NGOs and academics in the choice, design and implementation of programs and projects that genuinely help poor people in Third World countries to increase their incomes and family living. Because the circumstances (local and national) are highly varied, collaboration among academics and practitioners is needed. Together they can pay attention to issues like incentives, tradeoffs (and help for those hurt by certain needed policy reforms) and possibilities for synergy across programs.

Easterly, William. 2002. *The Elusive quest for growth: Economists' adventures and misadventures in the tropics*. Cambridge, Massachusetts: MIT Press. Despite the best intentions, massive economic programs intended to fix global poverty have had but a marginal impact. Easterly analyzes why foreign aid, population control and aid loans have not worked as intended. He reveals that such programs have been ineffective due to their misunderstanding of how incentives work, and offers new insights in poverty elimination.

Landes, David S. 1998. *The wealth and poverty of nations: Why some are so rich and some so poor.* New York: W.W. Norton. This monumental book attempts to answer the question, Why was Europe the location of the first sustained growth in living standards? China and the Middle East were far ahead of Europe in terms of technology and living standards during the Middle Ages. But, beginning with the sixteenth century, a gap opened up and continued to widen through the Industrial Revolution and well into the twentieth century between Western and non-Western living standards. Landes focuses on the roles of cultural values and geography.

Rivoli, Pietra. 2005. *The travels of a T-shirt in the global economy: An economist examines the markets, power, and politics of world trade.* Hoboken: John Wiley & Sons. This book takes a unique approach to trade issues by focusing on the international textile and clothing market. Readers follow the "story" of a T-shirt from its beginning in a cotton field, through factories, on to the retail market and finally to used clothing and rags. Along the way we are required to rethink trade as "exploitation" and discover trade as "opportunity." While recognizing the long-term benefits of freer trade, we also witness the short-term political "profit" from government intervention.

9

WORK AND VOCATION

What Is in Your Hand?

"Who am I . . . ?" (Ex 3:11). That was the first question Moses asked God when God told him to go to the pharaoh of Egypt and to bring the Israelites out of slavery into a land flowing with milk and honey. It is an unavoidable question for everyone considering whether a particular assignment, job or career is his or her "calling" from God. In the story of Moses at the burning bush, the conversation continues with more questions from Moses about his competence for the task that God calls him to undertake: Suppose they (the Israelites) ask me for the name of the God who sends me to them? What if they do not believe me?

Most of us do not experience our calling to serve God through our profession in such a dramatic way. However, we too pose important questions: Is this really God's voice calling me into a career in management, scientific research or teaching? What if someone thinks I am mistaken and asks for proof that God has called me to such a job, place or task? Our conversation with God about these matters takes the form of prayer and discerning fellowship with other Christians. We should pose questions in order to understand and confirm God's call.

At first, Moses protests, "What if they won't believe me or listen to me? What if they say, 'The LORD never appeared to you'" (Ex 4:1). But God replies with a question of his own: "What is that in your hand?" (Ex 4:2). It was a staff that God used miraculously by turning it into a snake when Moses threw it on the ground. Surely, this would convince any doubters that Moses was sent by God (Ex 4:3-5)! Nevertheless, Moses still had to be persuaded.

Clearly, when asked by God (or parents, teachers and friends) about what is in our hands, we would not answer "a staff." But as Christians prayerfully explore possible careers (or career changes), they must ask a similar question:

What are the gifts, talents, passions and opportunities for service with which God is presenting me?

In this chapter we consider vocation, that is, the sense of one's calling from God into the world of work, whether paid or unpaid. We do so with the conviction that the unique set of gifts with which God endows each of us represents the hand of providence. Scripture is clear that the array of New Testament spiritual gifts is meant for building up the body of Christ, not for individual pride or ecstasy. By implication the church teaches that God endows us each with special gifts. Using those gifts, we collaborate with others through our professions by producing knowledge, goods and services to meet human needs and fulfill dreams.

What is the nature of work? In this chapter we consider labor markets in terms of changing supplies and demands. We discuss wage rates—whether they should be determined by law or largely by market forces. We describe ways that wage rate changes help inform and orient people so they can better serve the interests and needs of the general public. Throughout, we consider these matters in the light of God's promise to meet the needs and deepest desires of the world through a vast multitude of callings.

What is in your hand?

A BIBLICAL VIEW OF WORK

Meaningful work is a gift. In the Genesis account of creation, work ranks very high, next to strolling with God in the cool of the day. God instructed Adam and Eve to "tend [the garden] and watch over it" (Gen 2:15). Just as God had created the universe, the only creatures he made in his image—men and women—were told to imitate him through their creative work. God commanded them to multiply and to bring forth fruit from their labor in the garden with its plants and animals.

Care of that lush garden, thus ordained by God, hardly sounds like work—recreation, perhaps, but not work. Between that story and today, sin and its consequences intervened. After expelling Adam and Eve from the garden, God said to them and their descendants:

> All your life you will struggle to scratch a living from [the ground]. . . .
> By the sweat of your brow
>   will you have food to eat
> until you return to the ground
>   from which you were made. (Gen 3:17, 19)

Now that sounds like work as we know it!

Nevertheless, this chapter presents a view of work that has the potential to become re-creation. After the Fall, the rest of the biblical story is an account of redemption and restoration, in which God takes the initiative. Those who receive the gift of new life are drawn back into a relationship with God and others that is creative, fruitful and delightful (though not without its hardships).

Unlike Greek and Roman elites, who held the mind's work in highest esteem, the Bible and the church proclaim that all work is worthy of honor. Through work, we take care of our families and ourselves; we collaborate with others by working together to create good things. Today, more than ever before, our work depends on a vast web of collaboration. Work supplies the physical, psychological, artistic and religious needs of communities extending to the ends of the earth. Furthermore, through work, we create abundance out of which we help meet the needs of others.

During the Middle Ages, despite the sheer drudgery of physical work, unaided by sophisticated tools and technology, the church proclaimed, "Their work is their prayer" (based on Ecclesiasticus 38:39, Latin Vulgate). Thus, no matter how humble, the work of our hands may be lifted up in continual thanksgiving to God. Redeemed by Christ, work becomes our collaboration with God's creative purposes—not unlike the work of Adam and Eve in the Garden.

During the twentieth century, several Roman Catholic documents took up the creation view of work, pointing to Jesus' work as a carpenter, through which the value and essential nature of human work are affirmed. Today, the Catholic Church now teaches the doctrine of vocation for all believers—a doctrine that Reformers Calvin and Luther drew from Scripture centuries earlier.

Prior to the Reformation the notion of a vocation or calling was restricted to members of religious orders, like priests and nuns, who were called to special ministries. But Calvin taught that everyone received a special calling to a work for which he or she received the necessary gifts. In this tradition, no morally acceptable occupation is unworthy or less godly than another. Nevertheless, full awareness of our calling requires knowledge of our interests and skills, and of the need for those skills in a variety of settings. Hardy (1990), writing in the Reformed tradition, explains that "we have a duty to use our talents and abilities for our neighbor's sake. Therefore we are obligated to find a station in life where our gifts can indeed be employed for the sake of our neighbor's good" (p. 66). The social standing of our profession is not the issue, but rather its suitability as an instrument of service.

Many sincere students, reflecting on future career possibilities, might understand Hardy's words about service for the "neighbor's good" to mean that Christian vocations must take the form of nursing, counseling, missions and the like—wherever the dimension of "service" is foremost. A spirit of service, however, is foundational for virtually all professions.

Management, for example, is a career that may not appear to be about service to needy people. But, in a recent article, Klay, Lunn and TenHaken (2004) demonstrate that the role of managers (even those far from the top of an organization) is essential in the modern world and is especially suitable for Christian service. They point out that modern economies require large organizations in order to accomplish very complex tasks, and they depend on extensive coordination across great distances and among people with different training, professional perspectives and experience. Furthermore, the virtues that make for good managers are among those that faithful Christians should always cultivate, such as "patience, care, prudence, self-restraint, disciplined tenacity, humility, and trustworthiness" (Klay et al. 2004, p. 130). According to Christian management professor Steve VanderVeen (2005), John Calvin taught that God calls Christians to specific professions as God's agents, transforming work into a place of blessing for all those involved.

Later in this chapter we will return to the theme of work as vocation. Monetary rewards enter the picture, but we must keep in mind that work is an activity continually open to the deepest Christian reflection.

First, though, let's look at the labor issue that has generated the greatest public debate over the centuries: "fair" wages. Our discussion of this issue moves through several subsequent sections, because judgment about what constitutes fair wages depends on a clear understanding of how labor markets function. For that purpose we first build a framework for looking at work in terms of productive services, whose uses are coordinated by interactions of workers and employers in labor markets.

THE PRICE OF WORK—A LIVING WAGE?

Economies function well for the good of their participants only if they have strong "institutional" foundations. By institutions, economists mean not just organizations like central banks, but the basic systems by which a society is coordinated, including markets. (For more on the subject of markets as social institutions, see North [1990].)

We have shown that the free market system is one such essential institution—both because free markets are responsive to an immense variety of human wants and needs, and because their capacity to do so is greatly enhanced by competitive pressures to produce efficiently (i.e., without unnecessary waste). Economists use the term *wants* to refer to human desires generally, rather than trying to distinguish between needs and desires for goods and services that exceed the requirements for basic subsistence.

Among the resources that are in scarce supply, and therefore require markets to promote efficient utilization, is labor. There simply are not enough dentists, software engineers, managers, plumbers, teachers and apple growers for society to waste their time and skills on doing things that could as easily be accomplished by people without their unique training, talents, practical wisdom and passions.

During the relatively simple but harsh times of our biblical, medieval and pioneer ancestors, the choice of what work to do was simple. A person followed in his father's or her mother's footsteps. Most were farmers, a few specialized in commerce, some were priests or soldiers, and a very tiny minority enjoyed prosperity as rulers (and their entourages). Throughout history the overwhelming majority of workers were poor—not because nobody cared but because people worked in isolated regions (too far from one another to be in continuous contact for purposes of exchange), and they used very simple tools, like hoes. Food production grew very slowly—sometimes too slowly to support short population growth spurts—hence, the dismal history of frequent conquest, disease and famine, until modern times. Only since the early nineteenth century have economic conditions and institutions changed enough for the masses (in advanced economies and increasingly in some Third World countries) to produce a better life for themselves. Until then, the average person lived only to the age of twenty-five and spent all his or her years working—no matter how young or old (Cameron and Neal 2002, pp. 27, 41).

Over the intervening centuries, transportation and communication improved dramatically. This led to the gradual extension of markets from local to national and then international scope. Larger markets made it possible for people to specialize in certain trades because they could depend on meeting most of their needs by buying from those who were proficient in producing other things. Furthermore, legal innovations in nineteenth-century England began to provide incentives for the development and application of new ideas to improve labor efficiency. For example, the establishment of patent rights made it possible for individuals (and companies) to dedicate the time, intelligence and money needed to invent new machines and manufacturing processes. Patents gave them temporary exclusive rights to any profits from successful innovations (usually preceded by many unsuccessful attempts and losses, before they become commercially viable). As a result, a person no longer needed to be either a monk or an independently wealthy intellectual to bring radically more productive technologies into service.

As a result of extensive labor specialization in larger and more capital-intensive markets, the vast majority of people living today in advanced economies like the United States, the European Union, Australia and Japan enjoy a material standard of living far superior to that of even kings of old. Although most of us do not have servants doing our bidding, we do have hot, running water to bathe in daily, opportunities to travel around the country and the world (without armed guards), easy access to the works of the greatest writers of all time, the expectation of seeing our grandchildren reach adulthood, and medical care unimagined by the bloodletting barbers of old.

Along with modern abundance comes the opportunity for each new generation to consider a range of careers that has expanded significantly since the time when their own parents found work. Many jobs today in marketing, publishing, banking, engineering, medicine, biological research, airline mechanics, plastics and recycling are almost unrecognizable compared to twenty (or even ten) years ago.

As every college senior knows, the opportunity to choose a career is an exciting adventure. It involves not only getting the formal training required, and the first job, but also shaping one's career path for the next forty to fifty years. Making these momentous choices is also anxiety-producing. Seniors wonder, *What if I have made the wrong choice after four expensive years in college? What if I can't find a job in my career that keeps me near family? What if concentrating on further education reduces the likelihood that I will find a husband (or wife)? What if the market for my skills shrinks drastically over the next few years (perhaps becoming "outsourced" to engineers in India), or I find myself graduating during a recession?*

The feeling of adventure is real and so are the questions. What is the nature of labor markets—the ring into which virtually everyone throws their hat at several points in their lives? As is the case with markets for other resources, such as oil and physical capital (i.e., machines, patents and production facilities), labor markets are driven by conditions of supply and demand. However, unlike machines, labor cannot be sold outright; it can only be "rented," which is what a person does who offers an hour's work for a certain wage.

Because labor cannot be separated from the person who performs it, markets for labor are rightly the concern of individuals, governments, churches and other organizations. (During times when slavery was legal, workers were indeed bought and sold as property.) Workers are not cogs in machines; they must not be treated as means to an end (however laudable the purpose). As much as possible, they must be afforded choices over their working conditions, wages, the degree of active collaboration with others in their work, skill development, time for family and so on. Workers are *actors* in their own right, not just recipients of orders.

Who or what can insure humane treatment for workers is the subject of much debate. In this book, we argue that government is only one of the forces able to protect workers. More important, for the billions of situations (many into which the public and the law do not, or cannot, see) where workers may be treated well or badly is a widespread social commitment to the extraordinary value of each human being—creator, employee, family member, decision-maker and the supreme object of God's love. Thus moral and cultural institutions in every society bear a responsibility to assist those whose work choices are limited by lack of skills, prejudice, disability and so forth. (See chap. 10 for more discussion about gaps in income opportunities for certain disadvantaged groups and potential remedies.)

Social activists and theologians are often suspicious of markets—especially labor markets—claiming that justice requires laws to regulate market conditions. Over centuries the Christian church taught the principle of a "just wage." The fear was that workers would be "exploited" by their employers, who could force them to work at dismally low wages, for long hours and in terrible working conditions. Thus the church held out to employers the moral obligation to pay a just wage.

Despite the devout and painstaking intellectual work of some of the best minds of all time, including Thomas Aquinas, no one has ever given a satisfactory answer regarding what determines a just level for wages. After all, sometimes harvests were good and food prices therefore low, so that a low wage rate could adequately provide for a worker. In other times the opposite was true. When harvests were poor and many were desperate for work, money wage rates in cities inevitably fell to the point where life was precarious, even when everyone in the family worked. This is inevitable in any economy with low productivity—today the Third World, then the entire world.

So far, we have referred to workers in large towns and cities. But throughout human history most people have been self-employed in agriculture, shifting over time from self-sufficiency to production for local and then wider markets. For farmers the issue of a just wage was irrelevant. What they needed was a good price for their produce. Was there also a "just price" to be discerned here? That too became a centuries-long concern of theologians. With a little reflection, though, it becomes clear that a just price for farmers, during a bad harvest (when market forces drive up prices), could appear very "unjust" to poor workers buying food in nearby towns.

Over time, even theologians were forced to accept a rule of thumb, agreeing that something like the "prevailing local wage" was the just wage, and the "prevailing local price" the "just" price. Under such moral rulings an unjust wage was possible only if an employer took advantage of a worker's ignorance (e.g., that only five miles away, he or she could get a better wage). Of course, as communication, transportation and education improved (and as laws began to allow for freer movement of labor beyond one's birthplace), it became less and less likely that an employer could get away with paying unjust wages.

By leaping across the intervening centuries we arrive at the present, where the idea of a just wage now goes by a different name—a "living wage." Beginning with Baltimore, in 1994, many U.S. cities and other entities enacted living wage laws, based on an estimate of the wage rate necessary for a full-time worker to support a family of four. Some of those laws cover wages paid only by companies providing services to the city (county, university, etc.), while others cover employees of all businesses with government contracts, subcontracts, tax abatements or financial assistance. A few cover businesses, like restaurants and hotels, even though they may have no special relationship with the city government.

Campaigns for living wages are local movements, designed to supplement federal and state minimum laws. The U.S. federal government enacted the first minimum wage in 1938, set at 25 cents per hour, and has continued to raise it periodically by Congressional action. When initiated, the federal minimum was intended to achieve what was then considered to be necessary for "life." By 2006 the minimum wage was $5.15. Living wage rates are higher, ranging from $8.19 to $12 per hour.

To the average person, opposition to minimum wage rate increases, or to living wage laws, seems mean-spirited. As a result, it is exceedingly rare to hear a politician express reservations about such laws. Economists, on the other hand, are almost uniformly opposed to any law that would artificially determine wage rates apart from market forces.

WORK ORGANIZED IN LABOR MARKETS

Before we investigate wage controls further, it is helpful to look behind the scenes to see how wage rates—the price of labor—are determined in market systems. Imagine that you have just finished your freshman year of college and are looking for a summer job. Among the jobs you consider is one at a lawn-care company. The company was just started by a senior fraternity brother, Zach, who hopes to use profits from the new business to pay for graduate school.

Because Zach is a friend of yours, he tells you how he decided what rate to pay his workers. He knows a few local kids who would work for very little— maybe two dollars an hour. One just wants out of the house, where he would otherwise have to baby-sit his five younger siblings. Another wants to be able to pay for a trip with his youth group to Adventure Land this summer. There is also a guy in the residence hall whose family is putting him through school and does not really have a financial need to earn money this summer. He would be willing to work with Zach for "fun money" and rent (he is sharing a house with four others)—maybe $4 per hour. He would much prefer to work with Zach and other friends than to take any job now available on campus. Finally, a good friend of Zach's is willing to work for only $5 per hour. What this friend wants from the job is to learn business and personnel skills from Zach in order to buy the business when Zach leaves for graduate school in two years.

Zach estimates that, given local market conditions, he could keep four teams of four workers each busy for the summer. He needs to pay a wage that is (1) high enough to attract high-quality workers, yet (2) low enough so that his business can attract customers, now and into the future. Zach can hire as many as five workers for practically nothing, but will have to attract the other eleven with a wage rate that compensates them for turning down other opportunities, like painting, working in the local movie theater or washing dishes for the college food service. So he puts up posters offering to pay $7 per hour and a bonus of $1 per hour, payable at the end of August, for everyone who sticks with him for all three summer months.

Although this is a simple example, it illustrates several points about labor markets. First, several people who are willing and able to work for much less than $7 per hour (assuming they are reliable and have the right skills) actually earn much more than their "reservation wage," the lowest wage each would have been willing to accept for the job. That reservation wage varies from person to person, depending on individual alternatives. So when Zach eventually hires the sixteen workers, virtually all of them will receive more than the minimum they would have accepted. Only Carol—whose next best alternative is $7 per hour, but working in an ice-cream parlor for a humorless boss—does not receive a premium above her reservation wage.

What we just considered was the workers' side of the market and workers' willingness to supply labor over a range of wage rates. Zach and all other potential local employers represent the demand side of the labor market. Given the revenues businesses receive by selling goods and services, they estimate the value of each hour of labor to them. If each company were on its own, we could represent its decision-making as similar to Zach's. But since the local going wage for inexperienced, physical labor is about $7 dollars per hour, their decision revolves around how many workers to hire (not what to pay). Some will pay to have groceries carried to the car at that rate; most will not, because even loyal customers will not pay a significant price premium for such amenities. Local manufacturers will not hire as many as they did last year if the local economy has not yet recovered from the latest recession and the furniture market, for example, is still weak. Furthermore, year-round factory workers who are still employed after the latest cutbacks will be shifted from the production of lower to higher-end products. They will not be given a raise, despite the fact that their output per hour is worth more to their employers now than it was last year (given high prices companies can still charge at the luxury end of the furniture market).

From this simple introduction to labor markets, we can extract the following principles:

1. Individual workers are generally paid more than the minimum they would be willing to accept (their reservation wage).

2. Workers' choices and eventual jobs are affected by the number and quality of options available to them, which in turn are determined by

   - The *size of the market*. For example, the landscaping market is largely local, and the size of the town therefore matters. On the other hand, for some high-tech skills, like aeronautical engineering, the labor market is global.

   - The *tastes of workers*. Family circumstances and personal tastes vary regarding teamwork versus independence, regular or flexible hours, fixed wage-rates or commissions, outside or indoor work, length of commute and so forth.

- *Consumer demand for the services and goods produced by workers with particular skills* relative to the availability of those workers. In neighborhoods where landscaping is highly valued but there are few people willing to do that work, wage rates and other job-quality dimensions rise to meet market conditions. School teachers in a university town may be paid what a good gardener earns in Palo Alto, California.

- The *difficulty and expense of acquiring the skills* needed for a given labor market. For this reason (among others), doctors earn more than child care workers—not because children are less important than sick people.

- The *rarity of certain, highly valued, intrinsic traits*. For example, labor markets pay a premium (other things being equal) for beauty, male height and raw athletic or artistic talent (for which no amount of training or makeover can compensate).

- The *riskiness of the work*. A study about injury risks and wage rates found that, on average, women who face nonfatal job risks receive a wage premium of 1.9 to 2.6 percent of the hourly wage (amounting to $408 to $563 annually). For men, the premium was found to be about 5 percent of their wage. (We might be inclined to say that the difference represents discrimination against women. However, the job-injury incidence rate for women was found to be only 71 percent that of men.)

- *Changes over time* in the market. These include the business cycle (locally, nationally and internationally), changing production technologies, improvements in transportation and communication, rising or falling populations, and changes in other factors that influence either output demand or worker productivity (e.g., rising education levels).

With this lexicon of choices and forces active in labor markets, we return to the related matter of just minimum or living wages. Suppose the local market for landscape workers is one in which there is little demand for such services, yet there is an abundance of people willing and able to do the work, even at $5 an hour. Is this low rate an unjust wage? From our previous example, it appears that Zach could hire several workers for that wage—some of whom would be willing to work for even less (e.g., the kid who wants to get away from corralling his siblings all summer).

If Zach is willing to start smaller, with only one team, should his pastor or his activist sister object to his paying only $5 an hour? Should the federal government insist that he pay either $5.15 or fold up his best plan to pay for graduate school? Should local citizens vote for a living-wage law—requiring $10 an hour—even though it would mean at least sixteen fewer summer jobs being created? Should the young teenager who wants to get out of the house, the student who likes hanging out with friends in town for the summer, the teen who wants to go to Adventure Land with his youth group and everyone else he prevented from getting lawn-care jobs, simply because $5 an hour cannot feed a family of four? If, by law, these jobs are eliminated, has injustice simply taken a different form—namely, unemployment?

These are precisely the arguments that economists have presented for decades against laws that would set a floor level for wage rates—be they minimum wages or living wages. Another sort of minimum wage emerges when government agencies are themselves legally required to pay "prevailing wages"—set at the local union rate—even though they may hire nonunion contractors. Unfortunately, the effect of such laws is either to destroy existing jobs or to reduce the rate of job expansion that would otherwise occur.

The visible "winners" are those whose wage rates are nudged up by wage laws. Less visible are the losers. They include workers who are let go, communities who lose businesses to other areas without such laws and taxpayers (who must now pay more for services contracted by the city or other government body). The majority of losers, though, are invisible to the public, because they are people who will not be able to get a job or the job of their choice. Furthermore, they are predominantly people who are so disadvantaged—by their youth, lack of education and experience, family responsibilities, and so forth—that they are dying for just a chance to work at $5 an hour.

The terrible irony of all minimum-wage laws is that they hurt the very people who are most disadvantaged, for example, teens and minority workers (Klay and Lunn 2003a). Those are the people least able to defend themselves against well-meaning legislators who support such laws at their expense. Not all legislators and public groups are ignorant of the perverse outcomes. For example, unions are very strong supporters of minimum-wage rate increases, even though their members' wages are far above that level. But unionized workers benefit indirectly from higher minimum-wage rates because the higher rate makes it more expensive for employers to replace one union worker with two minimum wage employees. As we wrote these lines, the Michigan legislature was passing a law that would raise the state's minimum wage. Since then, student employment has fallen at our college because the increased rate per hour, without any change in departmental budgets, has necessitated a cutback in student hours hired. Few students expected that a raise in the state's new minimum wage would adversely affect them.

Some people reason that if the total amount of additional income earned by those whose wage rates rise (in response to a wage law) is greater than the income lost by those who lose their jobs, then the law is justified. This kind of reasoning has always been suspect among economists. Public policymakers are not in clear moral territory when they support laws that would (1) equate the 50 cents extra per hour, earned by every ten workers whose wages rise from $5.15 to $6.65 (an annual amount of about $1,000 each), with the loss of a $10,300-per-year job (a similar total dollar amount), by one marginal worker who no longer has a job; and (2) substitute their own notion of what is fair for choices made by workers themselves, whose multiple reasons are unknowable by unions, city leaders and social activists.

USEFUL ROLES FOR GOVERNMENT IN LABOR MARKETS

Having made a strong argument against governments setting minimum-wage rates, we should consider other labor market policies that might appear necessary. For example, laws require that a worker be paid if he or she has been hired and has worked for an employer. There is a process for redress—either through the state labor department or through the courts. This "enforcement of contract" role for governments in labor markets is essential where the law is the final protector of property and persons.

There are other sorts of laws in labor markets that require certain safety standards be in place, where the risk to life and limb is significant. Clearly, if workers cannot be expected to be aware of risk to themselves in taking a certain job—in mining, for example—there may be a case for governments setting some standards. The difficult balance is for governments to require safety precautions that are not so costly as to wipe out whole industries and to do so in a way that allows for workers to still choose some blend of risk and reward that fits their own circumstances.

There is no way to make every job perfectly safe. Should government, however, impose rules that would make trucking as safe as being a receptionist in an office? Doing so might mean that truckers should be prohibited from working more than eight-hour shifts, travel at no more than fifty-five miles per hour and have top-of-the-line laser systems for viewing road conditions over the next ten miles ahead. Instinctively, we know that this is going overboard. It would make the cost of transportation soar, lower GDP and reduce living standards.

If government regulations insured that there were no safety (and other job-quality differences) between office work and trucking, the current wage premium in favor of truckers would be eliminated. As it is, this wage premium is the market's way of drawing people freely into an occupation that involves more risk than many others.

We will not here try to carefully assess the "correct" level of government involvement in worker safety. The public and economists disagree among themselves about this. In chapter three we considered cost-benefit analysis for government projects, which could inform worker safety policy.

EARNING A LIVING OVER A LIFETIME

One of the themes of this book is the Christian calling to exercise *reasoned hope*. This applies to all of life, especially to the matter of making choices about a possible career. Each choice marks out a path that will likely not bring one back to the same point. Without perfect insight about current alternatives, and lacking perfect vision regarding future circumstances, the choices we make are always risky. Christians must do their best to assemble good information about career possibilities in light of their own interests and abilities, while resting in the firm hope that God will provide opportunities to develop and use them for God's glory and their delight.

Consider Emily, who is now in her junior year of high school and is considering the next step beyond graduation. She has done very well in school and loves to learn but is completely open about a future career. Based on this information alone, we expect that Emily can, and should, go to college, although some exceptional circumstances might dictate otherwise. For example, Emily may live in a remote village in Nepal and lack the family resources or other connections needed to take that step. If she lives in the United States but comes from a poor family, most of us would be inclined to advise her to try for scholarships or to work and save money for college in a year or two.

Sometimes economists sound like they pay attention only to what the money says, regarding a given choice. Advising Emily that she should look for the career that "promises" the most money is only a caricature of economic reasoning, however. Since the founding of modern economics, upon Adam

Smith's ([1776] 1981) masterpiece *The Wealth of Nations*, all economists avoid taking a money-grubbing view of human decisions about their work. Economists often say that higher wage rates in certain professions (or jobs) attract workers away from other professions. What they mean is that, if the only difference between profession A and B in the minds of many people is the wage rate, workers can be expected (on average) to choose the better-paying profession (or job). But all else is not equal across persons, generations, places, families and values.

Suppose you see college teaching as your likely vocation, despite the fact that the overwhelming majority of your future students (and their parents) will have lifetime earnings in excess of your own. Would economists say that you are "crazy"? Definitely not! Your decision is completely rational and well understood by economists. Any one of the following may be the basis for your decision: you love to see the light go on in the eyes of students; you enjoy being in a place where they pay you to keep learning; you are fascinated by physics and want to help expand the frontiers of knowledge; you want a job that has flexible hours suitable to raising a future family.

If many people, like you, have the potential to be either professors or engineers but prefer flexible scheduling to fixed hours, then the earnings of engineers will exceed those of professors. Economists call this wage premium a "compensating differential." It is required in order to attract some people away from academic life into less preferred jobs in industry.

In a deeper sense, all the reasons for choosing a college-teaching career, taken together, represent important ways that Christians sense God's leading in one career direction or another. We can trust that God has placed particular gifts, interests and opportunities at our disposal, and that these are meant to delight and guide us into certain vocations. We bathe the matter of work and career in prayer, and we consult with those we trust (family, teachers and mature Christian friends) about our strengths and weaknesses. Then we trust the freedom God gives us to choose one direction or another.

We highly recommend a book that provides foundational and practical suggestions about discovering one's vocation, *The Fabric of This World: Inquiries into Calling, Career Choice, and the Design of Human Work*. Its author, Lee Hardy (1990), writes:

> Some experimentation, then, may be required in the process of career choice. If several occupational options lie before me, and they all look equally valid and interesting, rather than allowing myself to be *paralyzed by the lack of a deciding fac-*

tor, it would be better simply to choose one and pursue it. In the course of pursuing that occupation I will inevitably learn something I couldn't have known prior to its pursuit. I may become convinced that I had in fact made the right choice. On the other hand, I might find out in no uncertain terms that I made a "wrong" choice. Not to worry. I can still benefit from that. I have learned something about myself. Besides, career decisions are rarely irrevocable. Most people nowadays go through four or five career changes in the course of a lifetime. (p. 87, emphasis added)

After a tentative career choice, other important decisions follow; for example, whether to attend graduate school, what work to seek (in industry or education), where to reside and much more. None of these should be made on the basis of salary offers alone.

Robin remembers facing similar decisions when she was finishing a Ph.D. in economics. Her professors in Princeton University expected most of their doctoral "products" to take positions at major research universities. She was not feeling called to that possibility herself. Throughout Robin's study of economics, what sparked her greatest interest was that market economies could afford poor people chances to make better lives for themselves than were possible for their parents. She specialized in international economics and labor, and finished a dissertation on seasonal farm labor (among the lowest-paid sectors in the U.S. economy). She dedicated her dissertation to César Chávez—leader of the first national farm-workers union—with whom she volunteered while in graduate school.

Robin was also actively involved in a fellowship of Christian graduate students from all over the world who sought to deepen their Christian faith and find opportunities for service, while preparing for careers in astrophysics, Japanese studies, statistics, philosophy, economics and other areas. She had studied French, just for the fun of it, and had some experience living abroad. So when she saw an ad for economists willing to go to French-speaking Africa to teach and do research at a university, she was immediately intrigued.

That opportunity turned into a life-changing experience in Cameroon, West Africa, where Robin taught and conducted research, and also participated in Christian fellowship with Catholic and Protestant students, hospital patients and young men who sold vegetables in the municipal open-air market. Since then, she has taught at two Christian colleges, where the accumulating mix of her skills, interests and new opportunities still serves as confirmation that her vocation is from God. Throughout, God has used and blessed her beyond anything she might have conceived while finishing a degree at Princeton.

Each step in a career involves choices that can be both exciting and somewhat nerve-racking, even for those who entrust themselves to God. Furthermore, many people have second thoughts about their careers at various points. They must ponder the new situations (with the help of new information and the wisdom of others) and take stock of changes in their interests, skills, passions, obligations and opportunities since the previous decisions were made.

One of our colleagues wrote an essay in which she presents a reassuring analogy to those who worry about whether they are making the "right" decisions about their majors, careers and faith. She says that God is at least as good with us as Los Angeles traffic planners! LA engineers build roads and exit/entrance ramps in such a way that no matter how many wrong turns drivers make, they can reorient themselves and get to their destinations. This analogy can serve as an encouragement to those who are afraid of making a "wrong" career choice, fearing they could become trapped in some corner of the labor market from which they might never escape. Both because God keeps his promises to guide us and because labor markets continually make new opportunities available, being trapped in a career is not a great risk for most people. This is especially true for those who complete college degrees, on which graduates can always build new skills.

MORE ABOUT CAREERS AND LABOR MARKETS

While they are aware of the unique, personal considerations involved in any person's career choice, economists are interested in issues that affect workers generally. For example, they analyze the evolution of earnings over lifetimes (from entry point to retirement) in given professions, the earning ratios of one career relative to another and changes over time in both of these. All other things being equal (namely, preferred bundles of nonmonetary characteristics that figure in the career decisions of many people), we can expect that one type of work will pay better than another if it requires: more physical effort, longer and more-expensive training, a greater tolerance for risk and high income variability, or rare artistic, athletic and managerial talents. We also expect people who do not mind waiting for their rewards, and who work hard, to be more likely than others to take jobs with low entry-level wages combined with opportunities for advancement. When people skills of a certain kind are rarer than technical skills, the former will pay better and vice versa.

Education is what economists call an "investment in human capital." By this, they mean that a major (but not the only) consideration, when taking the next step in one's schooling or training, is how additional education might affect future lifetime earnings, compared to what one can earn in a career available without more education. Furthermore, even if a postgraduate-school career earns (above the extra costs of getting the degree, in terms of tuition and foregone income) more over a lifetime than does a postbachelor's-degree career, the economic basis for more education is still not obvious.

Suppose you consider starting a career in management right after graduating with a bachelor's degree. You plan to save what you would have spent on graduate school. You expect to accrue interest on those savings over your working years in excess of $100,000. If the accrued interest on your savings is expected to be greater than the extra income to be earned in the alternative career (when both are compared at today's date), the choice not to attend graduate school makes economic sense. This is so unless the other career not only pays more but also provides more personal benefits than does the postgraduate career. Nevertheless, estimated personal benefits must be judged in the context of individual values, and there is no way to predict them perfectly. Thus some people who attend graduate school appear—from the outside—to have made poor choices. But economists are not professionally equipped to offer such a judgment, and neither are most others.

Those who do attend graduate school (or who add to their skills through significant on-the-job training and experience, such as in business) are generally able to earn more than those who stop their education much earlier. Their higher earnings represent a return on their investment in more training and education. The ratio of earnings of American college graduates to others has been rising, from 38 percent in 1979 to 71 percent in 1999 (*Economist* 2000). (We evaluate concerns about such gaps and related public policy in chap. 10.)

What can seem to the public like outrageously high earnings in some professions—like medicine, stockbrokerage or lucrative software development—can be explained by economic analysis. Relatively high earnings in these professions reflect both the high prices that consumers are willing to pay (i.e., the demand side) for the services these professionals provide, and the relatively small supplies of the needed skills—either because they are inherently scarce or because the required education is long and expensive.

In the next section, we see not only that there is little reason for any resentment by those who have made lower-income career choices but also that virtually everyone is better off when some people earn more than the majority of workers. Skilled people whose productivity is exceptionally high are drawn into fields that meet human needs and wants, in part because they can earn much more than workers with average abilities.

WAGE RATES AS SIGNALS

Implicit in our earlier discussion of the wage rates needed to attract unskilled workers to jobs in local landscaping, manufacturing and ice-cream parlors is the idea that, other things being equal, workers are attracted by higher wage rates. Furthermore, the price of labor is like the price of any good or resource, the higher it is, the lower the quantity demanded by employers (at any one point in time) and vice versa.

Labor is the costliest input in the production of most goods and services. When the salaries paid to those with strong computer skills rise, as happened over the last two decades, more people pursue college majors preparing them for careers in which computers are used extensively. Higher salaries also move people who already have computer skills from jobs where those skills are less useful (e.g., parts of manufacturing) into jobs where they can now earn a premium.

The training and movement of labor, in response to market signals (falling or stagnating wages versus growing wages), benefit the general public as consumers. It means that supplies of computers, software, entertainment, banking services, travel and so forth expand quickly in response to increased demand. It also means that the prices of these services fall over time, as producers find ways to raise efficiency by using more capital and newer technology.

Of course, the same trends that favor those with computer skills temporarily harm those without them. There are fewer jobs for typists and bank clerks, and fewer jobs in manufacturing, where some jobs are taken over by robots programmed by engineers (for whom demand rises). This too benefits the general public, and more so over time. Workers released from low-earning (low-productivity) jobs have an incentive to move into sectors where wage rates rise—just the signal needed to inform them of increased demand there. When this happens, most young workers are able to get retrained in expanding fields, like heating and air-conditioning or swimming pool installation. For those whose working lives stretch far ahead, it would be worthwhile to continue formal education in preparation for careers that are now expanding, like health care. Middle-age workers may be able to successfully relocate to regions where their skills are still in relatively high demand. Older workers are hurt the most by labor market changes that leave them without the jobs they had for most of their lives. Some of them retire rather than retrain or relocate. For the poorest and least healthy among them, the church is called to reach out with practical compassion and understanding.

Job losses are not totally unpredictable. For example, the U.S. steel industry was in decline for more than a decade. In the 1990s those who voluntarily left the steel industry to seek better, long-term options were not around when large steel plants finally turned out the lights. Given the much more rapid rate of change in today's labor (and other) markets, people must become more farsighted and nimble throughout their working lives than they were in the past.

To recap, our message here is that wage rate changes act as very powerful signals that labor is "needed" more in some sectors and less in others, and that demand for some skills has risen while demand for others has fallen. Without such signals it would be extremely difficult, costly and time-consuming for anyone (including government) to acquire enough information to guide workers from one industry or region to another, or students from one career into another. As a result, our standard of living would look more like that of Russians at the end of the Soviet era, because their system suppressed the power of prices and wage rates to convey accurate information about changing needs for goods and resources.

Even though high and rising earnings never constitute a complete map for anyone who is exploring God's calling into a career, they do provide necessary and very important information about the social value and availability of various job horizons. Suppose, for example, that you are independently wealthy and never need to earn a dime from the career you enter. All you want is to be at the place where, by the grace of God, you can do the most to love and serve others in Christ's name. Is salary then irrelevant to you? Perhaps. But salary levels and trends may provide very useful information about needs in certain professions and jobs that would be hard for you to get otherwise.

Suppose, for example, that your intellectual abilities and interests make you indifferent about becoming a librarian or a chemist. As you consider God's will for your life, it may be highly relevant for you to know that, in the years from 1990-2001, the salaries of new librarians averaged only two thirds those of chemists with a bachelor of arts (Heylin 2000, p.49; and Terrell and Gregory 2003). What this tells you is that more people are willing and able to go into jobs as librarians than jobs as chemists. As a result, society today is not lacking (generally, at least) in people to fill librarianships, but it is harder to fill openings in chemistry. Consequently, if your own values include an appreciation for the needs that are met through chemical research, it makes practical and spiritual sense for you—and for society—to seriously consider careers in that field.

Considerations of society's "need" for certain skills do not trump all other criteria to be evaluated in the discovery of one's vocation. Perhaps you know that a ministry in a remote part of Alaska (or a city slum) is in need of a librarian. They are not likely to be able to pay anyone the going rate for professional librarians. In such a case it is quite possible for you to sense God calling you to be a librarian, not a chemist. After all, God cares for those who are disadvantaged, and access to a professionally organized library may be the ticket by which youth there become equipped to support themselves and serve others in God's name.

On the other hand, another dedicated Christian student could, with a clear conscience, pursue a career in chemistry. First of all, she may not know about the mission option. Second, if not independently wealthy, she needs to earn an income. Based on self-knowledge, the student may expect later to be called into married life with children. In such a case the premium paid to chemists would make certain things possible for her or her family: to live near ailing parents, to educate her future children in Christian schools or to personally fund research into a cure for a particularly nasty medical condition in the tropics, where she grew up.

For two reasons our budding chemist follows certain market signals during her career, while also turning a deaf ear to other signals. She *could* earn more by plowing future savings (out of an expected high salary) into the stock of a company developing longer-lasting botox treatments. Instead, she wants to study a serious medical condition that does not affect many people in advanced countries, because she cannot expect funding for her project to come from the Western pharmaceutical industry. By undertaking a risky project for which demand in high-income countries will never be large, our chemist chooses to overrule certain market signals. On the other hand, she exercises sensitivity to market realities (without abandoning Christian values) when, in future research efforts, she hires experienced scientists, instead of training neighborhood dropouts to do the lab work. Market signals matter. But they do not answer all questions about one's calling.

CHANGE: THE NATURE OF LABOR MARKETS

Economists are not oracles who can predict with precision the future directions of labor markets and careers. Looking backward, we can see that while manufacturing jobs came to replace agricultural work during the twentieth century, in today's advanced economies, relatively high-paying service jobs are now taking the place of those in manufacturing. (The agriculture-to-industry process is now occurring in many Third World countries.) Furthermore, precisely because twenty-first century workers in the United States are aided by billions of dollars of physical capital (robots, computers, etc.), U.S. workers are more productive and therefore earn higher annual incomes than did their parents. As the average education level rises, here and elsewhere, those with less education will experience slower increases (or even decreases) in their incomes than those with more education (especially in high-demand sectors, like engineering).

During 2003-2004, when the U.S. economy was only slowly recovering from a recession, many people complained about the "outsourcing" of American jobs. They pointed to some types of software jobs, for example, that were shifting from the United States to India. They blamed outsourcing not only for high levels of unemployment but also for a widening gap between the incomes of low-skilled and high-skilled workers, which had developed over the previous couple of decades. Economic studies, however, show that the greatest factor causing these widening gaps (see chap. 10) is the adoption of new technology.

During the nineteenth century, intellectuals and ordinary citizens feared that machines would replace humans in the workplace—witness the Luddites in England, who organized riots to smash machinery. Today, few politicians advocate holding back technology to save jobs, although many ride political waves of resentment against outsourcing. They do so despite the fact that new technology accomplishes the same thing as foreign sourcing of inputs; namely, it provides for cheaper means to produce the goods and services that make up our high standard of living.

Whatever the cause—displacement of jobs by technology or by foreign workers—history shows that fears about falling demand for workers are highly exaggerated. Computers replaced large numbers of telephone workers, secretaries, student assistants, travel agents and technicians, but other jobs have grown by leaps and bounds in industries that simply did not exist a few years ago: home saunas, MP3 players, marketing U.S. goods in China, satellites launched by private companies, computational biology and so on. The same will be true of jobs "lost" to India; they will be more than offset by different jobs in economic sectors where the expertise and productivity of U.S. workers (per dollar of wages paid) outstrip those of foreign workers.

Constant change in markets—especially in labor markets—is both a tribute to human ingenuity and a challenge to the human spirit. On one hand, we would still be living like medieval serfs if markets had not grown, education expanded, new technology developed and economies become energized by strong incentives to discover and produce. On the other hand, it is natural for steelworkers in Pennsylvania (as well as farmers in Iowa and sociology professors) to resent the lack of good prospects for their sons and daughters to get high-paying jobs in identical industries.

In advanced economies, like those of the United States, the European Union and Japan, job-change rates have been increasing, at least since the mid-1970s. In the United States, for example, the median years of job tenure for men between the ages of fifty-five and sixty-four fell from about fifteen years (in 1983) to about eleven years (in 1998). For younger men, aged thirty-five to forty-four, average job tenure fell from about seven to a little over five years. Increased turnover results from more work being contracted out, greater use of temporary workers and more competition from small service firms (with fewer layers of management, compared to large manufacturing companies). These changes provide both new opportunities and new challenges. In 1999, during the latter part of the long business boom, new jobs in the United States were being created at the rate of more than 100,000 per month, but first-time unemployment claims were still high—especially for poor, low-skilled workers (*Economist* 2000).

There are some modern writers (like poet Wendell Berry), social activists and theologians who suggest that the best Christian response to the uncomfortable speed and mobility of life today is to shun painful change in favor of returning to "simpler" lives in the village, where everyone knew each other and nobody was without work. (Even the village simpleton provided comic relief on dreary days.) We have already explained why this would mean a radical reduction in living standards everywhere. Furthermore, it is impossible to extract oneself from the intricate web of specialization, interdependence and change that characterize the modern world. Who would buy Berry's books if communication were by talking drums or Pony Express? Who would have time to write poetry if others did not specialize in producing food for sale? Who would even know about the "world out there," to critique it (like those theologians who are skeptical about markets) if the only transportation were by foot?

Christians believe that God's gifts of mind, talents, interests, communities (and even their limitations—consider Paul's "thorn in the flesh") are meant for our good, the benefit of others and God's glory. We believe that God has been at work throughout history, that he inspired those who consciously shaped the greatest parts of human culture and guides the processes (mostly unconscious and invisible) by which economic interconnections grow through expanding markets.

We know a God who cares for the lilies of the field, but much more for each of us. It should not, therefore, be a matter of deep shame, resentment or suspicion that we find ourselves today in a world of abundance and opportunity unimaginable two generations ago. (See chap. 8 for discussion of the potential for Third World peoples to experience similar improvements within the next half century.) This is as true in labor markets as in markets for goods and services. Thanksgiving should continually rise from the lips of those who recognize God and his creative genius, as he calls and equips people for their vocations.

What is in your hand?

FOR FURTHER READING

Kennedy, Robert G. 2006. *The good that business does.* Grand Rapids: Acton Institute. The author discusses the role of business in society and especially its contribution to the common good through markets.

Novak, Michael. 1996. *Business as a calling: Work and the examined life.* New York: Free Press. The author shows how much business depends on the practice of virtues such as courage, honesty and cooperation. Furthermore, entrepreneurs have a high calling. Their intimate knowledge of workers, market needs and productive resources makes good jobs and rising standards of living possible. In addition, their gifts are important sources of support for the work of nonprofit organizations on behalf of public welfare.

10

RICH MAN, POOR MAN, BEGGAR MAN, THIEF

Attending to the Poor or Worrying About Income Gaps?

In chapter nine, "Work and Vocation," we discussed the fundamental reasons why markets reward some people with higher incomes than others. Good choices count, whether they are to get more education or to or put off consumption today in order to save for tomorrow. Other reasons include the luck of the draw: a rare beauty or talent; a fortunate time, location and family of birth; good health and high energy levels; few family responsibilities; a better network of connections. In this chapter we consider income and wealth gaps across individuals and among certain social/ethnic and professional groups. At what point are these gaps a moral concern? What are the measures available through government, markets and private/voluntary action to mitigate suffering and to increase opportunities for those at the short end of market rewards?

RICH MAN, POOR MAN: WHEN IS POVERTY SCANDALOUS?

Anyone who reads the Bible knows that the plight of poor people is a special concern of God. God commands his people to make caring for the poor a top priority. The theme is introduced in a powerful and dramatic way with the liberation of Israel from Egypt. In giving the law, God repeatedly calls the Israelites to demonstrate true gratitude by "[sharing] freely with the poor" (Deut 15:11) in their midst—especially widows, orphans and strangers who were without other support.

Specifically, the law called Israel to institute certain practices to meet the immediate and longer-term needs of the poor. They were to set aside certain parts of their fields for harvesting by hungry people, tithe a portion of their grain for distribution to the poor, give jobs to the needy and cancel debts that would otherwise result in the enslavement of debtors. Furthermore, a Jubilee was ordered for every fiftieth year, during which the lands (over which the "owners" were called to be God's stewards) would revert to the original families. This was intended to break the cycle of poverty, by restoring land to poor families who had lost their lands due to bad circumstances or bad choices. With access to land they would again be able to take care of their basic needs, without resorting to begging, borrowing or indenture.

The Old Testament prophets railed against wealthy Israelites who sat in the lap of luxury, ignoring the crying needs of the poor at their doorsteps and selling the "poor people for a pair of sandals" (Amos 2:6). Judging in part by the prophetic witness, many scholars doubt that the Jubilee was ever practiced in Israel. We do know that many other measures were carried out, such as gleaning fallen grain, which the young widow Ruth (great grandmother of King David and ancestor of Jesus) did in the fields of Boaz.

Jesus brought the message forward in his teaching. The parable of Lazarus is among the strongest condemnations possible of those who ignore the needs of poor people at their literal doorsteps. Furthermore, Jesus identifies service to those who are hungry with serving him. Mother Teresa correctly described care for the needy as serving "Jesus in His distressing disguise" (Eagan 1986, p. 57). The apostle Paul also urged the urban churches he founded to collect funds for the purpose of relieving poor believers in Jerusalem (Acts 24:17).

There is no way for Christians to get around the biblical principle that care for the poor is an obligation, not an option. Economists—whether Christian or not—have made the study of poverty a special concern throughout the history of their discipline. In fact, the best-known economics textbook, prior to the 1950s, made poverty the center of its study. Its author, Alfred Marshall (1925), wrote:

> The conditions which surround extreme poverty, especially in densely crowded places, tend to deaden the higher faculties. Those who have been called the Residuum of our large towns have little opportunity for friendship; they know nothing of the decencies and the quiet and very little even of the unity of family life; and religion often fails to reach them. No doubt their physical, mental and moral ill-health is partly due to other causes than poverty; but this is the chief cause.
>
> Although then some of the evils which commonly go with poverty are not its necessary consequences; yet, broadly speaking, "the destruction of the poor is their poverty," and the study of the causes of poverty is the study of the causes of the degradation of a large part of mankind. (pp. 2-3)

Marshall was relatively optimistic, believing that a reduction of extreme poverty was likely, based on the "steady progress of the working classes during the nineteenth century" (p. 3). He cited certain evidence:

> The steam-engine has relieved them [the lower classes] of much exhausting and degrading toil; wages have risen; education has been improved and become more general; the railway and the printing-press have enabled members of the same trade in different parts of the country to communicate easily with one another, and to undertake and carry out broad and far-seeing lines of policy; while the growing demand for intelligent work has caused the artisan classes to increase so rapidly that they now outnumber those whose labour is entirely unskilled. (p. 3)

Given the progress that Marshall documented in England at the end of the nineteenth century and much faster increases in average living standards during the twentieth century for advanced economies, why are the "poor still with us," as Jesus said (Mt 26:11; Mk 14:7)? Answering this question is not possible without an understanding about what qualifies as poverty. There is an important distinction to be made between two common but very different measures of poverty. One measure is an estimate of the market value of a minimum "basket" of goods judged necessary for life in a particular economy. Alternatively (usually in addition to the first method), income data are collected across a population, and those who are in the bottom fifth or tenth of the income spectrum are considered "poor."

The U.S. government employs both approaches. When the federal government first established a "poverty line" for purposes of determining access to public assistance, they used the basket approach. After collecting data on a minimum budget for food (e.g., for a family of four), they multiplied this number by three, because at the time families spent about one third of their incomes on food. Since then, data have been reported about progress against poverty in terms of the percentage of U.S. families with annual incomes below the official poverty line. That line differs by family size and is periodically adjusted upward to take into account cost-of-living increases.

Governments in many other countries make similar calculations. Their definitions of poverty—for the purposes of establishing a "poverty line"—differ, however, because the public's sense of what constitutes poverty depends on the average standard of living in each country. Thus in the year 2000, in Egypt 17 percent, India 29 percent and Thailand 13 percent of their populations were living below national poverty lines. Because the poverty line differs across countries, data are now being collected to determine what shares of the population in poor countries have incomes below $2 per day—a sort of world poverty line. This allows for somewhat better comparisons across countries. In the year 2000, figures for the countries just mentioned were: Egypt 23 percent, India 35 percent and Thailand 33 percent. Thus, whereas Egypt appears to be poorer than Thailand, when judged by national poverty lines (17 and 13 percent, respectively), it is clear that by the international $2 standard, Egypt's poverty is greater than that of Thailand (44 percent versus 33 percent were living on less than $2 per day). By the $2 standard, poverty in India affects even more (81 percent) than when calculated using the national benchmark (World Bank 2006, pp. 278-79).

In table 10.1 we present data on average poverty levels over six years, during the 1990s, in the United States, Canada and four European countries.[1] The following observations can be made:

- Poverty rates (in terms of the percentage of individuals whose disposable household incomes were below 50 percent of the median—another proxy for poverty line), prior to taxes and transfer payments, range from 20 to 37 percent (with the United States at the low end). Poverty rates after taxes and transfers range from 6 to 20 percent, with the U.S. rate being second highest (next to the United Kingdom). This indicates that the U.S. tax and transfer system accomplishes less reduction in poverty rates than do the systems of the other five countries. Thus, the U.S. post-taxes/transfers poverty rate falls by only one-fourth, compared to a fall of one-half to three-fourths in the other countries.

- Long-term (six year) poverty rates (after taxes and transfers) are much lower than annual rates—ranging from 0.8 percent to 6.1 percent, with the United States ranked second highest next to the U.K. For the majority of people who are ever poor, the experience is temporary (2-3 years).

- However, the percentage of populations that experience poverty (before taxes/transfers) at *some* point over the six-year period is much higher—ranging from 32 percent to 54 percent (with the U.S. at the low end).

The study from which the data of table 10.1 were taken offers a unique perspective on the poverty experience in these countries, with respect to family characteristics and events that accompany transition into and out of poverty. Although the poverty level data differ substantially among the six countries

---

[1]The data here and following are from Oxley, Dang and Antolin (2000).

Table 10.1. Poverty Rates in Six Advanced Economies over a Six-Year Period

		Poverty rates (percentage)[a]	Percentage of population[b]		
		Average over the period	Poor through-out the period	Poor at least once over the period	Average years in poverty
POST-TAX AND TRANSFERS					
Canada	1990-95	11.4	1.8	28.1	2.4
Germany	1991-96	10.2	1.8	19.9	2.4
Netherlands	1991-96	6.1	0.8	12.1	2.2
Sweden	1991-96	7.4	1.1	11.9	2.4
United Kingdom[c]	1991-96	20.0	6.1	38.4	3.1
United States	1988-93	14.2	4.6	26.0	3.0
PRE-TAX AND TRANSFERS					
Canada	1990-95	26.3	14.3	42.0	3.8
Germany	1991-96	26.5	14.4	38.0	3.8
Netherlands	1991-96	22.8	13.5	32.2	3.8
Sweden	1991-96	34.5	19.0	45.4	4.2
United Kingdom	1991-96	36.8	23.1	54.4	4.2
United States	1988-93	19.5	8.3	31.5	3.4

[a]Poverty rate is the number of individuals having equivalent household disposable income below 50 percent of median equivalent household disposable income, calculated using an equivalence scale of 0.5.
[b]The same includes all those individuals interviewed in each of the six years.
[c]Data for the United Kingdom are less comparable to the other countries because they do not include taxes.

SOURCE: Oxley (2000)

studied, the dynamics of poverty and the associated characteristics are quite similar across all six. The results can be summarized as follows:

- Getting or losing a job, or experiencing a divorce are the two most prominent characteristics of those moving into or out of poverty—jobs being the more important. Furthermore, poor families who get a second income-earner experience a bigger drop (20 percentage points in the United States and Canada) in the persistence of poverty than do families whose head of household alone gains employment (5-6 percent).

- Using data for the United States, the duration of poverty is greater (compared to a poor, prime age, single, male poor person with at least a high school education who was not working at the time of his being in poverty) for those who were poor once before (7 percent), or who were single parents (6 percent), disabled (5 percent), less educated (6 percent) and nonwhite (9 percent). When these conditions overlap, the results are much worse. Thus, compared to those without any of these characteristics, people in poverty who are nonwhite, with low education levels and single-female household heads with children experience 25 percent longer periods in poverty.

- Although the percentage of the population experiencing long-term poverty is quite low across countries (3 percent in the United States), these people represent the greatest fiscal burden, in terms of assistance programs. In both Canada and the United States, the cumulative number of years in poverty of those who experience long-term poverty represents about 50 percent of the total populations' time in poverty. This means that policy changes that could significantly reduce long-term poverty would make a big difference for the overall experience of poverty and the cost of "treating" it.

- Because a sizeable share of the population (pre-taxes/transfers) experiences poverty at least once over a six-year period (almost one in three in the United States), taxes and transfer payments to assist them constitute a social safety net, which receives voter support probably due to the inevitable randomness of events that cause poverty.

What we have learned so far is that there are various ways to measure poverty that tell different things. A society could concentrate primarily on measuring poverty in terms of what number (and percent) of the population have incomes below the poverty line, in terms of the dollars needed to buy a basic basket of goods. If so, remedies would be called "successful" if the numbers (and percentages) declined over time. The study of six countries just described suggests that with their largely market-driven economies effective remedies would have to attend to the needs of those who are "caught" in long-term poverty, including many in single-parent families and with little education. Education and jobs would appear to be keys for poverty reduction.

Notice, however, that the study worked with a special definition of poverty, namely, that a person is poor if his or her income, at one point in time, is less than 50 percent of the whole population's median income. This is not a basket measure. And any progress against poverty affecting those with incomes below 50 percent of median income might not simultaneously reduce the percentage of people with incomes below the national poverty line.

DOES INCOME INEQUALITY DESERVE THE SAME ATTENTION AS POVERTY?

Often, concern for poverty gets confused with the issue of income inequality. Thus critics of American social-economic policy like to say that the average U.S. worker has gotten poorer over time, while the gap in earnings between those with college education and those with high school education is increasing. The intended conclusion is that economic life in the United States has gotten less fair over time, especially during the last couple of decades. Less concern would presumably arise if critics believed that the widening gap were simply the result of average earnings of lesser-educated persons having risen at a slower pace than those of more educated workers.

A closer look at earning data would surprise the critics. Kosters (1998) shows that earnings of both high school and college graduates have continued to rise, although more slowly since 1980 (p. 27). For example, between 1980 and 1997, total compensation for the average U.S. worker rose by 15 percent. Although the wage advantage of being a college graduate, compared to finishing high school (p. 39) has doubled (from 25 percent in 1978 to more than 50 percent in 1995), interpreting this as evidence of polarization in the labor force is misleading. At least half of the increase in the college wage "premium" constitutes a recovery from its temporary squeeze during the baby boom bulge when many new workers entered the labor force. Furthermore, the increased premium for completing college has worked the magic that we expect from labor markets: increased college enrollments, since 1980, almost exactly parallel the rising material incentives for attending college. Finally, there is an extensive overlap between the earnings distribution of college versus high school graduates. Thus, one fifth of high school graduates earn more than the average college graduate. Education, though important, is not everything when it comes to explaining earning differences.

One way to put income distribution (the result of pay differences coupled with savings rate differences) in perspective is to consider a hypothetical case in which *everyone* has the same income experience at each stage of life and makes the same choices about saving. First, assume that everyone earns $10,000 per year in their twenties, $20,000 per year in their thirties and on up to $50,000 in their fifties (followed by zero income after that). Second, assume that everyone saves 10 percent of disposable income (judged to be anything over $5,000). In this hypothetical world where everyone is treated equally, national income is, nevertheless, very unequal. Thus the top 17 percent of income earners have incomes that are five times those of the bottom 17 percent (Sowell 1995, pp. 52-53). This is a cautionary tale against overly interpreting national income differences—at one point in time—in terms of "exploitation" and "unfair treatment" by the rich of the poor; some inequality is the result of income changes over the lifetimes of virtually everyone.

In a nonhypothetical example, one factor that has affected the relative wages of skilled and unskilled workers (and therefore income inequality) is a return to higher immigration rates into the United States since the mid-1960s. In addition to their greater numbers, the newer immigrants have lower educational levels, on average, than those who came prior to the 1960s. Thus immigrants in 1970 represented about 10 percent of all workers across most of the spectrum of education from zero to twenty years; by 2000, they dominated (80 percent) among workers with two to six years of education, but represented only about 10 percent of high-school educated workers, and soared to 25 percent of those with doctoral degrees (Heckman and Krueger 2005, p. 246).

Whether immigration, as a source of income inequality, should be a matter of concern depends on many things. Some applaud the relative openness of the United States to new immigrants, since the newcomers earn more than they did in the generally poor countries they come from, while they add flexibility and competitiveness to the U.S. economy. Others are concerned about the social consequences of an income gap in which foreign-born persons are very poor relative to most native-born workers—especially for newcomers who are unskilled. Regarding education spending, for example, opponents of larger-scale immigration argue for raising the earning potential of the children of native-born poor workers rather than shifting funding to programs that would help close the educational gap between immigrants and native-born school dropouts (estimated to cost a total of $170 billion over a decade—much higher than any human policy development policies now being considered in public discussions [Heckman and Krueger 2005, p. 248]).

There is no single, right, Christian answer to the question of immigration. It is an issue that deserves widespread, value-clarifying discussion in which attention is paid to both economic and social gaps as well as the costs of any possible remedies. Like all discussions about what is right and feasible, distinct roles for public and private spending must be considered. For example, we might argue that relatively open borders are just, given the relative rich U.S. economy. If so, a corollary might be that a greater share of education—at least for those in the middle class and above—should be paid for by parents (combined with lower taxes). If this were the case, a combination of public and private spending (including by immigrant families themselves) might relieve many social-economic concerns about income inequality related to immigration.

Because earnings data suggest that no gaping hole now separates the U.S. labor force into haves and the have-nots, based on education, any concern with income inequality per se must be linked to some value other than caring for poor people. Throughout this book, we have said that poverty *is* a matter that must motivate Christians to action. However, it is not clear to us that income inequality by itself ought to be a special concern of Christians. We expect to find Christians legitimately defending differing opinions about income inequality.

Some Christians insist that equality of persons before God should be reflected in relative economic equality. They usually favor government intervention, aimed at not just "ending poverty" but also reducing gaps between the rich and the middle class. They usually support relatively progressive taxes, for example, whereby people pay a higher percent of their income in taxes the greater their incomes.

On the other hand, many Christians believe that income differences reflect free choices people make about education, risk-taking, flexible schedules and leisure. They are simply the result of people exercising their gifts, opportunities and responsibilities before God in different ways and to different degrees. Recognizing that some outcomes are *not* the result of choice, most Christians favor active engagement through the private/voluntary sector to help those in dire need. They would prefer, however, that government measures (using taxation and transfers) not be used to close income gaps per se. After all, income rewards are simply one set of rewards that accompany certain choices. As we showed in chapter nine, responsible choices may be made in favor of a lower-paid career or job—for the sake of family, special service or sheer delight. It does not, therefore, make moral sense—after the choices have been made—to seek government remedies for income gaps that result largely from choices. Why should we, professors at a Christian college, for example, begrudge the parents of families who send their children here just because their incomes are generally much higher than ours?

There is still room for Christians to dialogue about the matter of income inequality. We believe, however, that disagreements should be resolved primarily in favor of private-sector action (not higher taxes and more government programs, which are funded by all citizens, no matter what their views on inequality) to reduce income inequalities that result largely from choice. Thus Christians who believe that the economic status of all Christians should mirror their equal status before God must make sacrifices to achieve a narrowing of income differences, using their own time and funds (e.g., funding scholarships at colleges for those whose parents are only high school graduates). They might also support programs to encourage saving, family responsibility and the benefits of entrepreneurship, or create local alternatives for people who would otherwise have very different consumption patterns given their different earnings.

RICH MAN, POOR MAN: ARE EXECUTIVES PAID TOO MUCH?

The business press often decries the huge salaries paid to CEOs of top U.S. companies. When total compensation packages of U.S. CEOs are compared with those of other advanced economies, the differences are, indeed, striking. According to Abowd and Kaplan (1999), in 1996, U.S. CEO compensation packages were 1.8 times those of Canadian and U.K. executives, and 3.1 times those of Japanese executives. Alternatively, comparisons may be made between the ratio of CEO compensation to that of manufacturing operatives. Data for 1996 show that the highest ratio of executive to worker compensation is in the United States—about 16 times, compared to 10 and 11 times in the United Kingdom and Canada respectively, and only 8 times in Japan.

It is tempting to cry "unfair" when examining such gaps. However, research on executive pay shows that there are reasons for boards of directors to set executive salaries so high. The compensation numbers do not "speak for themselves." Thus, for example, greater risk associated with the long-term incentive portion of an executive's salary (i.e., stocks and stock options) makes it worth only 50 cents on the dollar, compared to straight salary. There is no such long-term component in the compensation packages of executives in several advanced economies, including Japan; and where it exists, such compensation is a much smaller share of the package than in the United States—ranging between 14 percent in Switzerland to 17 percent in Canada, compared to 29 percent in the United States (1996 data).

This portion of a CEO's compensation package is designed to link the chief executive's rewards to the company's success. As a consequence it is not surprising that "firm performance, as measured by the realized shareholder return, is strongly and positively correlated with managerial remuneration"; so too is firm performance in terms of the growth of sales. Further, upper-level executives (not just CEOs) work harder when their bonuses are linked to their performance evaluations (Abowd and Kaplan 1999, p. 159). Incentives work.

This information does not assure us that all high compensation packages of U.S. CEOs are "justified" in both company success and moral terms. It does suggest that they have the intended effect of encouraging executive efforts to increase productivity in ways that ultimately prove valuable to stockholders as well as consumers. To the extent that there is competition to attract the investment funds of stockholders (needed to finance business operations), competition in markets for their products and services and competition to hire top executives, it is efficient to pay executives a lot more than what it takes to hire a line worker. In a largely market-driven economy like ours, this means that, overall, people enjoy a higher material standard of living as a result of such efficiency. Were any society to decide that these compensation gaps are unjust, they would have to consider carefully to what degree they would be willing to forgo growth in average living standards in favor of smaller compensation gaps.

Sweden is such a country, where the tax and transfer system is much more extensive than that of the United States. It is not surprising, therefore, to find that GDP per capita in Sweden (tied with Belgium for the lowest ratio of CEO compensation to factory worker, at less that 4 times) is only about 68 percent that of the United States (data taken from GNP in purchasing power dollars for 1999). Apparently, the Swedish electorate has opted for less inequality of compensation (and incomes), accepting a somewhat lower standard of living as a necessary price for their social values.

It is not possible to identify which social policies (all involving trade-offs) are uniquely Christian. Some Christians argue for the United States to follow the Swedish example. Others believe that the role of government with regard to compensation and income gaps should be relatively minimal, with an emphasis on guaranteeing disadvantaged individuals and groups improved access to opportunities to succeed. They do not support government measures that are aimed primarily at diminishing compensation and income gaps per se. Instead, they urge private voluntary institutions to actively work to minimize the distress of those who are poor, thereby, raising the floor for living standards.

RICH MAN, POOR WOMAN: WHY DO WOMEN EARN LESS THAN MEN?

Wage and job opportunity gaps between men and women were widely debated during the late twentieth century. For three decades, between 1955 and 1985, the ratio of female to male earnings by full-time U.S. workers hovered around two-thirds. Social critics who interpreted the data to reflect widespread labor market discrimination against women actively supported passage of antidiscrimination laws during the 1960s. However, economic studies have shown that gender wage gaps are not only or even primarily the result of discrimination. The picture is not only more complex but also markedly changed since the mid-1980s.

Based on average weekly earnings of full-time workers, the ratio of women's to men's wages in the United States rose rapidly during the second half of the 1980s. It continued to rise, though less rapidly, over the 1990s. By 2002 the ratio stood at 77.9 percent, having closed by only 1 percentage point since 1995. Interestingly, at the time of their entry into the labor force, each new "cohort" (meaning people in the same age group, e.g., ages 18-24, 25-43, etc.) has experienced an increase in the ratio of female to male wage rates (for full-time workers). For example, in 1978, women between the ages of 18 and 24 earned 82 percent of the wages of men in the same age group. By comparison, in 1998 the new cohort of 18-24 year olds earned 94 percent of the wages of men. This sign of progress, however, may be somewhat misleading. Evidence for the period from 1978 to 1998 shows that as they aged the youngest cohorts experienced a relative fall in their wages (by 6.9 percentage points between 1978 and 1998 for the cohort of 18 to 24 year olds) (Blau and Kahn 2000). This is likely due to the fact that young women, more often than older women and men, reduce their labor force participation for family reasons.

Economists use a variety of techniques to uncover factors giving rise to the overall gender wage gap. No study can fully explain it, but about 62 percent of the gap is attributable to human capital differences between men and women, in combination with occupational (including industry and unionization) differences. The remainder is likely due to unmeasured aspects of productivity as well as some discrimination.

Differences today between the human capital-based earnings of men and women are not due to different levels of formal education but to different amounts of on-the-job experience. At the beginning of the 1980s, according to Juhn, Murphy and Pierce (1991), the gap between men and women, in terms of average full-time experience, was 7.5 years. By the end of the decade the number had fallen to 4.6 years.

There are several interactive forces at work here. First, because women earn less than men, on average, they have had less reason to "invest" in more full-time experience and on-the-job training (during which knowledge, skills and contacts are further developed). Second, the still predominant expectation that mothers will spend more time at home with their children than fathers makes women less likely to choose occupations for which continuous, full-time experience is rewarded (like international management consulting, compared to teaching).

Finally, because employers have become accustomed to the greater mobility of married women into and out of the labor market (or between full and part-time work), some are less eager to promote women or to hire them into career paths for which uninterrupted, full-time experience is especially valuable. This is called "statistical discrimination" because it is based not on employers thinking less of women but on the average experience of employers with women compared to men. The problem for a married woman who presents herself for a full-time job is that, even if she plans not to leave full-time employment, the employer has no way of knowing that her "commitment" is firmer than that of the average, married, female employee. To the extent that the preferences and practices of couples regarding family responsibilities shift over time, statistical discrimination affecting the pay of married women versus married men will diminish.

All of these reasons for women's earnings being below those of men can and do change over time. Thus, because the full-time experience of women relative to men is increasing, gradually there will be less reason for employers to statistically discriminate. And because employers discriminate less, women will have more incentive to stay in full-time employment, which allows their human capital to grow. The combination of a modest increase in the rate of return on experience plus increased investment in experience has the effect of significantly raising the relative wage rates of women. This is precisely what accounts for most of the recent rise in full-time women's wages, from two-thirds to over three-fourths of average men's wages.

Improvements in women's wages relative to men are clearly related to changes in technology and to shifts in the labor market, generally, away from manufacturing and toward skilled services. As a result, education and training have become more important than sheer physical strength in determining pay.

Not education alone but also the choice of majors makes a huge difference in the earnings prospects of women relative to men.

We have discussed differences in human capital investments by women and men as a key factor explaining the gender wage gap. Women's progress shows up in an impressive increase in their attendance at professional schools. Thus the share of women graduating with degrees in medicine rose from 6.7 percent in 1966 to 37.7 percent in 1993; in law, from 3.8 percent to 42.5 percent; and in business, from 3.2 percent to 34.6 percent. However, there is some evidence that outright discrimination against women may not be strictly a matter of salaries. "Unexplained" differences in pay between male and female professionals of between 10 and 15 percentage points may reflect some continued discrimination (along with differences in productivity that are difficult to discern and measure).

Economists have argued for some time that in competitive markets any wage gaps that do not represent actual productivity differences tend to erode over time. This may sound naive to those who instinctively attribute virtually all gaps to discrimination—by gender, race, age and disability. However, the logic is sound. When firms compete in the same product or service market, their profits depend on getting the most out of their workers.

Any employer who might prefer to hire young, white, married men over anyone else has to "pay" for his discriminatory preferences by overlooking potential employees in other categories who are actually more productive. As a result, the discriminating firm must charge more for its output than nondiscriminating firms, losing some market share to their competitors or keep the same price in order to maintain its previous sales volume. In either case, discrimination means lower profits for the firm's owners, and this could make the company ripe for takeover by another firm willing to hire and pay workers competitively, independent of any social or gender category unrelated to productivity.

With the spread of deregulation in advanced economies over the 1980s and 1990s, we would expect differences between the pay of men and women to have diminished. This is because regulation tends to insulate firms from competition, allowing them to charge higher-than-competitive consumer prices in industries like transportation, utilities and banking. In an interesting study of the banking industry, Black (1999) confirms this expectation by showing that shrinkage of the pay gap between women and men in banking began in the mid-1970s, when deregulation shook up the industry.

The moral of this story is clearly that discrimination in hiring and wages, against any class of workers, tends to be less viable the more competitive the economy. As a result, increased competition from international trade and out-sourcing in the twenty-first century should further reduce pay gaps that are unrelated to productivity differences.

BLACK AND WHITE: WHEN GAPS REQUIRE MORE THAN LEGAL REMEDIES AGAINST DISCRIMINATION

Economists have for decades studied economic gaps based on race, using tech-niques similar to those employed to explore earnings gaps between men and women. The most common approach is to use data that measure differences in skills between the two groups (holding industry and occupation constant), related to their education and training as well as on-the-job experience. Any remaining differences between black and white workers' earnings are said to be unexplained. The unexplained portion constitutes a maximum estimate of the role of discrimination in causing earnings gaps, because some (as yet) un-measurable differences in skills, aptitudes and attitudes may account for a por-tion of the remaining difference.

In an interesting challenge to economists, well-known African American economist Glenn Loury (2002) has suggested that economists' studies of black-white gaps are incomplete. These studies may also provide unwitting ammunition to political conservatives who call for a "race blind" approach to public policy. Without condemning economists' professional focus on individ-uals (their wants and skills), Loury doubts that economic models based on in-dividuals can successfully capture the socially embedded history and nature of race views, relations and outcomes in the United States. (His focus is on black-white racial history and relations, but he calls for similar critical thinking about gaps between whites and other racial groups.)

We will follow Loury's analysis here because it differs from the approach we have just used for other gaps and sheds light on policy issues that go beyond the partial solution of increased market competition via deregulation and anti-discrimination laws. Furthermore, Loury is a Christian economist whose ideas and ideals confront Americans with their moral obligations to reduce racial gaps—obligations about which most whites are largely unaware.

There is more than overt discrimination going on when a significant por-tion of black Americans continues to experience poor economic and social outcomes. Discrimination is addressed in the law, since there are legal reme-dies for those who can demonstrate that they have been denied a job or promotion, or have been paid less than white workers with similar skills and responsibilities. Not every instance of discrimination can be eradicated in this way. However, a combination of legal remedies and increased market competition has certainly reduced the practice of outright racial discrimination in U.S. labor markets.

Nevertheless, a considerable black-white economic and social gap exists before and during the labor market experience of African Americans. It takes the form of fewer opportunities for blacks to acquire the resources needed to compete effectively in the labor market (and to function on a par with whites in other social domains). Loury does not separate out the issue of poor-quality schools in central-city neighborhoods that are predominantly poor and black. This is, however, a public policy issue of great importance to America if we wish to reduce race-based gaps that severely blemish our society. The charter school movement has many supporters in minority communities due to built-in incentives: they must attract students by offering better educations than traditional public schools.

Instead of focusing on equal access to high-quality precollege education as an issue, Loury refers more generally to many social networks that influence the lives of those African American persons who are most geographically isolated from the rest of American life and opportunity. These networks include family, church, school, public safety (or the lack of it) and community organizations (for youth, health, housing and culture).

It has become popular with some conservative commentators (including a few high-profile blacks) to hold the African American community itself responsible for its problems. The line of reasoning is: If there are still economic and social gaps between whites and blacks, even decades after the passage and implementation of civil rights laws, central-city blacks must not be applying themselves to legitimate opportunities afforded them. Instead, they are opting for crime and drugs over jobs, and unprotected sex over marriage and family. They are failing to adopt a disciplined approach to life planning (including education, saving, staying out of trouble, etc.), without which success for anyone is impossible.

In every segment of society there are needs for further self-development, including greater sense of personal responsibility and the willingness to sacrifice for the sake of achieving genuine greatness. Organizations within black communities continue to make a difference on these fronts. However, Loury challenges claims that the historic stigma attached to the descendants of former slaves has nothing to do with weaknesses within the black community. To believe such is to be blinded by the common American assumption that there are no *real* (nonself-imposed) limits to "pulling oneself up by his bootstraps."

In reality, subtle mechanisms exist by which assumptions about race differences continue to adversely affect the chances of African Americans to succeed—especially those who are socially isolated in central cities. Most often these mechanisms are not consciously known or directly observable. Here is a helpful example from Loury (pp. 29-30):

> Imagine a group of employers who harbor the a priori belief that blacks are more likely than others to be low-effort trainees. Suppose they observe the number of mistakes any employee makes on the job, but not the effort exerted by that employee during the training period. Let employers have the option of terminating a worker during the training period, and suppose they find it much more difficult to do so later on. Then employers will set a lower threshold for blacks than for other employees on the number of mistakes needed to trigger dismissal, since, given their prior beliefs, they will be quicker to infer that a black worker has not put in enough effort to learn the job. Mistakes by black workers early in their tenure will provide evidence of the employers' worst fears, more so than an equal number of mistakes by other workers. Employers will, therefore, be less willing to extend the benefit of the doubt to blacks during the training period.

But how will black workers respond to such behavior by employers? It is costly to exert effort during the training period, and the reward for doing so can only be realized if an employee escapes termination. Knowing they are more likely to be fired if they make a few mistakes, an outcome over which they cannot exert full control, more blacks than other workers may find that exerting high effort during the training period is, on net, a losing proposition for them. If so, fewer of them will elect to exert themselves. But this will only confirm the employers' initial beliefs, thereby seeming to confirm employers' racial stereotype that "blacks tend to be low-effort trainees."

Several features of this example stand out. First, whatever the basis (or lack of it) for employers to begin behaving in this way (giving white trainees more benefit of the doubt than black trainees), once the practice becomes relatively common, reality starts to conform to biased expectations; that is, potential black employees do not expend as much effort as whites, due to the lower probability of their being rewarded for it. Thus the feedback between the employers' practice and the behavior of potential black workers causes employers to feel confirmed in their practice. This is so, even if most employers do not personally believe that African Americans are less human, skilled, dedicated or worthy than workers of any other group. The problem is that no disconfirming evidence presents itself, because any employer who applies equal standards to both black and white trainees may be penalized by having to deal with more demotivated black trainees, even though it is not built into their "nature" that blacks expend less effort than whites on any given task. (The relative success of black athletes in many sports attests to the significant role of effort in domains where they are likely to be rewarded.)

Economic gaps that are not due to clearly irrational, illegal or immoral acts are difficult to eradicate. This is even more so when the processes are less visible and are the result of interactions among individuals and groups, such that no one person can be held responsible. Economist Loury argues that these gaps will persist unless and until leaders and ordinary citizens are prepared to protest sizable and persistent racial gaps. Consider a few examples of possible gaps totally unrelated to race. Suppose that data were widely published showing that teenage girls routinely are much more likely to attempt suicide than teenage boys, that blue-eyed persons are much more susceptible to cancer than those with brown eyes, that middle-aged women are much more likely to be denied loans than men in the same age group, and that third-generation farmers are much more likely than third-generation teachers to be infertile.

If any of these results became known, we could expect a public outcry: "This is not tolerable in America! We must take action to remedy unequal outcomes, because these gaps have little to do with real differences in the inherent worthiness, choices, efforts and value of individual members of the groups represented." The reaction would be widespread, not just among the "disadvantaged" groups—teenage girls, blue-eyed people, middle-aged men and third-generation farmers. There would be no obvious "us" and "them," because "they" would be our children, mothers, neighbors, fathers and friends. The sense of crisis and commitment to action would be a "we" thing, and the solutions would require multiple, mutual and sustained efforts, until the gaps had virtually disappeared. Anything less would be considered a failure of America, and evidence of moral, spiritual, intellectual and political disaster.

Unfortunately, most white Americans do not immediately interpret persistent black-white economic and social gaps in the same light. When they look at current rates of black versus white imprisonment, broken families, educational achievement and unemployment, they often think, *Well, this is about right. The averages have improved somewhat since the civil rights era. The remaining gaps probably reflect poor choices by those who should know better— dropping out of school, dealing in drugs, being promiscuous and so on. After all, some blacks have "made it" in politics, business, education and entertainment. The rest just need to try harder.*

Loury insists that, having achieved most of the purely legal changes needed to reduce outright discrimination in hiring and pay, our common task is to end racial inequality—economic and otherwise. He writes:

> More important is the fact that too many African Americans cannot gain access to anything approaching equal terms to social resources that are essential for human flourishing, but that are made available to individuals primarily through informal, culturally mediated, race-influenced social intercourse. It follows that achieving racial justice at this point in American history requires more than reforming procedures so as to ensure fair treatment of blacks in the economic and bureaucratic undertakings of private and state actors. . . .
>
> A broader and more comprehensive *moral vision* is required of us—the vision I have called race-egalitarianism. On this view, achieving the elusive goal of racial justice requires that we undertake, as a conscious end of policy, to eliminate the objective disparity in economic and social capacity between the race-segregated networks of affiliation [churches, clubs, neighborhood associations, schools, museums, etc.] that continue to characterize the social structure of American public life. (p. 169 emphasis added)

Loury challenges Americans in general and Christians in particular to catch this moral vision and hold onto it. As long as large social-economic gaps persist, white Americans must resist the convenient temptation to say that certain groups have achieved "enough" progress. Significantly lower-than-average graduation rates, higher-than-average incarceration rates, higher unemployment rates and lower health status provide evidence of persistent disadvantages—some of which are largely unrelated to the character and efforts of individual members of disadvantaged groups.

There in no single best route to reducing the disadvantages. Our individual, family, church and community involvement with these issues must be deep and generations long. Soup kitchens and help for the homeless are good, but not enough. School voucher programs are good, but not enough. Mentoring and scholarships are good, but not enough. Progress will be stunted and slow until white Americans (and certainly white Christians) are as outraged by racial disadvantages as they would be if similar disadvantages routinely affected their own families, neighborhoods and places of employment. Until white Americans work on these issues alongside friends and neighbors who are members of disadvantaged groups, the gaps will persist and cry out judgment against them for their lack of concern.

RICH FAMILIES, POOR FAMILIES: TAXES, SPENDING AND INCOME GAPS

In all advanced economics (rich nations), governments play a significant role in relieving poverty through the fiscal system. Tax rates that vary with incomes, assistance payments made to disadvantaged persons and families, and public spending on everything from education and housing to transportation and health all affect the incomes of poor people and their access to necessities. It is very difficult to capture the total effect of all government interventions on income-inequality. Progressive federal and state income taxes (where a greater percentage of income is paid in taxes by those with higher incomes) are largely offset by regressive federal payroll taxes and regressive state and local property and sales taxes (where those with lower incomes pay out a greater share in taxes than do those with higher incomes). As a result, the American tax system is quite flat, with families across the income spectrum paying similar tax rates overall.

On the other hand, government transfer payments (everything from Social Security to unemployment benefits) and public consumption—including government spending on education (50 percent of total public consumption spending at all levels), transportation (plus housing, community services and natural resources, 20 percent), and health (12 percent)—are highly progressive. As a result, when both taxes and government outlays are taken together, income groups from the lowest through the sixth decile[2] receive net benefits (equal to 70 percent and 50 percent of income in the poorest two deciles, and falling to 12 percent and 4 percent for the fifth and sixth deciles). The four highest income groups (seventh through tenth deciles) pay out more in taxes than they receive in transfers and other benefits (equal to 1 percent of income in the seventh decile, and rising to about 15 percent in the top two income groups). Wolff and Zacharias (2004) provide even more details.

It is especially interesting to note that racial income disparities are much smaller than they appear when one looks only at incomes before the effect of taxes, transfers and public consumption spending. For example, after making

---

[2]Deciles are groupings of income from the first-highest 10 percent to the tenth-lowest 10 percent for a given population.

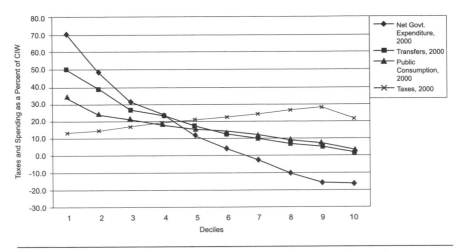

Figure 10.2. Net government expenditure as a percent of wealth-adjusted comprehensive income (CIW) by CIW Decile, 2000 (from Wolff and Zacharias [2004, September 28])

adjustments for those impacts, the ratio of nonwhite to white family incomes in 2000 was 87 percent, having risen from 85 percent in 1989. (However, the ratio is lower—dropping to 78 percent—when further adjustments are made for family size, because families are generally larger among nonwhites.)

Most if not all Americans would undoubtedly argue that the net effect of government overall does, as it should, enhance the opportunities of relatively poor families, at the expense of those who are relatively well off. On the other hand, many questions remain.

Whether governments at all levels are doing enough to reduce gaps in economic opportunity (especially important in a free market system) for American families continues to be a matter of intense discussion. That discussion comes to bear on the design of reforms in taxes, education, Social Security, Medicare and Medicaid (just as it did on welfare reform during the Clinton administration). The questions include:

- Should more help overall be provided to the long-term poor or to those who are poor only for short periods?

- In what form should help be provided, for example, through vouchers for education, housing or health (to be spent as families choose), or in the form of government-owned programs (like public schools, public housing and public health clinics)? Or should benefits instead be paid out in cash that can be spent on anything?

- What should be the work requirement, if any, to continue receiving benefits?

- Should benefits be targeted to needy groups or built into systems to which people of all incomes have access—as is now the case for Social Security, Medicare and public education.

- How quickly should direct assistance (e.g., welfare) be reduced as earned income increases? If aid drops quickly, so that for every additional dollar earned, the benefits contract by 80 cents, the program's costs are lower than if the benefits contract by 20 cents. However, incentives are heavily weighted against finding employment (and taking other healthy initiatives) when the cutback rate is over 50 cents on the dollar.

In addition to these questions regarding fairness there are those of efficiency. Is direct government provision of housing, education or health care likely to deliver more or fewer benefits per dollar of expenditure than would private sector provision? Anyone who has stood in line to get a license, tried to contact their Medicaid worker or urged their school district to increase academic standards has reason to question the ability of government agencies, without competition from for-profit and not-for-profit organizations, to meet the wide spectrum of needs and wants of citizens. This problem lies at the heart of many tax-and-benefit reform proposals being discussed in the early twenty-first century. They include everything from creating personal Social Security retirement accounts (thereby handing control over investment decisions to individuals) to expanding use of nonprofit (including religious) organizations in delivering health care, housing, employment assistance and other services.

There remains one important consideration about whether governments should do more than they do now to relieve poverty. Would any new or expanded assistance program actually reduce freedom at the expense of short-term security? In the Bible the story of twins Jacob and Esau comes to mind. Esau was tricked into selling his birthright for a meal. Wisconsin Assembly member John G. Gard has written about this question, using his state as an example.

Wisconsin's welfare reform (a model for federal reform under President Clinton) aimed to help families achieve long-term independence through work, and to support those efforts with generous childcare and health benefits. The good news is that the state's welfare load dropped from 52,000 before reform to 10,000 in 2004 (this, despite the recession of 2001). Wage rates earned

by those who went to work rose from $7.30 to $8.10 per hour over one year.
That, plus more hours worked, raised the family incomes of recipients (including earnings and benefits) from $12,100 to $14,800.

Sounds like success, but Representative Gard is concerned, because Wisconsin achieved these results with a greater tax burden than that of neighboring states. As a result:

> There is less money left in a Wisconsin worker's paycheck than in any of our neighboring states. That fact hurts every worker in Wisconsin, but it hits those just making the jump from poverty to the world of work the hardest. . . . Without change, more and more of our job creators [businesses] and our best workers will simply vote with their feet and take their jobs, skills, wealth, and ideas to states with more reasonable tax climates. (Gard 2005)

Gard argues than when love of neighbor is extensively replaced by citizen-financed government programs, then freedom and individual initiative may be compromised.

> True compassion springs from recognizing the inherent human worth and dignity of every individual and encouraging each individual to maximize his or her potential in a free society. Our goal should be to display that kind of compassion by working to end the cycle of dependency, reforming welfare, and reducing the tax burden so all citizens can enjoy the maximum economic benefit from the work they do. If we achieve these goals we can ensure that we have a properly functioning social "safety net"; one that helps those who have fallen bounce up and not one that keeps those striving to rise tied down. (Gard 2005)

The difficulty of providing help without weakening initiatives and without impairing a state or nation's ability to compete for entrepreneurs and workers is one reason why moral and cultural institutions are needed. They can reach out, with voluntary human and financial resources, to alleviate poverty and encourage steps toward independence. Furthermore, they can do so while tailoring help to meet the immensely varied needs of poor people. One family may need budgeting assistance, another help getting into a training program, another information about care for a disabled father or sick child. When government tries to be all things to all people, programs are often bundled in ways that adversely affect independence, self-respect, and joining churches and other groups that promote mutual care and responsibility.

FROM MEASURING GAPS TO PERSONAL AND SOCIAL ACTION

In this chapter, we have argued that some income and opportunity gaps are more important than others. Wherever the principle reason for such gaps is primarily a matter of personal choices about education, careers, family, saving and so forth, gaps are less disturbing than where they result from outright prejudice. Markets generate economic incentives and rewards that are important for personal freedom and material well-being. Both tend to erode economic gaps over time. Under the best competitive circumstances, unwarranted prejudice gives way to market rewards that enhance productivity. As a result, government initiatives to dramatically reduce such gaps cannot usually be justified.

On the other hand, when economic gaps result from pernicious social barriers that persistently limit access to productive resources (like education, relative safety of persons and property, and social networks that teach and support personal, family and social values), much more than legal reforms and policy interventions are needed to reduce those gaps. In chapter eleven, we discuss the importance of "social capital." We will see that all communities—separated by race, generation, education, wealth, health status, religion and the like—require extensive investments in building networks that affirm human dignity and enhance access to resources for economic success. This is the grassroots level where we live most of our days and are challenged to make a real, sustained difference.

FOR FURTHER READING

Blank, Rebecca M. 2006. Was welfare reform successful? *Economists' Voice.* 3(4). Also available through the Brookings Institute website <www.brook .edu/es/ccf/20061116blank.pdf>. This is an excellent, brief summary of U.S. welfare reforms in the mid-1990s and their outcomes.

Morse, Jennifer Roback. 2003. Making room in the inn: Why the modern world needs the needy. In Doug Bandow and David L. Schindler, eds. *Wealth, poverty, and human destiny* (pp. 179-212). Wilmington, Del.: ISI Books. The author is concerned about the way modern society has "marginalized the needy" by making individual autonomy a high virtue. In touching and convicting ways, Morse calls for a recovery of human dignity based on the love of God, not the individual "usefulness" to society. Taking care of children, the mentally ill and the elderly is a test of any society's true greatness.

Sider, Ron. 1999. *Just generosity.* Grand Rapids: Baker. This book provides a good survey of biblical teaching about care for the poor. It also explores a variety of concrete suggestions regarding ways to alleviate poverty, including possible partnerships between governments and faith-based organizations. Though not all equally sound, the author's suggestions should provoke good discussion and further analysis.

Yuengert, Andrew M. 2003. *Inhabiting the land.* Grand Rapids: Acton Institute. In this excellent monograph, economist Yuengert shows how the Christian natural law tradition treats the human right to migration.

11

GOING BEYOND MARKETS

Renewing Neighborhoods,
Reconciling People and Restoring Hope

People do not live by bread alone" (Mt 4:4). This Old Testament quotation was Jesus' answer to Satan's suggestion that Jesus exploit his divine power to satisfy his forty-day hunger by turning a stone into bread. Jesus refused the temptation, explaining in the same verse that we must feed on "every word that comes from the mouth of God." This is one of the hard sayings of Jesus. God answers our prayers for daily bread and challenges each of us to take in spiritual food. Thus, despite markets' amazing capacity to supply us with bread and other good things, they cannot directly meet our deepest needs.

Feeding on the Word of God grows in us the capacity to make responsible choices as consumers, workers and neighbors. More than the words of Scripture, more than the sacred bread of Communion, this Word is the very One who redeems sinners. His Spirit enables Christians to be the hands, feet and heart of Christ for others. Doing so requires that we make good choices.

One of the key economic lessons illustrated in this book is that we must make choices about how best to use time, money and other scarce resources. However, the basis for all choices is a set of values. Thus Sarah's convictions and values become evident when she chooses to buy pornography or a contract to freeze her brain—trusting in a scientific resurrection long after her death. José reveals his values when he becomes a big brother for a kid without an intact family instead of working more overtime hours. The Vander Nats expose their values when they and their children join their church a few Saturdays every year to build houses with Habitat for Humanity.

Our decisions about buying, working and spending leisure time are billboards for our values. Movie companies and other businesses produce "clean" products when there is a sufficient demand for them. Markets are not to blame if they merely respond to consumers' tastes for dirty products and services. Rather than point the finger at markets, those with strong personal and social values are called to exercise individual and collective choices consistent with their values. Christians accept their God-given duty and delight to walk in the light with their words and deeds. In so doing, they become open books from which neighbors and fellow workers may feed on every word of God (Mt 4:4).

In this chapter we observe the powerful influence Christians can have when they join hands with others to tackle social and moral challenges that do not lend themselves to lasting solutions by either markets or governments alone. We begin by exploring the roles played by moral and cultural institutions, since they provide fundamental social relationships based on mutual trust and care.

WHY MARKETS AND DEMOCRATIC GOVERNMENTS ARE NOT ENOUGH TO HOLD SOCIETY TOGETHER

Democracy and free markets may be counted among humanity's greatest social inventions! But the effectiveness of both of these extraordinary institutions and the well-being of society depend on the presence of dynamic moral and cultural institutions as well. Such institutions produce social glue that unites and equips people for common action based on shared values. This is the topic we explore in this chapter. But first we review why free markets are not sufficient for societies to thrive.

Throughout this book we have discussed the advantages of markets for organizing the production and allocation of goods and services. Markets are efficient—producing the most highly desired mix of goods and services possible—whenever many informed buyers and sellers compete and all the costs and benefits fall directly on them alone rather than neighboring consumers and producers. When these conditions are weak or missing, markets do not necessarily deliver the best deal for society. For example, when negative costs of producing paper fall on neighbors in the form of foul-smelling air, paper is underpriced. Its price should be higher in order to reflect the total cost to society of all resources used—including clean water and air—in making the product. But low market prices encourage people to buy too much paper, resulting in pollution that makes living downwind very unappealing. In the case of pollution, partial remedies include government measures to regulate (or provide incentives for) polluting firms to reduce waste volume and toxicity.

Beautiful orchards pose the opposite problem—too few people are willing to plant fruit trees. If orchards are enjoyed either by passing motorists or neighbors, then markets fall short of delivering the socially optimal number of orchards. Only if a system can be introduced that rewards producers for benefits to others will orchards be planted at socially optimal levels. Interestingly, the fact that bees pollinate fruit trees and also produce honey has led to informal market arrangements between beekeepers and orchards to their mutual advantage, even though selling fruit is the fruit rancher's primary source of income.

In chapters three through five we discussed useful roles governments may play in discouraging pollution, and we discussed settings in which governments are better equipped to deliver the goods than firms. Governments tax residents to pay for public goods, like national defense, that would be underfunded if left completely to the market or voluntary contributions. There is also a potential role for governments to encourage activities that produce benefits for society in excess of the monetary returns earned in competitive markets. For example, a government might pay subsidies to businesses that include GED instruction with training programs for new employees.

The market and government sectors of a society are not equally competent in all activities, however. We have mentioned the importance of strong moral and cultural institutions for filling needs not met by the first two sectors. According to the social tripod analogy we developed in chapter one, a thriving society requires three poles: free markets, democracy and strong moral and cultural institutions. Each of the three sectors must be strong, without attempting to take over functions best accomplished by another sector. For example, some efforts to protect environmental quality are best addressed through voluntary gifts to organizations that spend donations on such things as buying up development rights to rain forest (thereby enhancing species preservation or reducing global greenhouse pressures).

One of the strengths of moral and cultural institutions (sometimes called "private voluntary organizations" or PVOs) is that they provide individuals with outlets to speak and act on behalf of their own values without forcing the hands of those who may not hold identical values. When a government uses tax funds to buy up and manage land for environmental purposes (instead of leaving such activities to privately funded groups) or to solve social problems, three problems arise:

1. *All citizens are forced to participate*, no matter their incomes, values or personal trade offs. Should poor families in Detroit be taxed to protect national forests they will never visit?

2. Depending on the mechanism used, *governments sometimes mismanage* public resources to such an extent that environmental or social goals are unmet, or are extremely costly relative to what the same revenues could have achieved elsewhere. For example, large forest fires occur primarily on government lands, not privately owned lands. Because private firms need healthy forests to keep their industry going, they more actively remove dead trees and brush, which are deadly fire hazards. Furthermore, many government attempts to manage wilderness have also backfired. For example, the early years of Yosemite National Park (America's first national park) were disastrous. Government mismanagement repeatedly led to species elimination. Upon reflection, it seems that there is really no such thing as "managing wilderness."

3. Finally, when a government undertakes to provide a public service, like cradle-to-grave care for the poor, the *result can be less total help*, because private individuals may assume that their moral duty to help those in need is adequately covered by their taxes. "I gave to the poor at the IRS office" might be their reply to an organization asking for their donations.

In this chapter we take up a number of issues regarding moral and cultural institutions. We argue that they perform some functions especially well and they undergird the workings of markets and governments. This they do by teaching and sustaining values, without which material, social, political and spiritual standards of living would be lower. As noted by Wilkinson and Bittman (2002):

> no matter how complex and distant some social institutions have become, that *[sic]* the roots of any just political system still lie deep in the ground in real social relationships based on trust and care. . . . [I]t is here, in the webs of social connections and the compassionate impulses which support them that the potential to renovate democratic practices and renew our sense of citizenship really lies. (p. 2)

The basic values needed for effective social action are taught and practiced in the context of moral and cultural institutions, beginning with families. Strong values become deeply rooted, however, only when individuals commit themselves to living them out.

VIRTUE AS A PUBLIC GOOD

The Christian church teaches that God both demands and is the perfect model for virtue. God calls us to live out our faith according to the highest moral and spiritual values. He offers grace needed to practice virtue, and forgiveness to those who repent and want a new chance to do right. Patience in doing good is reinforced by God's promise that evil will be punished, that good ultimately triumphs and that Christ joins us in daily sacrifice and struggle.

Thus, although humans have some basic instincts about what is right (see Rom 1), churches and other organizations build up wisdom about how to live a righteous life. They also provide many occasions to practice virtue, both within and outside the group. This dedication to building up the capacity for virtue fascinates economists because the practice of virtue produces benefits for society at large, in addition to the rewards enjoyed by virtuous persons. Greater honesty, kept promises and the gift of confidence in another person or their group—taken together—enhance the benefits from social interaction.

Sellers, for example, who develop and practice trust with their customers and suppliers accomplish tasks that would otherwise require the costly services of attorneys, accountants and courts to enforce. Hence, as Baron (1998) indicates, trust may be viewed as a public good that can lead to higher productivity and better quality at lower costs. Firms that have a reputation for honesty and responsibility within a community earn goodwill, which may enable them to undertake riskier (but highly productive) investments without burdensome interference from skeptical regulators and private suits.

Governments too can spend more on direct services and less on expensive oversight in a society where the practice of trust and other virtues is widespread. Thus the effectiveness of public services and the benefits of market transactions are both enhanced in societies that engender relatively high levels of virtue.

The problem with the supply of virtue is that human beings are often self-centered and nearsighted. Markets and governments can channel self-interest into socially useful endeavors, but they cannot provide the moral and spiritual basis for a society in which people enjoy deeply satisfying personal lives and strong social relationships. If all education, health services and environmental care were left to for-profit ventures, backed by government rules, enticements and tax money, we would expect too little of these services to be provided.

VALUES THAT SUSTAIN INDIVIDUALS AND THEIR SOCIETIES

Economists have just begun to explore the relationship of moral and cultural institutions to economic and social progress. Previously, they focused on the need for physical capital, education and technology as keys to economic growth. Religious beliefs, values and practices were assumed to be beyond their professional expertise. Although it is difficult to measure and scientifically model the impact of religion on an economy, we explore some likely connections in this section.

Christianity is not the only religion teaching values that are useful to society and important to those who practice them. Important values—like love, honesty, patience, hard work and respect for life—are encouraged within many religions. However, we concentrate here on the church of Christ—one spiritual body, made up of denominations, congregations and religious authorities at many levels.

Traditionally, the Christian church has taught seven fundamental virtues. Four of them are referred to as *cardinal virtues*, based on *cardio*, the Latin word for "hinge," because all other virtues pivot on them. They are prudence (wisdom), justice, temperance (moderation) and fortitude (courage). The *theological virtues*—faith, hope and love—round out the total to seven. Wisdom, moderation and courage are virtues whose practice is very important in market economies.

Wisdom is the virtue that guides our choices. In daily life wisdom implies careful reasoning before undertaking a project. This is the essence of Jesus' teaching about "counting the cost," but also the basis for successful entrepreneurship. As Klay (1986) illustrates, economics provides tools for prudently matching effective means to desired ends. For example, economic analysis shows how firms can enhance revenues and reduce costs, thereby increasing profits. It also encourages families and larger groups to consider alternative means for realizing both lowly goals and lofty dreams.

Moderation implies that one should not spend all effort and income on the immediate satisfaction of physical and psychological appetites. Such constraint is at the basis of saving and giving. Saving builds up productive capital—through investment in machines, skills and ideas. Giving has the potential to relieve distress, support the activities of moral and cultural organizations, and provide for the development of values that strengthen spiritual, social and economic life.

Courage in some contexts is called "guts." Entrepreneurs, savers and workers all exercise courage when they undertake actions based on prudent expectations, but in the face of real risk. They must sacrifice and endure reversals along the road to success.

We practice *justice* by giving all persons their due as humans, made in God's image. In labor markets this includes paying people their agreed-upon wages, based on the value they contribute to production. In product (and service) markets sellers have an obligation to accurately represent products regarding their content, safety and durability. We have argued that competitive markets do a lot—not everything—to assure that justice in exchange prevails. But justice does not encompass *all* that is required for optimal personal and social interaction, which is why love is the last of the virtues we discuss.

Consider now the meaning and social significance of the three theological virtues. *Faith*, in the Christian tradition, is not a matter of assenting to a list of beliefs. Instead, it is lived out when people *entrust* themselves to Jesus Christ in all of life. Without faith, we are on our own—the only author of our fate. If we have many personal, psychological, social and economic resources, we may expect to do well. However, if these resources seriously fail us, we may find ourselves trapped in despair to the point of contemplating suicide.

So, how does faith affect economic life? Christians and Jews may quote the Bible here, "Unless the LORD builds a house, / the work of the builders is wasted" (Ps 127:1, where the remainder of the verse says that cities also depend on the Lord for safety). They expect the full value of their work (and all their daily activities) to be realized—now and eternally—only through a continuous relationship of trust in the Lord. Such trust is a source of vision and energy that could not be sustained without God.

Hope is one of the least well understood of the virtues. The word is used today to suggest everything from a silly wish upon a star to a vague, subrational desire for something good to happen in the future. By contrast, hope as described in the Bible is an *anchor* (see Heb 6:18-20) for believers, an openhearted and open-minded confidence in the promises of God. Those promises are powerfully summed up in God's words "I will never fail you. I will never abandon you" (Heb 13:5, quoting Deut 31:6, 8). The promise of his presence is complemented by promises of forgiveness, daily sufficiency, the power to love others and more.

Is there a benefit to society that many people hope in God's promises? Surely yes, if that hope holds out for them a vision toward which they orient their work, play and love. Successful entrepreneurs have a vision of what they want to accomplish. That vision must have the weight-bearing capacity to inspire collective effort and sacrifice. It must not be built on flimsy logic, failure to consider the risks, inadequate resources, preening leaders or purely selfish ends. Their visions must have the capacity to build something of lasting value.

Love. The apostle Paul says that without love, we are only making meaningless noise like "a noisy gong or a clanging cymbal" (1 Cor 13:1). Competitive labor markets regularly pay people their due in a material sense. They may or may not support the practice of love between workers and employers. However, experience confirms for most of us that the quality and fruitfulness of relationships among fellow workers and between managers and workers is greatly enhanced where all are valued as full persons. At its best, that valuing includes love.

Will products be better when love is practiced at work? Possibly. Will the company have more success at attracting the best people into its work force? Quite probably. The employment decisions made by workers are based on much more than salary. Will treating people with love overcome laziness, lack of skill and poor marketing? No. Will love—together with the practice of other virtues (with or without a foundation in religious faith)—make life more rewarding and society healthier? We have no doubt that the answer is a resounding yes!

Believers are called to practice additional values that affect the workings of an economy and the whole of society. These values may, but need not, be gathered under one of the seven virtues just described. Who would like to live in a society where other values like honesty, trust, peace and humility were largely absent?

In Banks and Stevens (1997) we read, "Character is influenced by habits, and habits are formed by choices. The virtuous life is a life in which the acquired habits are in harmony with one another." Developing and practicing virtue requires a lifetime investment of faith in God, openness to God's spirit and active participation in the Christian community. One of the main duties of the church is to recognize and call out of Christians the gifts needed to exercise virtue in service to God and others. Thus the gift of hospitality is an outlet for practicing love. And the gift of discernment (wisdom) is necessary for the practice of peace. Such gifts are present to different degrees in individual members of a group. For that reason the church helps ensure that the gifts are combined to better serve the world as the body of Christ.

Congregations are examples of small groups that make up the web of moral and cultural institutions. Their smallness, compared to most government entities, makes them especially fertile places for virtues to be taught and practiced.

THE ABILITY OF SMALL GROUPS TO ACHIEVE GREAT ENDS

The early 1970s book *Small Is Beautiful*, by E. F. Schumacher (1973), attracted a lot of attention to the idea that being small is sometimes better than being big. There were no "Supersize It!" ads then, but it was an uphill battle to persuade Americans that anything really progressive could be offered on a small platter. Schumacher showed how small technologies, considered obsolete in the West, were still of great potential value in the Third World, where big and expensive technologies were out of reach. For example, biosand water filter projects in Mexico (see pp. 231-32) are a beautiful illustration of a technology hundreds of years old being used in a simple design that is affordable and removes 95 percent of water impurities (which account for millions of deaths annually in the Third World).

To economists small is beautiful whenever the advantages of large-scale operations are more than offset by the advantages of personal insight, attention and motivation. Thus family farms in certain crops will not likely be overtaken by megacorporations, because each farmer's intimate knowledge of the land, crop and microclimates is invaluable.

Neither are high schools likely to be organized with ten thousand students under the same roof. Why not? Because the touted advantages of larger schools—in consolidated administration, curriculum diversity and bulk purchase of supplies—do not exist. Furthermore, large size makes for less student participation in school activities and a weaker sense of community, with the result that academic achievement is lower and disruptive behavior more common. Small size means that students frequently express care for others and feel valued in the setting of a face-to-face community. Studies show that students fare better academically and socially in high schools with a total of about four hundred students in grades 9 through 12. Not surprisingly, the only high schools in the United States where a majority of low income, minority students achieve at high levels are small schools (Noguera 2002). According to Sommers (1997), a small school produces an "atmosphere [that] is warmer, more cohesive, and safer. It creates in students the desire to belong, to participate, to contribute, and to achieve" (p. 10) Sommers notes that cost advantages presumed to exist in large high schools do not materialize. First, central administration actually grows as a share of the budget for larger schools. Second, purchasing cooperatives can achieve the same cost advantages in buying supplies that a larger school enjoys.

Furthermore, a key advantage of smaller units is the possibility for creativity and accountability. Why are congregations not the size of Fortune 500 firms? Firms depend on some hierarchical organization, fitting the layers of administration into a sort of pyramid. Some companies have switched to more lateral coordination and less top-down command. Even so, a power pyramid exists. As a result, all companies must find ways to motivate everyone in the organization to do their part—not as cogs in a wheel but as thinking, feeling, collaborating men and women and their teams. Businesses have one advantage over churches, namely wages, salaries, promotions and dismissals.

Congregations (in most denominations) also hire and manage a team with several levels of responsibility. We might think that members of the congregation are like a company's customers, in which case, the coordination problem is just one of selling the religious "product" to a growing number of happy consumer/members. But the Christian church—as a whole, as denominations and as congregations—has never seen itself as a consumer-oriented organization. The church is not its pastors, bishops or councils. It is the people of God. Consequently, the organizational problem for churches is not identical to that of firms.

Firms pay for services. But churches do not pay their members for services (although some churches hire organists and even pay professional choirs). Instead, they "call" members to certain tasks, which are accomplished under the direction of the Holy Spirit and with the guidance of clergy. Without the committed involvement of members, churches would be bare skeletons and performance venues, not organs of Christ and bodies at worship.

As a result, the average U.S. congregation has two to four hundred members, even though there are some megachurches with ten thousand members. The advantage of having at least several hundred members is the ability to support at least one pastor, a secretary and a building. The advantage of several hundred members, compared to over four thousand, is that face-to-face participation makes it more likely that most members will actively commit their time and resources to do the work of the church, within and beyond the building walls. This is the way that churches handle the generic "free rider" problem of group activity. They stay small enough to actually minister to each other, and they invoke the name of God, who calls out from people gifts they may never have realized existed.

IDEAL SOCIAL CONSTITUTIONS AND RULES

Moral and cultural organizations do not function in a social vacuum. The most obvious rights needed by moral and cultural organizations are to freely assemble, believe, speak, recruit, fund themselves and own property. This seems obvious in America, which has long been described as a place where once a problem is identified a group immediately forms itself to deal with it. See, for example, Tocqueville (2000). However, such freedom cannot be taken for granted.

Until the last decade of the nineteenth century the French actually had a law forbidding nongovernmental organizations to provide social services. Although the law was changed, France still lags behind England and the United States in terms of the financial size and scope of nonprofit organizations and their activities. If you have traveled in France (or other countries in continental Europe), for example, you know that virtually all major art museums are owned and operated by governments, not by nonprofit boards supported by private donations.

In the United States, private, nonprofit organizations do not have to pay income taxes on contributions or property taxes on land and buildings. Furthermore, donors themselves do not have to pay income taxes on their gifts to charity. Some critics have argued that since churches are major beneficiaries of tax exemptions, we have a case of unconstitutional mixing of religion and state. The picture they paint is that nonreligious taxpayers are forced to carry a greater tax burden than religious ones.

Economists are not professional experts on the constitutionality issue. Historians and legal scholars have more to offer in that domain. However, economists do affirm that fiscal favor toward nonprofit organizations (in the form of tax advantages) is generally consistent with the argument that societies *need* them. These organizations support the practice of virtue, whose benefits spill over onto the rest of society and each subsequent generation—a clear case of positive externalities (see chap. 3).

Thus virtue is a "public good," whose benefits to society are optimal only if some public resources are used to subsidize the activities of those who extend the practice of virtue. Such is the nature of a tax exemption. Broad tax exemptions for nonprofits in general would seem to overcome accusations of state-support for religion, since all taxpayers may select from among many nonreligious and religious organizations to receive their donations.

Some political scientists would agree with the notion that private voluntary organizations, including religious ones, deserve some government support. According to Black, Koopman and Ryden (2004), "Rather than enervate social institutions, the government should effectuate, energize, and engender civil society" (p. 280).

At the beginning of the twenty-first century, many societies are asking themselves whether certain state functions can be better accomplished by voluntary organizations. There is no absolute answer to that question. Some activities now undertaken by governments fully accomplish their goals only when there is close personal attention, local knowledge, development of motivation, instruction in virtue and abiding hope that transcends the moment and the situation. These include work with troubled youth and help for poor families to meet their immediate needs and develop skills required for their long-term independence.

We expect Christians and other concerned citizens to be of different minds on this issue. Some worry that the private, voluntary sector is not fully equipped to handle such enormous and expensive tasks. A partial remedy, widely practiced in America for decades, is to provide some taxpayer funds to subsidize these activities.

President George W. Bush introduced the term *faith-based initiatives*. So far, it has been implemented by means of presidential directives to federal agencies. Accordingly, federal government agencies must ensure that funds handed out for social services are made available to religious organizations as well as other private agencies. Since President Johnson's tenure the federal government has increasingly funded religious organizations to provide social services. The trend increased under President Reagan, and state and local governments (with or without federal dollars) have increasingly relied on nonprofit agencies, including religious ones, to deliver services to those in need of education, health, housing or other care. In the late 1990s major partners with the government in social service delivery included Catholic Charities (receiving $1.3 billion, two-thirds of its budget, from government), and Lutheran Social Services (receiving 92 percent of its revenue from government) (Black et al. 2004).

Critics of this approach challenge it from opposite positions. For some, the greatest danger is that religious organizations will misuse the funds to proselytize. For others, the most serious problem is that religious organizations dependent on some state funds will be forced to deliver services without the moral and spiritual meat that helps families and communities overcome deep problems and sustain wholesome life.

An alternative is to offer tax-funded vouchers to people who desperately need social services (e.g., access to low-cost health care, organized after-school activities, life-skills training, housing, vocational counseling, etc.). Most commentators agree that the Supreme Court's 2002 decision in favor of school vouchers *(Zelman vs. Simmons-Harris)* opened the door to using vouchers for the delivery of social services by religious organizations (Black et al. 2004, pp. 241-44). (Their constitutionality requires that clients have access to nonreligious as well as religious providers.) This approach has the virtue of not forcing religion on those seeking help, providing them with choice among programs and harnessing a competitive model in areas that could benefit from innovation, cost containment and volunteer energy.

Still others argue that vouchers may result in too much state control over services. Some church-organized programs that provide temporary housing refuse government monies because governments limit the choices organizations make regarding the type and duration of assistance provided. We might expect them to also refuse to participate in a voucher system, if the conditions for doing so were a level of government oversight that is too burdensome and restrictive in the pursuit of their service to needy families.

Better still would be restoring income to taxpayers in the form of lower taxes. That way, more donations would increase the ability of moral and cultural institutions to serve society in practical and lasting ways.

PERSONAL APPLICATIONS

We have focused on the moral foundations and social institutions responsible for making society flourish materially, socially and spiritually. It is easy to get caught up in descriptions and fail to make personal applications. Ultimately, the success of markets, governments, and moral and cultural institutions depends on individuals making good decisions. We may learn about what is good within our families, neighborhoods, schools, clubs and churches, but will never be the salt and light the world needs, without personal conviction, change and whole-hearted commitment.

If we do not tell our employers the truth and get to know our neighbors, no other person or group can do it for us. For all their importance the police cannot protect our neighbors and us if we do not look out for each other. If my neighbors cannot read English and do not hear about a new school that could help their child, who will tell them, if not me? If someone falls victim to a beating in a place where you are a tourist, and everyone else turns away, who will come to his aid, if not you?

Let's consider three concrete examples of the power of individual initiative and strong collective action to improve communities and restore personhood. After all, the neighborhood is usually the place providing the greatest opportunities for putting values to work.

RENEWING COMMUNITIES

Markets are dynamic, with feedback effects that can lead to upward steps toward success or downward spirals of failure. An example of the latter case is an older neighborhood from which many people are moving as their incomes and opportunities expand. The inflow of families that follows is more likely to keep the neighborhood strong if those coming in are homeowners, not renters. On average, people take better care of their own property—including houses they live in—than of things they rent or use without compensation.

However, the inward flow will include poorer families whose priorities do not always include renovating their homes and mowing their lawns. In this case, there is a strong possibility that a concerted effort to plant new families in the neighborhood, who are likely to remodel and keep up their houses, could set in motion an upward spiral of renewal. This is a challenge and an opportunity waiting for vision and action.

Holland, Michigan, is a small city along Lake Michigan, where Hope College is located and we teach. Over the last two decades the city has changed in ways that have vastly improved the private and social lives of residents. Concerned individuals and groups have renovated the downtown, built a Boys and Girls Club in a needy neighborhood, and constructed seventy-five houses through Habitat for Humanity. One organization, Good Samaritan Ministries, enlists the collaboration of many churches in meeting local needs for housing, training, language assistance, transportation, childcare and more.

Of course, in all these endeavors, markets play a part. For example, some humanitarian organizations receive donated cars and make them available for sale to needy families through the services of another organization. However, because the staff at Good Samaritan does not include any former car dealers, they leave the task of matching the right car to the right family to others. They sell donated cars, and use the revenue to support activities in which they have recognized expertise.

Although organizations serving the community use markets extensively (buying supplies and hiring managers), they also depend heavily on volunteer time and gifts donated directly to them and to collaborating institutions, like churches. They serve effectively only if many of us join them in expressing our values through personal service, prayer and financial support.

One striking initiative in Holland is taking place well below the public's radar screen. This is the renewal of some neighborhoods near the college campus by creating incentives for college employees to live there. The program is called "Walk to Work." It helps locate houses for sale in the immediate area of the college, providing incentives for Hope College people to buy, renovate and make their homes there.

Like other places where Christians often built colleges shortly after establishing pioneer communities, Holland's college is located in the middle of the city's densest housing. These neighborhoods now contain the lowest-cost houses in town. As expected, the houses are priced low because they and other houses in the immediate neighborhood have not been well kept. Nevertheless, attractive houses (and houses with real potential) regularly come up for sale in these neighborhoods.

Hope College is interested in maintaining the quality of surrounding neighborhoods for both practical and moral reasons. For example, student housing in these blocks cannot continue to be safe if the neighborhoods deteriorate further, and families will not choose to send their sons and daughters to Hope College if the neighborhoods look rundown. Furthermore, as a Christian college, the administration, faculty and staff have long been committed to serving neighbors' needs through help in many forms, including tutors, physical and financial support for organizations that help children at risk, and full-tuition scholarships plus mentors for area minority students wanting to become teachers.

One anonymous philanthropic benefactor became concerned about physical and social deterioration in Hope's neighborhoods, and committed funds in to the college to launch and maintain the Walk to Work program. This gift makes it possible to offer a $7,000 grant for needed remodeling of houses bought by Hope College faculty or staff members within a few targeted blocks of the college. This investment in their neighborhood has the potential to improve the community for residents and for the college.

RECONCILIATION: BRIDGING GAPS THAT DO NOT GO AWAY

In chapter ten we noted that income and opportunity gaps sometimes persist for long periods of time even in democratic, market-oriented societies. Many social, economic and racial gaps result from unequal access to quality education and weakened families, as well as poor life choices about marriage, drugs, friends and more. Most of the time the factors are so interconnected that it is impossible to determine what are the original causes. None of them lend themselves to quick, uniform or cheap solutions.

Any large gaps that persist over generations are a direct challenge to Christians because we are called and equipped by God to persistently and sacrificially love our neighbors and enemies. Followers of Christ should not easily go to bed on full stomachs and expect sweet dreams without committing themselves to specific outreach aimed at enhancing the limited physical, social and spiritual resources available to others. The "others" may be persons of a different age, health, economic or social status, but they are still our neighbors by the grace of God.

So this is the challenge. But what are the means, and where is the vision? God's great promise is to supply us with all we need to serve him and others in his name. Our job is to *notice, care* and *act*.

More than half of what keeps most of us contentedly on our side of a gap is failing to really see our neighbor. That was the case for several travelers who quickly passed by a man left for dead along a Palestinian highway. Jesus' parable reports that several travelers just looked the other way—even crossed to the other side of the street—to avoid noticing the man. Only the foreigner—a despised Samaritan—looked at the man, stopped and did what he could to save the man's life (Lk 10:30-37).

Based on lifetimes of practice, we two Christian economists offer the following guidelines and prompts to noticing, caring and acting on behalf of neighbors, all of whom are so loved by God that he has put us within shouting distance of their neighborhoods.

1. *Get to know your immediate neighbors.* Some are financially needy or new and disoriented, having moved away from their hometowns. Others need opportunities to interact with others, so that by giving of themselves, they may regain a sense of purpose. Furthermore, neighbors have something to offer you! They may be able to tell stories of courage and God's care as they fled war, famine or persecution.

2. *If you now find yourself in a neighborhood where most people appear to be doing very well materially and are self-sufficient, get to know those neighbors too.* They may have children overloaded with gadgets but drowning in a sense of purposelessness. You may not have the gift of evangelism, but you do have the Spirit of God within to enable you to receive that neighbor as a God-given friend.

3. *If you are at a point in your life when you are moving to a new house, neighborhood, town or country, carefully consider your choices.* No doubt, price, proximity to work and other matters are important. However, this may be an ideal time for you to "choose your neighbors" in a way that was never before possible. With some research—using realtors and Christian organizations, and looking around on your own—you should be able to find a place where your gifts and experiences (and those of your family) would be especially useful. At one extreme you might choose to live in a gated community—offering safety, wealthy neighbors and all the amenities. That could be the place God is calling you to, but for most Christians it likely is not. A careful reading of the Bible—from Jonah in Nineveh to Jerusalem and finally to Paul's churches in Asia—the message is that God is in the business of breaking down "the wall of hostility that separated us" (Eph 2:14), and so Christians are called to do likewise.

4. *Seriously consider joining a church that has a very active outreach in its own neighborhood* (or is laying the groundwork for it)—especially when the neighborhood's needs are obvious and neighborhood people are active in the church. Long-distance "neighboring" is fraught with problems, due to lack of intimate involvement with these people as friends, not just "objects" of ministry.

5. *If, because of age (too young or too old) or other circumstances, making big changes in your neighborhood or church is impossible, look for ways to become involved with groups whose vision and practice is reconciliation and bridge-building.* Reconciliation may cross religious and other barriers. For example, we have delighted in praying and working across divides between Catholic and Protestant Christians. Built up during eras when they were "needed" to protect the true faith and the faithful, barriers among Christians are growing obsolete today. The divide seriously detracts from Christian ministry of all kinds. Secular challenges today are God-given opportunities to heed Christ's prayer that we be "one" in him.

6. *Create a neighborhood where none exists.* One of us, Victor, belongs to a Lutheran congregation that has joined with many other churches to create Greater Grand Rapids Interfaith Hospitality Network, IHN (part of a national network of IHN, headquartered in Summit, New Jersey). They open their doors to homeless families a week at a time, rotating with about fourteen other churches. Their place of worship becomes a home and neighborhood for families. Members of the congregation act as volunteer hosts during the evenings, providing families with food and childcare.

An independent study of government and private voluntary programs assisting homeless people in Grand Rapids, Goggin and Orth (2002) found that IHN compares favorably to other local programs for homeless families. They take in families rejected by others, including those who have had problems with substance abuse and mental illness. They are appropriately flexible when circumstances warrant allowing a family to exceed the normal thirty-day limit. Guest families enjoy greater trust and reliance on each other, instead of tensions common in other programs. And after only a week in any given church, many longer-term relationships develop between former "guests" and church members. The people of IHN achieve this without accepting government funds, because applications for funds require too much of their time and allow too little flexibility to meet the needs as they see them.

RESTORING HOPE IN THE "LEAST OF THESE"

In markets, what counts are personal skills, knowledge, contacts and resources one brings to the table. In the kingdom of God, however, the "least of these" are especially beloved and singled out for mercy (Mt 25:31-40). All are sinners, but these are in prison. All are born naked, but these need clothes. All fall short of the glory of God, but these are prospective saints.

Especially for intellectuals it is easy to look out over the world and believe that severe problems of poverty and violence are either without solutions or require turning things upside down through radical social revolution. Even Christians face such a constant barrage of bad news that they often feel hopeless and paralyzed by the sheer enormity of the problems. Added to this, some Christians are overwhelmed by the presence of sin and sickness in every social venue, including the media's emphasis on the benefits of looking out for one's self above all else. In addition, crime, family dissolution and suicide appear rampant.

Jesus did not live at a time when the ills of the entire world were brought into every home. Nevertheless, his words are more important than ever for us to hear; his deeds are still supreme examples for us to imitate. Like Jesus, we are to receive prostitutes and visit the sick, including mentally ill people, who are often either socially isolated or living on our streets. Those who are making a living along on our streets or held as prisoners in our jails are brought near us by God—to be noticed and ministered to in Jesus' name.

Indeed, Mother Teresa's order, the Sisters of Charity, with a presence far beyond India, serves as a contemporary example of Jesus' ministry. The sisters and volunteers bring dying people off of the streets and into their refuge, where they are lovingly bathed and fed. In the dying, the sisters see the face of Christ in his "distressing disguise."

Who could be less relevant to markets than people who are about to die or will never leave prison? But these are the people Jesus calls us to notice and serve. What labor market is more repugnant to Christians than that of prostitutes, but these are the ones whose stoning Jesus refused to sanction.

For some reason, despite their apparent uselessness in our society, those who are very ill, troubled and degraded are the apple of Jesus' eye. He sees past their present physical or moral ugliness to their future wholeness. Apparently, they are not forever lost to him, nor should they be to us. If some of Jesus' followers and witnesses were former prostitutes and lepers, how can we call anyone unclean?

Recently, Robin met Francisco, an Italian man who owns a restaurant just off the beach of Puerto Escondido in southern Mexico. As Robin sat with a Hope student at a table in the lively Italian cafe, "Franco" was just returning from a trip to a prison an hour away. He has a ministry there with prisoners. The first thing out of his mouth was, "The Christian men there are more free than people strolling the beach in front of us."

Nobody knows this better than Franco. He came to Puerto during his twenties to enjoy one of the three best surfing locations in the world. Becoming a "surf bum," he got heavily involved with drugs and attempted suicide. God then took him from self-destruction on the streets into a new Christian community. That community was itself the fruit of God's call upon a successful Canadian businessman and his wife, bringing them to evangelize in Puerto Escondido fifteen years ago.

Even after a late night back from his ministry with prisoners, Franco cheerfully serves customers at tables that are beautifully painted with images and words that allude to Jesus, like "The Lily of the Valley." He wears a T-shirt sporting a drawing of the Lion of Judah. When asked about the Lion, he beams and shoots back over his shoulder, "Es mi Señor!" (He is my Lord).

The story of Puerto Escondido, a town of about thirty-five thousand, is one of God's miracles in the making. Once said to be beyond help by a Mexican evangelist, Puerto Escondido is now the location of many churches who are very successful, evangelizing and discipling new Christians and their families. The fruits are now being realized in civic life as well.

Despite decades of extreme tension and mutual mistrust, more and more poor Catholic and Protestant families are collaborating with each other in small groups to build houses for each other. Habitat for Humanity's Mexican staff and volunteers work with families to build trust, hope and a new future for people who previously saw each other as strangers and even enemies. They pray and read Scripture together, then go out to mix cement and lay bricks side by side.

As we were finishing writing this book, some Hope College faculty and students were creating the first ever vocational internship program in Mexico. Because some volunteers listened to the stories of people living in Puerto, there are now prospects for sending Hope College students on many projects. These include engineering majors working with the mayor's office on installation of septic systems, biology students testing new low-tech water filters and political science students studying a delicate jurisdictional dispute between two municipalities.

We share this account of Puerto Escondido because it illustrates the power for change that develops when Christians put themselves in places where they are able to see God's vision. Hearing God's call anew, they eagerly respond and create partnerships with the people who need a helping hand.

Miracles occur when Christians make themselves available to serve God in the presence of people who have been treated as so much social garbage. Restored by God, those same people become beacons of hope for others—not just those in similar circumstances. Hearing their stories and sharing their lives may be the only effective antidotes to discouragement and paralysis that afflict First World people who lack no material benefit, but wring their hands about the world's problems.

WHEN SOCIETY AND ITS FOUNDATIONS BREAK DOWN

Any consideration of the importance of the social fabric, built up in society through moral and cultural institutions, can benefit from a look at a society suddenly bereft of either. Such was the case for a POW camp first immortalized in the 1957 movie *Bridge on the River Kwai*. The movie tells the story of Ernest Gordon (2002) and has been recently reprised in another film, *To End All Wars*.

At the height of World War II, Ernest Gordon was taken prisoner by the Japanese and sent to a POW camp in Thailand, where other Scottish sailors and allied prisoners spent more than two years. Chungkai was, "a place of shadows in the dark valley" (p. 72). According to Gordon, when they first arrived, the atmosphere was one of free enterprise at its worst, with all the restraints of morality gone. Our captors had promised to reduce us to a level "lower than that of any coolie in Asia." They were succeeding all too well.

Although we lived by the law of the jungle, the strongest among us still died, and the most selfish, the most self-sufficient, the wiliest and shrewdest, perished with the weak, the generous and the decent. (pp. 73-74)

At his worst, Gordon found himself lying in the death house, "whose atmosphere was . . . anti-life; over it all was the miasma of decay, the promise of nothingness." Reason whispered to him, "You too are part of this. There is no escape." However, two fellow prisoners—one Catholic and one Protestant— ministered to him by sharing their meager rations, bathing his wounds and encouraging him to put his hope in the living God. Replacing his inner voice of despair, another voice urged, "The battle between life and death goes on all the time. Life has to be cherished, not thrown away, I've made up my mind. I'm not going to surrender" (p. 87).

An amazing resurrection of the spirit occurred throughout the camp following Gordon's recovery of the will to live. It started with private resolve, but soon led to big changes in the lives and attitudes of the prisoners. Instead of stealing from each other, they began to sacrificially help one another. Some men literally laid down their lives for their brothers in the camp, taking blows for the mistakes of others. Prayer services were conducted in a jungle clearing. The sick were bathed and cared for. Gordon writes:

Generosity proved to be contagious. Once begun, this charity soon extended beyond regimental loyalties to include any man in need. Men started thinking less of themselves, of their own discomforts and plans, and more of their responsibilities to others. . . . It was dawning on us all—officers and other ranks alike— that the law of the jungle is not the law for man. We had seen for ourselves how quickly it could strip most of us of our humanity and reduce us to levels lower than the beasts. . . . Death was still with us—no doubt about that. But we were slowly being freed from its destructive grip. We were seeing for ourselves the sharp contrast between the forces that made for life and those that made for death. Selfishness, hatred, envy, jealousy, greed, self-indulgence, laziness and pride were all anti-life. Love, heroism, self-sacrifice, sympathy, mercy, integrity and creative faith, on the other hand, were the essence of life, turning mere existence into living in its truest sense. These were the gifts of God to men. (pp. 105-6)

What follows this passage in Gordon's book is his account of sweeping changes throughout the camp. The love of God, which transformed men, became the genesis for a jungle university, whose courses included philosophy, math and nine dead and living languages. "They [the courses] helped us to see that our minds could work only on what they received from education, from experience, above all from faith. It was faith, I felt, that enabled us to transcend our environment" (p. 133).

The renewal of spirit in Camp Chungkai did not end suffering and death, but it forever changed the POWs' perspectives on life. "In the light of our new understanding, the Crucifixion was seen as being completely relevant to our situation. A God who remained indifferent to the suffering of His creatures was not a God whom we could accept. The Crucifixion, however, told us that God was in our midst, suffering with us" (p. 119). At a later point the grace prisoners received was extended to their captors. A group of newly released allied prisoners bathed badly injured Japanese soldiers who had been left to rot in a hot railroad car. It is hard to imagine a greater picture of forgiveness in action!

We have told his story, following a discussion of moral and cultural institutions, because it distills much of what we have noted about the importance to society of groups forming themselves to encourage virtuous and self-giving lives under much less austere circumstances. Even in a POW camp, it was within human capacity, by the grace of God, to turn a jungle into a university, and mistrust into sacrificial love. Any society that forgets or ignores the importance of sustaining spiritual and social life does so at its peril. There are more lessons to be learned from POW camps.

SOCIAL AND MORAL COLLAPSE AND REGENERATION

In the prisoner of war experience the "law of the jungle" took over when all normal social structures and moral foundations had broken down. For a long time the Japanese authorities were successful in their attempts to reduce the men to animals. This they did in many ways. They separated men from their units in different sections of the camp, and took away officers' ability to control their subordinates. They humiliated or executed anyone who stuck his head above the masses.

Gordon describes the utter chaos that resulted from social breakdown. Prisoners robbed each other, stole from corpses and betrayed men to the prison authorities in hopes of getting a better deal for themselves. Wanting to save their own skins, men risked being shot to buy food from villagers—using money and anything of value they could get their hands on in the camps. This was a dog-eat-dog world.

What we see in Gordon's account is an entirely believable and vivid demonstration of the importance of all three pillars of society. Without some structure to induce prosocial behavior, all hell breaks lose. In this case (as in much of China under Mao), the normal rules are turned upside down by the authorities. Betrayal is rewarded. Mutual help is punished. Random acts of violence are used to completely demoralize the prisoners. As a result, some POWs go crazy (rather few, considering the circumstances). Others stare into space and refuse to eat until they die, usually within a day of giving in to utter hopelessness.

What happened after the spiritual resurrection of a few men, spreading through the camp, was a reversal of the process of social breakdown. Not all men discovered God, but everyone benefited from the dramatic changes that a contagious recovery of hope made possible. Whereas men had been shot for lesser things, the Japanese guards, noticing positive results, eventually tolerated prisoners' embryonic efforts at self-help.

Revival of this decaying society, undertaken under extreme conditions, took many forms. The "university" began—first near the death house, so as not to call attention to themselves. Concerts were organized, using a hodgepodge of Western and makeshift instruments. Prisoner chefs concocted a Christmas pudding, using rice, fermented with bananas, limes and palm sugar, wrapped in palm leaves. Officers began serving their men, which improved organization and boosted morale. Previously, the bush market had been used to enhance individuals' survival chances. Men still risked death, but now used their meager provisions to bargain for eggs to save the lives of extremely malnourished fellow prisoners.

Although the spiritual lesson of the story is obvious, there are others. If the camps had never reinstated a capacity for self-governance, men would have died at their own hands, as well as those of prison guards. With increasing self-governance, incentives to cheat diminished. Social orderliness allowed men to think less about protecting themselves and more about using their limited freedom to exercise personal initiative.

As a result, POWs discovered solutions to previously intractable problems. For example, a few men designed and crafted artificial limbs for amputees, using scrap metal and local fibers. By contrast, their captors had no use for the maimed, since they could no longer work. For the Japanese guards, prisoners who were wounded and weak no longer deserved any respect. The Japanese code of ethics required that a vanquished warrior commit suicide. Only a coward hung around to be looked after.

With greater orderliness in the camp, specialization developed. This raised productivity and lifted life above bare survival. Small, private efforts by disparate, unorganized men quickly congealed. With the help of a tight community, a makeshift clinic, classes, worship services, art studios (using pigments extracted from native plants) and debate clubs sprang up.

One of the lessons learned from reading Gordon's account is that it was not money that destroyed lives and morale in the camp. Instead, money became a useful way of spreading resources around so that a variety of personal needs could be met. After camp renewal, money was used for both personal and group enjoyment, and sometimes given to others in need, but never employed for survival at the expense of others.

Neither did competition weaken the social fabric, as is often feared. Instead, newly motivated men took it upon themselves to compete with a deadline set by their captors for finishing the Thai-Burma railroad. Prisoners who previously were barely adequate soon had the organizational wherewithal to overcome seemingly impossible odds. Under terrible conditions—fighting mud, disease, lack of sleep and malnutrition—POWs finished the railroad in less than half the time ordered.

Under less harsh conditions, social networks were rebuilt in an Italian POW camp during World War II. Markets and money evolved out of nowhere as men found that cigarettes were acceptable in payment for anything they wanted from other POWs (e.g., a tin of beef or tea). Except for production of goods and services, the camp became a fully functioning economy, where even credit became available. Instead of resenting intrusion by market values, POWs there (as in Thailand) found that a reliable system of exchange allowed everyone to enjoy a higher standard of living than was possible without trade or with limited barter.

What we see in these brief accounts about POW camps in Asia and Europe is a combination of human spirit and its marvelous capacity for organizing people to meet social and personal needs. We witness the tragedy of totalitarian governments and war. But neither had the final word. Markets that initially served selfishness were harnessed to match skills and resources with needs and delights.

Humans, who are capable of great evil and pettiness, may choose to practice mundane mercies and costly love. We respond to both legitimate material incentives and the highest callings. Our personal commitment to God and our neighbor is the foundation for exciting, fruitful lives in all times and everywhere. No society can thrive without the gift of ourselves. By his example God teaches us to care for brothers and sisters across the street, around the world and in generations yet to be born. God's final word for us, in all of life, is that he so loved us that he sent Jesus Christ to be our Savior and firstborn Brother! Hence the marching orders of Jesus, "Go into all the world" (Mk 16:15).

FOR FURTHER READING

Dean, Judith M., Schaffner, Julie A., and Stephen L. S. Smith, eds. 2005. *Attacking poverty in the developing world: Christian practitioners and academics in collaboration*. Waynesboro, Ga.: Authentic Media. Written by Christian scholars and practitioners, this book explores many aspects of poverty reduction—domestic and international. They evaluate the effectiveness of various approaches and policies in terms of their impact on the poor—ranging from education and trade to debt relief and global policies.

Fukuyama, Francis. 1995. *Trust: The social virtues and the creation of prosperity*. New York: Free Press Paperbacks. This is a tour de force treatment of social capital across time and cultures. The author abundantly illustrates the impact of trust, or the lack of it, on the chances of economic success in both industrialized and developing countries, as well as on expectations placed on their governments.

Morisy, Ann. 2004. *Journeying out: A new approach to Christian mission*. Harrisburg, Penn.: Morehouse. Written in a down-to-earth manner, this book challenges congregations to more effectively engage with community needs. While doing so, members become more open to trusting in God and discover their vocations as Christians.

Oster, Merril J., and Hamel, Mike. 2003. *Giving back: Using your influence to create social change*. Colorado Springs: NavPress. Chronicles the experiences of a variety of social entrepreneurs who have made a lasting impact. A helpful read for anyone thinking about beginning a new ministry to the less fortunate among us.

Rundle, Steven L., and Steffen, Tom A. 2003. *Great commission companies: The emerging role of business in missions*. Downers Grove, Ill.: InterVarsity Press. This book provides striking examples of businesses established by Christian businessmen and women in parts of the world where the Christian witness is weak. Readers will be encouraged to consider the possibility of applying entrepreneurial skills to supply valuable goods and services while also witnessing to God's love in the marketplace.

EPILOGUE

Nine Big Ideas from Economics
That Can Help You Be a Good Steward Every Day

Throughout the course of this book, we have shared a few ideas from economics that we cannot imagine living our lives without. We summarize nine of them here:

1. **For everything you do, there is something you are choosing to leave undone** (opportunity cost, chap. 4). Attending one church means you cannot attend another one at the same time. Giving your money to the poor in one nation means that you will not be giving it to the poor in another. There are lots of good things we could be doing, but we cannot accomplish them all simultaneously. Choose carefully, and choose prayerfully.

2. **The anticipated social benefit of any policy proposal must be seriously weighed against every likely social opportunity cost** (optimal policy choices, chap. 4). Where either positive or negative externalities arise, carefully designed and implemented public policy has the potential to nudge suboptimal market outcomes toward more socially preferred ones. However, policy action should be undertaken only in instances where the anticipated social benefit exceeds the possible social opportunity cost. Careful and wise stewardship of our resources demands it.

3. **Actions speak louder than words** (rational expectations, chap. 7). The nature of a person's true values is expressed in his or her actions, not in words. Just like rational expectations means that the public will learn about the Fed through its actions over time, people will learn what you value most highly from observing your actions too. Economists sometimes call this idea—that we can learn what is in someone's heart from observing his or her actions—"revealed preference." Be known for your fruits, not merely for big talk.

4. **Markets move precious resources from less-valuable to more-valuable uses** (price incentives, chap. 2). When new business ventures succeed, consumers are signaling that they really like the ways in which entrepreneurs are using society's resources. And when products like McDonald's Arch Deluxe or Coca-Cola's Surge soda fail, consumers have signaled that they would like McDonald's and the Coca-Cola Company to stop squandering society's precious resources making things few of us want. Markets continually transform resources from unproductive uses to productive uses. Do your part by letting your purchasing habits reflect what you hold in the highest moral regard, and encourage others to do so as well.

5. **Job creation is rightly viewed as a cost, not a benefit, of any initiative** (the labor game, chap. 3). People are precious, valuable resources—at least as precious as any other of God's creatures. And when they are doing one job, there is some other activity they are not doing instead (e.g., staying at home with loved ones, going to school, working in another job). Finding mere busywork for people is not an appropriate use of their creativity, talent or ingenuity. Instead, society should be more concerned with channeling individuals into their most highly prized uses—just like any other valuable resource.

6. **Free international trade is a proven way to help the world's poorest people** (globalization: mutual benefits of opening opportunities, chap. 8). Free trade by both rich and poor countries gives the poorest people access to employment and market opportunities that they would not have otherwise. Protectionist measures designed to defend the poor, while noble, do nothing but guarantee the impoverishment of the world's most destitute. Dislocations caused by changes in trade are temporary, can be offset by wise complementary economic policy, and are small compared to the large gains to be had through trade.

7. **Hope for a better future may require temporary discomfort today** (real business cycles and "creative destruction," chap. 7). College is not easy or cheap, but a college education holds great promise for the future. Chemotherapy is not easy or comfortable, but the treatment brings the promise of remission. Growth and change require temporary inconvenience. We cannot be so focused on remaining comfortable today that we miss out on the hope that tomorrow holds.

8. **Corrupt governments keep the poor down** (barriers to growth, chap. 8). When a government can take anything it wants from its citizens, there is

no incentive to work hard to create anything. Christians should continue to work for economic freedom and social justice throughout the global community.

9. **Sunk costs are sunk** (sunk costs, chap. 4). You cannot relive yesterday. Yesterday is gone. Begin living each day anew, and live each day as faithfully as God's grace enables you.

References

Abowd, John M., and David S. Kaplan. 1999. Executive compensation: Six questions that need answering. *Journal of Economic Perspectives* 13, no. 4:145-68.

American College of Physicians. 2003. Statement to the Practicing Physicians Advisory Council, Centers for Medicare and Medicaid Services, U.S. Department of Health and Human Services. Washington, D.C. [Online]. Available: www.acponline.org/hpp/ppac.pdf.

Badaracco, Joseph L., Jr. 2002. *Leading quietly.* Boston: Harvard Business School.

Balvers, Ronald J., and Thomas F. Cosimano. 1994. Inflation variability and gradualist monetary policy. *Review of Economic Studies*, 61:721-38.

Banks, Robert, and R. Paul Stevens. 1997. *The complete book of everyday Christianity.* Downers Grove, Ill.: InterVarsity Press. Also available online: www.ivmdl.org/cbec.cfm.

Baron, Jonathan. 1998. Trust: Beliefs and morality. In *Economics, values, and organization,* ed. Avner Ben-Ner and Louis Putterman, pp. 408-18. Cambridge: Cambridge University Press.

Bhalla, Surjit S. 2002. *Imagine there's no country: Poverty, inequality, and growth in the era of globalization.* Washington, D.C.: Institute for International Economics.

Black, Amy E., Douglas L. Koopman, and David K. Ryden. 2004. *Of little faith: The politics of George W. Bush's faith-based initiatives.* Religion and Politics Series. Washington, D.C.: Georgetown University Press.

Black, Sandra. 1999. Investigating the link between competition and discrimination. *Monthly Labor Review* 122, no. 12:39-43.

Blau, Francine D., and Lawrence M. Kahn. 2000. Gender differences in pay. *Journal of Economic Perspectives* 14, no. 4:75-99.

Bordo, Michael David. 1980. In memoriam: Clark A. Warburton, 1896-

1979. *History of Economics Society Bulletin* 1:16-19.

Bouma-Prediger, Steven. 1995. *The greening of theology: The ecological models of Rosemary Radford Ruether, Joseph Sittler, and Jürgen Moltmann*. Atlanta: Scholars Press.

———. 2001. *For the beauty of the earth: A Christian vision for creation care*. Grand Rapids: Baker.

———. 2003. Introduction to the theme issue. *Christian Scholar's Review* 32:346.

Brooks, Arthur C. 2006. *Who really cares: America's charity divide*. New York: Basic Books.

Cameron, Rondo, and Larry Neal. 2002. *A concise economic history of the World: From Paleolithic times to the present*. 4th ed. New York: Oxford University Press.

Carlisle, Tasmin, and Jeffrey Ball. 2005. Kyoto's reality begins to bite. *Wall Street Journal* (February 15): A16.

CIVICUS. 1997. *New civic atlas: Profiles of civil society in 60 countries*. Washington, D.C.: World Alliance for Citizen Participation.

Coffman, Michael S. 1994. *Saviors of the Earth? The politics and religion of the environmental movement*. Chicago: Northfield.

College Board. 2006. *Trends in college pricing*. Trends in Higher Education Series. Washington, D.C.

Couretas, John. 2003. Philosopher on the factory floor: The sacramental entrepreneurship of François Michelin. *Acton Commentary* (May 14).

Danner, Peter L. 1995. Personalism and the problem of scarcity. *Forum for Social Economics* 25:21-32.

De Pree, Max. 1987. *Leadership is an art*. East Lansing: Michigan State University Press.

De Vous, Phillip W. 2003. The new urbanism—Can it survive the company it keeps? *Acton Commentary* (July 16).

Dollar, David, and Aart Kraay. 2002. Growth is good for the poor. *Journal of Economic Growth* 7:195-225.

Donner, Arthur, and James F. McCollum. 1972. The Phillips curve: An historical note. *Economica* New Series 39:323-24.

Dvorchak, Robert. 1999. Home game: The inside story of how the Pirates were saved. *Pittsburgh Post-Gazette* (April 7).

Eagan, Eileen. 1986. *Such a vision of the streets*. New York: Doubleday.

Economist. 1999. Embracing greenery. (October 7).

————. 2000. Career evolution. (January 27).

————. 2003. Survey of water. (July 17).

Fires of Kuwait. 2001. Dir. David Douglas. Videocassette. Warner Home Video.

Fisher, Irving. 1926. A statistical relation between unemployment and price changes. *International Labour Review* 13:785-92.

Foreign Policy. 2004. Ranking the rich 2004: The second annual CGD/FP Commitment to Development Index ranks 21 rich nations on how their aid, trade, investment, migration, environment, security, and technology policies help poor countries. Find out who's up, who's down, why Denmark and the Netherlands are the top spots, and why Japan—once again—finishes last. (May-June): 46-56.

Foster, Richard. 1998. *Celebration of discipline.* New York: HarperCollins.

Gard, John G. 2005. Freeing those trapped in the net. *Acton Commentary.* (January 5).

Geisel, Theodor Seuss. 1971. *The Lorax, by Dr. Seuss.* New York: Random House.

General Motors. Reinventing the automobile with fuel cell technology. [Online]. Available at www.gm.com/company/gmability/adv_tech/400_fcv/index.html (accessed December 2, 2006).

Goggin, Malcolm L., and Deborah A. Orth. 2002. "How Faith-Based and Secular Organizations Tackle Housing for the Homeless." The Roundtable on Religion and Social Welfare Policy, Rockefeller Institute of Government, State University of New York. (October).

Goodstein, Eban S. 2005. *Economics and the environment.* 4th ed. Hoboken, N.J.: John Wiley.

Gordon, Ernest. 2002. *To end all wars.* Grand Rapids: Zondervan.

Graedel, T. E., and Paul J. Crutzen. 1993. *Atmospheric change: An earth system perspective.* New York: W. H. Freeman.

Grand Rapids Press. 2006a. Research finds conservatives are givers. (November 19).

————. 2006b. Fences really do make good neighbors. (November 27).

Gwartney, James D., Richard L. Stroup, Russell S. Sobel and David A. MacPherson. 2006. *Microeconomics: Private and public choice.* 11th ed. Mason, Ohio: Thomson South-Western.

Hardy, Lee. 1990. *The fabric of this world: Inquiries into calling, career choice, and the design of human work.* Grand Rapids: Eerdmans.

Hay, Donald A. 1991. *Economics today: A Christian critique*. Grand Rapids: Eerdmans.

Heckman, James J., and Alan B. Krueger. 2005. Comments. In *Inequality in America: What role for human capital policies?* ed. Benjamin M. Friedman, pp. 241-92. Cambridge, Mass.: MIT Press.

Heilbroner, Robert L., and Aaron Sincer. 1984. *The economic transformation of America: 1600 to the present*. New York: Harcourt, Brace, Jovanovich.

Heylin, Michael. 2000. 2000 salary survey. *Chemical & Engineering News* 14:46-53.

Hicks, John R. 1937. Mr. Keynes and the classics: A suggested interpretation. *Econometrica* 5:147-59.

Hillsdale College. www.hillsdale.edu (accessed on November 30, 2006).

Independent Sector. 2001. *Giving and volunteering in the United States: Key findings*. November. Retrieved from www.independentsector.org/PDFs/ GV01keyfind.pdf (accessed February 1, 2007).

———. 2002. *Engaging youth in lifelong service: Findings and recommendations for encouraging a tradition of voluntary action among America's youth*. Presentation given as part of Independent Sector's Giving and Volunteering Signature series. Washington, D.C. November 20. Retrieved from www. independentsector.org/media/mediaonly/engaging_youth.ppt (accessed February 8, 2007).

Jetcar. Retrieved from www.jetcar.de/english/ (accessed December 2, 2006).

Juhn, Chinhui; Kevin M. Murphy and Brooks Pierce. 1991. Accounting for the Slowdown in Black-White Wage Convergence. *Workers and Their Wages: Changing Patterns in the United States*, pp. 107-43. AEI Studies 520. Washington, D.C.: AEI Press.

Kelly, John. 2004. The tithe: Land rent to God. *Religion & Liberty* 14, no. 4:6-9.

Keynes, John Maynard. 1923. *A tract on monetary reform*. London: Macmillan.

———. 1936. *The general theory of employment, interest, and money*. New York: Harcourt, Brace.

Klamer, Arjo. 1989. An accountant among economists: Conversations with Sir John Hicks. *Journal of Economic Perspectives* 3, no. 4:167-80.

Klay, Robin Kendrick. 1986. *Counting the cost: The economics of Christian stewardship*. Grand Rapids: Ecrdmans.

Klay, Robin, and John Lunn. 2003a. Just remuneration over a worker's lifetime. *Journal of Markets & Morality* 6:177-99.

———. 2003b. The relationship of God's providence to market economies and economic theory. *Journal of Markets & Morality* 6:541-64.

Klay, Robin; John Lunn and Vicki TenHaken. 2004. Middle management as a calling. *Journal of Biblical Integration in Business*, fall: 118-37.

Kosters, Marvin H. 1998. *Wage levels and inequality: Measuring and interpreting the trends*. Washington, D.C.: AEI Press.

Kuhn, Thomas. 1970. *Structure of scientific revolutions*. Chicago: University of Chicago.

Levin, Andrew, and Steven L. S. Smith. 2005. Macroeconomic stability and poverty reduction. In *Attacking poverty in the developing world: Christian practitioners and academics in collaboration*, ed. Judith M. Dean, Julie A. Schaffner and Steven L. S. Smith. Waynesboro, Ga.: Authentic Media. Copublished by World Vision.

Lindblom, Charles E. 2002. *The market system: What it is, how it works, and what to make of it*. New Haven, Conn.: Yale Nota Bene.

Lomborg, Bjørn. 2001a. *Global crises, global solutions*. Cambridge: Cambridge University Press.

———. 2001b. *The skeptical environmentalist: Measuring the real state of the world*. Cambridge: Cambridge University Press.

Loury, Glenn C. 2002. *The anatomy of racial inequality*. Cambridge, Mass.: Harvard University Press.

Lucas, Robert. 1976. Econometric policy evaluation: A critique. *Carnegie-Rochester Conference Series on Public Policy* 1:19-46.

Lukas, Aaron. 2000. *WTO report card III: Globalization and developing countries*, Trade Briefing Paper Number 10, Center for Trade Policy Studies, Cato Institute (June 20). Available at www.freetrade.org/pubs/briefs/tbp-010.pdf (accessed February 1, 2007).

Lynn, Stuart R. 2003. *Economic development: Theory and practice for a divided world*. Englewood Cliffs, N.J.: Pearson Education.

Marshall, Alfred. 1925. *Principles of economics: An introductory volume*. 8th ed. London: Macmillan.

McKibben, Bill. 1998. A special moment in history: The future of population. *Atlantic Monthly* (May): 55.

Michelin, François. 2003. *And why not?* Morality and business. An interview with Ivan Levai and Yves Messarovitch. Trans. Marc Seblanc. Lanham: Lexington Books.

Mill, John Stuart. [1859] 1974. *On liberty*, ed. Gertrude Himmelfarb. London: Penguin Books.

Morita, Akio, Edwin M. Reingold and Mitsuko Shimomura. 1986. *Made in Japan: Akio Morita and the Sony corporation.* New York: E. P. Dutton.

Mueller, Dennis C. 1989. *Public choice II: A revised edition of Public Choice.* Cambridge: Cambridge University Press.

Murphy, Robert G. 2003. *Instructor's resources.* For use with Mankiw: *Macroeconomics.* 5th ed. New York: Worth.

Muth, John F. 1961. Rational expectations and the theory of price movements. *Econometrica* 29:315-35.

New York Times. 1993. Gulf found to recover from war's oil spill. (March 18).

Noguera, Pedro. 2002. Beyond size: The challenge of high school reform. *Educational Leadership* 50, no. 5:60-64.

North, Douglass C. 1990. *Institutions, institutional change and economic performance: Political economy of institutions and decisions.* Cambridge: Cambridge University Press.

Novak, Michael. 1982. *The spirit of democratic capitalism.* New York: Simon & Schuster.

Oxley, Howard, Thai Ghanh Dang and Pablo Antolin. 2000-2001. Poverty dynamics in six OECD countries. *OECD Economic Studies* 30:14-15.

Parkin, Michael. 2005a. *Macroeconomics.* 7th ed. Boston: Addison-Wesley.

———. 2005b. *Microeconomics.* 7th ed. Boston: Addison-Wesley.

Phillips, A. William. 1958. The relation between unemployment and the rate of change of money wage rates in the United Kingdom, 1861-1957. *Economica,* new series 25:283-99.

Radford, Tim. 2005. Two-thirds of world's resources "used up." *Guardian,* 30 March.

Rawls, John. 1971. *A theory of justice.* Cambridge, Mass.: Harvard University Press.

Rigobon, Roberto, and Brian Sack. 2003. Measuring the reaction of monetary policy to the stock market. *Quarterly Journal of Economics* 118:639-69.

Roberts, Russell. 2001. *The choice: A fable of free trade and protectionism.* Englewood Cliffs, N.J.: Prentice Hall.

Schneider, John R. 2002. *The good of affluence: Seeking God in a culture of wealth.* Grand Rapids: Eerdmans.

Schumacher, E. F. 1973. *Small is beautiful: Economics as if people mattered.* New York: Harper & Row.

Smith, Adam. [1776] 1981. *An inquiry into the nature and causes of the wealth of nations.* Indianapolis: Liberty Fund.

Sommers, Norman. 1997. Smaller schools: An ambiance for learning. *American Secondary Education* 26:9-14

Soto, Hernando de. 2000. *The mystery of capital: Why capitalism triumphs in the West and fails everywhere else.* New York: BasicBooks.

Sowell, Thomas. 1995. *The vision of the anointed.* New York: Basic Books.

Sterm, Nicholas. 2007. *The economics of climate change: The Stern review.* Cambridge: Cambridge University Press.

Tampering with Nature. With John Stossel. 2002. Grand Rapids. WZZM (ABC) (June 14).

Terrell, Tom, and Vicki L. Gregory. 2003. *A Look at Now and Then: Salaries of Academic and Research Librarians.* Association of College & Research Libraries Eleventh National Conference, Charlotte, N.C. (April 10-13).

Tocqueville, Alexis de. 2000. *Democracy in America,* trans. and ed. Harvey C. Mansfield and Delba Winthrop. Chicago: University of Chicago Press.

Tresch, Richard W. 2002. *Public finance: A normative theory.* Amsterdam: Academic Press.

Trumbull, William N. 1990. Who has standing in cost-benefit analysis? *Journal of Policy Analysis and Management* 9:201-18.

Tucker, Robert C., ed. 1978. *The Marx-Engels reader.* 2nd ed. New York: W. W. Norton.

United Negro College Fund. www.uncf.org (accessed November 20, 2006).

U.S. Bureau of the Census. 1975. *Historical statistics of the United States: Colonial times to 1970.* Part I. Series G. Washington, D.C.

———. 2001. *Statistical abstract of the United States.* Washington, D.C.

———. 2002. *Statistical abstract of the United States.* Washington, D.C.

———. 2006. *Statistical abstract of the United States.* Washington, D.C.

VanderVeen, Steve K. 2005. Personal conversation.

Viscusi, W. Kip. 1993. The value of risks to life and health. *Journal of Economic Literature* 31:1912-46.

Whelan, Robert, Joseph Kirwan and Paul Haffner. 1996. *The cross and the rainforest: A critique of radical green spirituality.* Grand Rapids: Acton Institute for the Study of Religion and Liberty; and Eerdmans.

White, Ben. 2005. Wall Street greets nomination with rally. *Washington Post* (23 October):D1.

White, Lynn, Jr. 1967. The historical roots of our ecologic crisis. *Science* 155:1203-7.

Wilkinson, Jennifer, and Michael Bittman. 2002. Volunteering: The human face of democracy. SPRC Discussion Paper No. 114, Social Policy Research Centre, University of New South Wales, Sydney. www.sprc.unsw .edu.au/dp/DP114.pdf (accessed February 3, 2007).

Wolff, Edward N., and Ajit Zacharias. 2004. An Overall Assessment of the Distributional Consequences of Government Spending and Taxation in the U.S., 1989 and 2000. Paper presented at the Levy Economics Institute conference, October 15-16, Bard College, Annandale-on-Hudson, New York. www.econ.nyu.edu/user/wolffe/wolff_zacharias_levy2004conf_paper.pdf (accessed February 3, 2007).

World Bank. 2003. *World development report: Sustainable development in a dynamic world: Transforming insititutions, growth, and quality of life.* Washington, D.C.: World Bank and Oxford University Press.

———. 2006. *World development report 2006: Equity and development.* Washington, D.C.: World Bank and Oxford University Press. Also available online at http://econ.worldbank.ort/WBSITE/EXTERNAL/EXTDEC/ EXTRESEARCH/EXTWDRS/EXTWDR2006/0,menuPD:477658~page PK:64167702~piPK:64167676~theSitePK:477642,00.html (accessed February 3, 2007).

World Health Organization. 2002. *The world health report 2002: Reducing risks, promoting healthy life.* Retrieved from www.who.int/whr/2002/en/ index.html (accessed February 3, 2007).

Author Index

Subject Index